LANGUAGE USE

SWANSEA STUDIES IN PHILOSOPHY
General Editor: D. Z. Phillips, Professor of Philosophy, University College of Swansea

Philosophy is the struggle for clarity about the contexts of human discourse we engage in. What we need is not theoretical explanation, but clarification and elucidation of what lies before us. Recent returns to theory in many fields of philosophy, involving more and more convoluted attempts to meet counter-examples to such theories, make this need all the more urgent. This series affords an opportunity for writers who share this conviction, one as relevant to logic, epistemology and the philosophy of mind, as it is to ethics, politics, aesthetics and the philosophy of religion. Authors will be expected to engage with the thought of influential philosophers and contemporary movements, thus making the series a focal point for lively discussion.

Recent titles:

David Cockburn
OTHER HUMAN BEINGS

İlham Dilman
EXISTENTIALIST CRITIQUES OF CARTESIANISM

John Edelman
AN AUDIENCE FOR MORAL PHILOSOPHY?

Martyn Evans
LISTENING TO MUSIC

Raimond Gaita
GOOD AND EVIL: An Absolute Conception

D. Z. Phillips
INTERVENTIONS IN ETHICS
WITTGENSTEIN AND RELIGION

Timothy Tessin and Mario von der Ruhr
PHILOSOPHY AND THE GRAMMAR OF RELIGIOUS BELIEF

B. R. Tilghman
WITTGENSTEIN, ETHICS AND AESTHETICS: The View from Eternity

Language Use

A Philosophical Investigation into the Basic Notions of Pragmatics

Pär Segerdahl
Lecturer in Philosophy
Uppsala University
Sweden

First published in Great Britain 1996 by
MACMILLAN PRESS LTD
Houndmills, Basingstoke, Hampshire RG21 6XS
and London
Companies and representatives
throughout the world

A catalogue record for this book is available
from the British Library.

ISBN 0–333–64611–8

 First published in the United States of America 1996 by
ST. MARTIN'S PRESS, INC.,
Scholarly and Reference Division,
175 Fifth Avenue,
New York, N.Y. 10010

ISBN 0–312–12864–9

Library of Congress Cataloging-in-Publication Data
Segerdahl, Pär.
Language use : a philosophical investigation into the basic
notions of pragmatics / Pär Segerdahl.
p. cm.
Includes bibliographical references (p.   ) and index.
ISBN 0–312–12864–9
1. Pragmatics.   2. Semantics.   3. Language and languages–
–Philosophy.   4. Linguistics.   I. Title.
P99.4.P72S44   1996
306.4'4—dc20   95–21529
                                                          CIP

© Pär Segerdahl 1996

All rights reserved. No reproduction, copy or transmission of
this publication may be made without written permission.

No paragraph of this publication may be reproduced, copied or
transmitted save with written permission or in accordance with
the provisions of the Copyright, Designs and Patents Act 1988,
or under the terms of any licence permitting limited copying
issued by the Copyright Licensing Agency, 90 Tottenham Court
Road, London W1P 9HE.

Any person who does any unauthorised act in relation to this
publication may be liable to criminal prosecution and civil
claims for damages.

10 9 8 7 6 5 4 3 2 1
05 04 03 02 01 00 99 98 97 96

Printed in Great Britain by Ipswich Book Co. Ltd., Ipswich, Suffolk.

'Say what you choose, so long as it does not prevent you from seeing the facts.' — **Wittgenstein**

Contents

Preface xiii

Introduction 1
Pragmatics and the calculus conception of language 1
Aims and methods of the investigation 6
The use of examples 9

PART I DEIXIS

1 Language and Context 15
  1.1 Deixis and the notion of language as an autonomous system 15
  1.2 The linguistic perspective in pragmatics 17
  1.3 The mastery of language involves the mastery of activities of life: an example 18
  1.4 How time-expressions have meaning 20
  1.5 To ascribe meaning is to establish a practice 22
  1.6 Concluding remarks 24

2 The Pragmatic Account of Deixis 25
  2.1 The notion of grammaticalization 25
  2.2 The pragmatic account of deixis projects the general description of a speech event onto the actual event 27
  2.3 Similar accounts of deixis in philosophy 28
  2.4 Concluding remarks 30

3 Context-Dependence 31
  3.1 The pragmatic notion of the difference between deictic and non-deictic expressions 31
  3.2 The way time-expressions refer depends internally on the organization of the context 32
  3.3 Effects of linguistically based methods of observation: the case of disambiguation 35

3.4	Effects of linguistically based methods of observation: the case of the compositional nature of meaning	37
3.5	Explanation of the phenomenon of context-dependence and other forms of functional dependence	39
3.6	A notion of context-dependence contingent on a misuse of linguistic terminology	40
3.7	Using ordinary things in communication	41
3.8	Concluding remarks	43

4 Ironical Use of Indexical Expressions 45
4.1	The pragmatic conception of irony	45
4.2	The utterance of a word is a part of a way of acting	46
4.3	Meaning and established uses of words	47
4.4	Irony is a modified language game	48
4.5	Concluding remarks	49

PART II CONVERSATIONAL IMPLICATURE

5 The Semantic Reading and Conversational Implicature 53
5.1	Meaning more than we actually say	53
5.2	The semantic reading is a technique of paraphrase	54
5.3	The pragmatic notion of conversational implicature	58
5.4	Some examples of how the theory of implicature works	62
5.5	Defeasibility of implicatures	64
5.6	Concluding remarks	65

6 Literal Meaning 66
6.1	Literal meaning: an instinctive attitude toward the semantic reading	66
6.2	Distinct uses of one sentence	67
6.3	The notion of literal meaning condenses distinct uses into one paraphrase	68
6.4	Does use follow from meaning?	70
6.5	Meaning is not grounded in linguistic structure	73
6.6	Concluding remarks	75

7 The Pragmatic Notion of Order   76
   7.1 The conceptual possibility of a reversed order of events   76
   7.2 How order in language is determined   78
   7.3 Can there be an independently defined notion of the order in language?   80
   7.4 The difference between explaining particular acts of language use and explaining the phenomenon of language use in general   82
   7.5 Concluding remarks   83

8 General Principles of Rationality as a Basis for Language Use   84
   8.1 The semantic reading is responsible for the phenomenon of 'meaning more than we actually say'   84
   8.2 The maxims of Quantity and Relevance, and the language game of evidence   86
   8.3 The maxim of Relevance and the use of a simple imperative   88
   8.4 The maxim of Quality and the idea of a general notion of Truth   90
   8.5 The notions of rationality and cooperation cannot ground our conduct   92
   8.6 Meaning-inferences   97
   8.7 Concluding remarks   98

9 Formal Pragmatics   99
   9.1 On some prevailing motives for formalization   99
   9.2 The calculus conception of the process of language use   100
   9.3 On the formal treatment of scalar implicatures   101
   9.4 Remarks on the applicability of the formal theory   104
   9.5 Concluding remarks   106

PART III SPEECH ACTS

10 The Speaker–Hearer Scheme of Communication   109
   10.1 Two approaches to meaning and communication   109
   10.2 The speaker–hearer scheme   113

	10.3	The method of philosophical analysis employed in speech–act theory defines the notions of communication in a logically reversed order	117
	10.4	Concluding remarks	119

11 Speech Acts versus Language Games   120
    11.1   John R. Searle's conception of the problem of communication and its solution   120
    11.2   The notion of a request is the notion of one move within a language game   122
    11.3   Remarks on the investigation of the game of requesting and passing toys   126
    11.4   The idea that speech acts are effect-independent   128
    11.5   Investigation of an intuitive justification of the speech–act conception of requests   131
    11.6   Remark on the notions of meaning and understanding   133
    11.7   Concluding remarks   135

12 Language vs Languages and Philosophy vs Linguistics   136
    12.1   Searle's conception of the relationship between language in general and particular languages: conventional realization of underlying rules   136
    12.2   A comparison: road signs   139
    12.3   First language learning versus second language learning   143
    12.4   If use is all that matters, why can I not invent words and expressions at the moment of speaking?   145
    12.5   A problem caused by a misuse of the linguistic notion of particular languages: the problem of linguistic relativity   147
    12.6   Philosophy versus linguistics   150
    12.7   Concluding remarks   152

13 Intentions and Beliefs as Conditions for Use   153
    13.1   The role of beliefs in making statements
    13.2   Searle's explanation of Moore's paradox
    13.3   Statements cannot be divided exhaustively into sincere and insincere statements: the normal use of ordinary sentences is neither sincere nor insincere   158

13.4	The role of intentions in making promises: speaker's intention to place himself under an obligation	161
13.5	The role of intentions in communication: Grice's analysis of meaning in terms of communicative intentions	165
13.6	Concluding remarks	169

14 The Semantic Reading and the Notion of Indirect Speech — 171

14.1	The notion of indirect speech in speech–act theory is a technical notion	171
14.2	Inventing different readings: the game of indirectness	172
14.3	The facts of use which the game of indirectness draws on	174
14.4	The differences between inventing readings in the game of indirectness and the employment of the semantic reading in semantics and pragmatics	176
14.5	An example of how the semantic reading misconstrues forms of use as indirect: metaphor	178
14.6	The relationship between the practice of semantic reading and theories of meaning	179
14.7	Indirect speech acts and idioms	181
14.8	Concluding remarks	

PART IV PRESUPPOSITION

15 The Notion of Presupposition in Pragmatics — 185

15.1	Presuppositions as background assumptions about the context	185
15.2	The identification of presuppositions in linguistic tests	186
15.3	Pragmatic versus semantic conceptions of presupposition	188
15.4	Concluding remarks	190

16 Presuppositions and Methods of Linguistics — 191

16.1	Description of a language game	191
16.2	A formal notion of precondition	193
16.3	A precondition for a linguistic practice belongs to the practice as a whole	195

16.4	Making inferences from isolated verbal utterances	197
16.5	Linguists 'overhearing' language use	198
16.6	The idea that presuppositions are inferences about the context	200
16.7	The idea that presuppositions are merely assumed to be true	202
16.8	The idea that utterances are inappropriate if the presuppositions are not mutually known	206
16.9	Concluding remarks	208

17 Defeasibility and the Projection Problem — 209

17.1	Examples of the property of defeasibility	209
17.2	The identification of the phenomenon of defeasibility is contingent upon a general way of reading presupposition triggers	210
17.3	Investigation of the examples: the first example	211
17.4	Remarks on the second example	213
17.5	Remarks on the third example	214
17.6	Remarks on the fourth example	214
17.7	Inferences from linguistic data versus features of actual use	215
17.8	The projection problem	216
17.9	Concluding remarks	217

Notes and References — 219

Bibliography — 227

Index — 231

Preface

If someone asks me what time it is, I will almost immediately raise my left arm, take a glance at my watch, and then report the time as indicated by the watch. This is a practical method, a routine that belongs to our uses of language. Nothing could be simpler than telling the time; nevertheless, it is something that children must learn to do, and not without difficulties. To us who know how to report the time by means of clocks, sentences like 'It's five o'clock' almost seem to radiate their meaning, but the relation between the sentence and the practical method that we learnt as children is not equally clear to us. It is tempting to think that the practical method *follows* from the meaning of words and from thoughts about the situation. For why on earth should I bother to take a glance at my watch and utter the sentence 'It's five o'clock', if that sentence did not *mean* a point of time that my watch can indicate, and if I did not *think* that the other person wanted me to inform him about the time? It seems to us as if the practical method was *illuminated* by meaning and quiet deliberation; as if the meaning of words, together with our thoughts about the situation, worked as a rationale for our way of acting.

The pragmatic notion of language use is a technical form of this way of thinking about the use of language. According to pragmatics, even our most basic forms of language use are *founded* on linguistic meaning and unconscious abilities to make inferences and deliberations. Our use of language is conceived of as though it were talkative in its very foundations. If I am right, however, pragmatic theory is not primarily an unprejudiced examination of the various uses of language, but an attempt to bridge a gap between a certain influential philosophical notion of language, and conspicuous facts about our practices of language use. Pragmatics thus fulfils a central mediating function within a widespread philosophical theorizing about language. This work is a critical examination of the mediating function of pragmatics, and of the notion of language use on which it is based.

I would like to thank my friends at the Departments of Philosophy and Linguistics at Uppsala University for their support. One person has been of vital importance to me, to my way of thinking and to the writing of this book: Sören Stenlund, whose works in the philosophy of language, of logic and of mathematics I count among the most important philosophical achievements made in these fields. Sören Stenlund, Juan Wilhelmi, Sven Öhman and many others have read the manuscript, and I am grateful to them for their comments. The author and publishers are grateful to Stephen C. Levinson and John R. Searle for permission to quote from, respectively, *Pragmatics* (1983) and *Speech Acts* (1969), both works published by Cambridge University Press. Work on this book was financially supported by Uppsala University, the Swedish Council for Research in the Humanities and Social Sciences, Anders Council for Research in the Humanities and Social Sciences, Anders Karitz's Foundation, and Knut & Alice Wallenberg's Foundation. Let me finally thank Sharon P. Rider who has corrected my English, and Oswald Hanfling who has checked my English in rewritten passages. It was not a part of their task to improve my style: any stylistic peculiarities are entirely my responsibility.

PÄR SEGERDAHL

Introduction

PRAGMATICS AND THE CALCULUS CONCEPTION OF LANGUAGE

In order to clarify the relevant sense of the term 'pragmatics' in this work, and in order to make the book comprehensible to readers who are not acquainted with pragmatics, I will give a rough sketch of the most basic ideas of pragmatics that will be investigated in this work.

Most of the research which is currently classified as pragmatics is on the border between empirical linguistics, sociology, ethnology and anthropology, and will not be a concern of this investigation. I shall not deal with, for example, empirical research into politeness strategies in Japanese, or turn-taking in the opening of telephone calls. Nor am I concerned with pragmatics in the merely schematic sense of Charles Morris's (1938) distinction between *syntax* (the study of 'the formal relations of signs to one another'), *semantics* (the study of 'the relations of signs to the objects to which the signs are applicable') and *pragmatics* (the study of 'the relation of signs to interpreters').

Pragmatics, in the sense relevant here, must be understood in relation to philosophical *problems* concerning the predominant notion of language in philosophy and linguistics during the past decades; a notion of language which is based on the techniques of logic and linguistics. Sören Stenlund (1990: 4–6) has characterized this notion as 'the calculus conception of language,' a conception according to which:

> a language is determined (or given) by its vocabulary (its lexicon) and grammar, or – through the influence of meta-mathematics and logical semantics – by its syntax and semantics. (Stenlund 1990: 6)

For reasons to be explained below, I will often call this conception the notion of language as an *autonomous system*. Pragmatics, as I will henceforth use this term, is an attempt to redefine and solve these problems concerning the calculus conception of language. I am thinking of four basic problems which might threaten the whole idea of language as a *system*, or as a linguistic *structure*, or as a semantic *machinery* that can be abstracted from its concrete use in ordinary situations of life:

1. The most striking problem is that the meaning of a sentence containing so-called indexical expressions (e.g., 'I', 'you', 'this' and 'that') is not fully determined by the linguistic structure of the sentence. The meaning of one and the same indexical sentence *varies* depending on the context of use. What is communicated by saying, 'If you give me that, I will give you this' cannot be understood from this sentence merely, but requires knowledge of the particular context of utterance.

2. Another problem is that the meanings of natural language expressions rarely correspond exactly to their literal meanings as the latter are accounted for by semantics. Take, for instance, the sentence 'Someone just walked up the staircase'. The literal meaning of this sentence is simply that *someone just walked up the staircase*. But what if the sentence occurred as a reply to the question 'Has Sarah come home yet?'? Then it would have an additional meaning, namely, that Sarah probably has come home.

3. A third problem is that sentences of natural languages do not merely express true or false propositions about the world, but are associated with a great number of different human acts such as promising, requesting and warning; acts that, moreover, play important roles in the lives of people. According to the calculus conception, however, the sentences of a language can only express propositions *about* the world: propositions cannot perform actions or change states of affairs.

4. The last problem concerns (or originally concerned) sentences containing definite descriptions, sentences such as 'The king of France is wise'. This sentence seems perfectly meaningful. But if it is meaningful, then it ought to say something that is either true or false about a certain individual, namely, the king of France. But since there is no king of France the sentence should lack truth-value. This is a problem for the calculus conception of language, for, according to this conception, a sentence cannot be meaning-

ful and still not express a true or false proposition. The property of having a truth-value does not, according to this conception, depend on the state of the world. It is merely *what* truth-value a sentence has that depends on the state of the world.

A number of features of our language, then, make it difficult and in fact even questionable to conceive of natural language as being in principle a calculus, or a formal system L that can be isolated from the situations in which it is used. These problematic features of ordinary language have always been recognized in the philosophy of language, even by formal philosophers such as Rudolf Carnap. But philosophers have instinctively felt that if natural languages differ from formal languages in certain respects, then so much the worse for ordinary language. Their inclination has been to replace, or regiment, or represent ordinary language expressions within some formal system, and they have instinctively felt that they have thereby transformed a half-blooded language into a full-blooded language.[1]

It seems that during the 1950s, a new approach to these discrepancies between formal languages and natural languages began to develop. One good example of this new approach is Peter Strawson's (1950) critique, in 'On Referring', of Bertrand Russell's theory of descriptions. In that article, Strawson introduces a new way of thinking about linguistic phenomena. He suggests that we should make a distinction between (i) a *sentence*, (ii) a *use* of a sentence, and (iii) an *utterance* of a sentence, and he tries to demonstrate that this distinction is not merely terminological, but is a way of *solving philosophical problems* about meaning and reference. According to Strawson's analysis, the sentence 'The king of France is wise' may be *used* in certain circumstances to make true or false assertions, but the sentence *itself* does not have a truth-value. At most, the sentence could be said to contain '*general directions* for its use in making true or false assertions.'

Strawson does not use the term 'pragmatics' in 'On Referring'. Nevertheless, his way of thinking in that article is pragmatic in the sense relevant to this study. He suggests that by making a distinction between *language* and *use*, fundamental problems concerning the calculus conception of language can be solved. In this respect, Strawson was later followed by Paul Grice (1975) who tried to demonstrate that by making a distinction between language and the use of language in conversation, well-known problems concerning the calculus conception of natural language expressions such as 'and', 'or', 'if ... then', 'not', 'all' and 'some' can be solved.

Although Strawson and Grice were probably inspired by J. L. Austin's investigations of language use (e.g., in 'Other Minds' (1946)), Austin was not a pragmatist in the sense pertinent to this investigation. Austin's attitude to the techniques of philosophical logic and theoretical linguistics was not, it seems to me, as respectful as Strawson's and Grice's, and discrepancies between a notion of language based on those techniques and facts of language use would not constitute a serious problem for him. It could be said that ordinary language philosophy *becomes* pragmatics when the attitude to logic and linguistics becomes reverential. Pragmatics can be characterized as a mediator between logical semantics and ordinary language philosophy.

The central idea underlying the pragmatic approach is that, seen in the light of the distinction between language and use, the four problems above are in fact not problems at all, but pragmatic phenomena of use, namely:

I. *Deixis.* Natural languages contain expressions that are designed to *interact* with features of the context of use. The meanings of these expressions *qua* expressions are constant, but very schematic. The meaning of the word 'now', for instance, could be paraphrased *at the time of utterance*, and the meaning of 'here' could be paraphrased *place proximate to the speaker*. When these words are used, however, their *uses* (or *users*) will refer to different points of time and to different locations, depending on the context in which they are uttered. The varying meaning of indexical sentences of which I spoke above (1) as a problem for the calculus conception of language is interpreted pragmatically as an external property of language; as a phenomenon of our *use* of language. Accounts of deixis of the kind relevant to this work are found in, for example, Bar-Hillel (1970), Levinson (1983), Kaplan (1989) and Wettstein (1991).

II. *Conversational implicatures.*[2] The speakers of a language often mean more than what is expressed by the literal meanings of the linguistic expressions they use. The additional meaning which I mentioned above (2) does not threaten the calculus conception of meaning because the additional meaning is interpreted pragmatically as belonging to the use of the sentence in conversation. It is interpreted as being a so-called conversational implicature; something that the *speaker* (and not the sentence) implies (or 'implicates') by using the sentence in a particular situation and in accordance with certain maxims of conversation. The notion of conversational implicatures was introduced by Grice (1975); the basic features of Grice's theory are described in Levinson (1983), and a formalized variant of the theory is presented in Gazdar (1979).

III. *Speech acts.* Speakers may use the same proposition with different intentions and thereby perform different speech acts. A speaker may *state* that it is raining, he may *ask* if it is raining and he may *warn* that it is raining. According to a pragmatic interpretation of problem (3), then, it is not propositions that perform these different acts that change states of affairs – but their *users*. The standard account of speech acts is to be found in Searle (1969).

IV. *Presuppositions.* In using sentences containing, for example, definite descriptions such as 'the king of France', speakers assume, or presuppose, that there is a king of France. If there is no king of France, that does not affect the meaningfulness of the sentence (qua linguistic expression): it is not the *sentence* that fails to be true or false (because sentences never are), but the *speaker* who fails to make a true or false assertion using the sentence. The problematic feature (4) above is, in this case too, redefined as an external feature of language; a feature of the use of language. For characteristic pragmatic accounts of presuppositions, see Kempson (1975), Gazdar (1979), Levinson (1983), Stalnaker (1991) and Soames (1991).

In sum, we might say that pragmatics is an attempt to *protect* the calculus conception of language by placing language – the autonomous language system – in a hidden zone beneath an overlay of uses, speakers and utterances. The invention of pragmatics is based on the discovery of the philosophical *usefulness* of the distinction between language and use. This distinction corresponds, in terms of disciplines of research, to the distinction between semantics and pragmatics. Thus, alternatively, we might say that the invention of pragmatics is the invention of a useful way of supplementing semantics with a pragmatic theory of uses, utterances and speakers.

AIMS AND METHODS OF THE INVESTIGATION

This work is divided into four parts, each corresponding to the pragmatic phenomena mentioned. Although the concepts and the problems discussed in these parts are different, the most basic ways of thinking that we will focus on are essentially the same. Among the themes that will recur in these four parts, the following three interconnected ones are central to the critical aims of the investigation:

A. Pragmatics does not question or reject the calculus conception of language, but modifies and *supplements* this notion in an attempt to make the problematic facts (1–4) fit into the general picture of language as a system that is conceptually independent of its concrete use. The fact is that pragmatics presupposes the calculus conception of language and its limitations with regard to our actual linguistic practices. The notion of conversational implicatures, for example, would lose its technical, pragmatic sense if the semantic technique of paraphrasing the alleged linguistic content of sentences did not meet problems of kind (2) above: it would not be possible to claim that speakers often mean more than what is expressed by the literal content of the expressions they use.

B. The calculus conception of language *can* be questioned on the grounds of careful descriptions of *how* our language is used; its practical methods. What is really problematic about the phenomena (1–4) is revealed only when we consider the concrete practices of language use to which they belong. Basic semantic concepts such as 'literal meaning', 'truth', 'reference' and 'compositionality' can then be seen to be misconstrued in at least two ways. Certain notions (e.g., 'compositionality' and 'literal meaning') describe features of *imposed* logical and linguistic techniques of representing our language, rather than features of our actual linguistic practices. Other notions (e.g., 'truth') have their intended philosophical application only on the basis of the very practices of language use for which they are intended to constitute a foundation.

C. Basic pragmatic notions, such as 'context-dependence', 'relevance', 'rationality', 'cooperation', 'intention' and 'pragmatic inference', can be questioned in very much the same manner as the semantic notions mentioned above; by looking more closely at details of the practical methods of language use. Certain notions (e.g., 'context-dependence') describe features of imposed, linguistic methods of representation, rather than features of actual use. Other notions (e.g., 'relevance' and 'pragmatic inference') presuppose the practices of language use for which they are intended to constitute a foundation.

In sum, the calculus conception of language is threatened by facts of our language use. Pragmatics is an attempt to protect the calculus conception from these facts. For various reasons, however, this attempt fails. Above all, the conceptual framework in terms of which pragmatics attempts to explain the problematic facts has its intended pragmatic application only on the basis of the very linguistic practices to which the problematic facts belong. An investigation into the practices of language use and into the basic notions of pragmatics shows, then, that pragmatic theory is circular, or logically reversed. Obviously, pragmatists are unaware of this circularity in their basic conceptual framework.

My presentation of pragmatics aims at being neutral on technical points where pragmatists tend to disagree. My investigation is concerned with the most fundamental ideas and the most central ways of thinking in pragmatics in relation to the problems (1–4) above. These basic ways of thinking are essentially the same in more technically sophisticated developments of pragmatic ideas, but they are generally more concealed there. For this reason I have made extensive use of Stephen Levinson's (1983) book *Pragmatics*, which emphasizes these basic patterns of thinking, especially on points where pragmatists explicitly or implicitly tend to make philosophical claims about the nature of language. For similar reasons my investigation of speech-act theory starts out from John R. Searle's (1969) book *Speech Acts*.

Some notions that I use as characteristic examples of the pragmatic approach to language use have been examined critically *within* pragmatics: they have been modified, and in some cases even rejected by certain theorists. It must therefore be kept in mind that the features of these notions that I focus on, and which I examine critically, are normally not even touched by the internal pragmatic critique, and they tend to reappear in the suggested alternative notions. Take, for example, the notion of a boundary between semantics and pragmatics. My characterization of this notion is often intentionally simplified, at least at the technical level, in order to bring out the problematic character of the very *idea* of such a boundary and the attendant distinction between language and use. Nevertheless, my characterization contains an idea that has been rejected by, for example, Sperber and Wilson (1986), and, following them, Carston (1988). This idea is that semantics determines the truth-conditional content of utterances independently of pragmatics; that semantics is *autonomous* with respect to pragmatics. According to the theorists just mentioned, truth-conditions are often underdetermined by linguistic sense, and a semantic component of a theory of meaning must sometimes have access to pragmatic information. What these theorists do, however, is that they replace a *simple* distinction between semantics and pragmatics with a *complicated* distinction between, on the one hand, two *kinds* of semantics, and two *roles* played by the pragmatic component, on the other; one role in determining the proposition explicitly expressed by an utterance, and another role in determining the implicatures. In each of these pairs, however, the semantic component is autonomous in relation to the pragmatic role with which it is contrasted. This is explicit in Carston:

> It seems then that we must distinguish two kinds of semantics, linguistic and truth conditional, ... Linguistic semantics *is* autonomous with respect to pragmatics; it provides the input to pragmatic processes and the two together make propositional forms which are the input to a truth-conditional semantics.... Natural language semantics, then, is autonomous and provides the input to pragmatics, which plays a major role in determining the explicature of an utterance [the proposition explicitly expressed] as well as determining implicatures,... (Carston 1988: 176–178)

I hope that this example suffices to demonstrate that a discussion of *competing* pragmatic ideas is not central to the purposes of this investigation, which rather tries to focus on what these ideas have in common. I am concerned with a *very* general way of thinking about our language which distinguishes language from its concrete forms of use, and which conceives of forms of language use as following from linguistic meaning and unconscious abilities to make inferences and deliberations. This general way of thinking is inexorably connected with the notions of language use suggested by, for example, Yehoshua Bar-Hillel, Gerald Gazdar, Paul

Grice, David Kaplan, Ruth Kempson, John Searle and Robert Stalnaker. The distinction between language and use, and the idea that forms of language use are based on linguistic mechanisms and general abilities to make inferences, seem to be fundamental in most of the contributions to Steven Davies's (1991) anthology *Pragmatics*, and in the contributions on pragmatic issues to the *Syntax and Semantics* series edited by Peter Cole and Jerry Morgan (vols 3, 9 and 11). This way of thinking about language and language use is brought out clearly in the first five chapters of Stephen Levinson's comprehensive *Pragmatics*.

THE USE OF EXAMPLES

The work presented here has a certain affinity with other recent studies in the philosophy of language which draw on Ludwig Wittgenstein's later work. In particular, many of my results are related to the ideas put forward by G. P. Baker and P. M. S. Hacker (1984) and by R. Harris (1981). But there is an important difference between my approach to these problems and theirs, one having to do with the central role which the investigation of examples and of particular cases plays in my work. Baker, Hacker and Harris participate in a general discussion in which examples – to the extent that they are employed – occur as illustrations of general points of view, or as evidence for or against certain general points of view. In my work, examples and investigations of particular cases of our language use are intended to *replace* these general views on language. Occasionally I use examples as illustrations too, but my examples are mainly chosen to exhibit such facts of our language as show pragmatic conceptions to be untenable. They are not chosen in order to support some alternative general conception of language.

Since my employment of examples differs from the normal philosophical employment, it requires some comments. Concerning a typical textbook example of what it is to be under an obligation, Bernard Williams remarks: 'To make the example realistic, one should put in more detail; and, as often in moral philosophy, if one puts in the detail the example may begin to dissolve' (Williams 1993: 180).

This is slightly surprising, for what is an example supposed to provide, if not independent facts that can be used as evidence for or against philosophical theories, analyses or conceptions? A more detailed and 'realistic' example ought to be an improved and more trustworthy example. Nevertheless, Williams's remark expresses a truth about the philosophical use of examples: the more the example manages to recall the everyday facts of life, the more difficult it becomes to relate the example to the philosophical conceptions between which the example is supposed to differentiate; the example dissolves in its philosophical function as support for a certain conception, or as a counter-example to a competing view. Another feature of the normal philosophical use of examples is that the examples almost immediately reveal their consequences for competing theories. The examples do their philosophical work by simply being mentioned or enumerated. To invoke an example in a philosophical discussion is akin to performing a well-defined operation in a calculus. Very often, then, philosophical examples are described in a schematic manner that relates to the basic conceptual framework which is *common* to the competing conceptions. They do not merely exemplify the phenomenon under consideration, but illustrate basic ways of thinking that are taken for granted in the background of the discussion.

In this work I will employ simple examples of our uses of language in order to examine the characteristic pragmatic schematization *of these very examples*. That is, my examples will be employed in an inquiry into the basic conceptual framework in terms of which the examples would be described even by opposing pragmatists. To use examples with such an aim, it obviously will not do simply to mention or enumerate the examples, expecting their implications for pragmatics to be obvious. The examples must be described more carefully, and in such a manner that they can work as *recollections* of familiar, everyday ways of acting which finally can be *contrasted* with pragmatic conceptions. To this end I will often use the notion of a language game, but it is important to keep in mind that the attitude in which I employ this notion is not that of theoretical explanation, but that of description and recollection. The reason why this notion is of such importance to my investigations is that it enables us to relate to our language in a simple and common-or-garden manner known to everyone; the manner in which we relate to ordinary games and to well-known ways of acting. The notion of a language game is used to *support* our memory of the various ways in which our language is used. It may come as a surprise that such an investigation into the trivial details of examples and particular cases can have important and *general* implications for pragmatics and philosophy of language.

In its approach, this investigation concerns a feature which pragmatics shares with tendencies in most current modes of philosophical thought. I am thinking of the tendency to philosophize according to a series of basic dichotomies such as:

> general conception / particular cases
> theory / examples
> general explanation / data
> principle of action / concrete ways of acting
> intellectual reflection / facts of practical life
> and so on,

which share the property that the notions on the left-hand side are considered more fundamental and desirable in that they are taken to subsume, or account for, or explain, or ground, or systematize the various facts on the right-hand side. In this manner, pragmatics employs a number of general notions such as 'rationality', 'cooperation', 'relevance', 'truth', 'meaning', 'sincerity' and 'belief' as though they could be combined in a theory and provide a foundation for our concrete practices of language use. I am questioning the tenability of these notions in their pragmatic employments according to the above dichotomies. Observe, then, that my use of the notion of a language game does not belong to the left-hand side of any of these dichotomies; neither do the examples I use belong to the right-hand side of any of the dichotomies.

Normally, my examples are not used as counter-examples to pragmatic ideas, since it is essential to my aims that the examples *could* be used by pragmatists to illustrate their own basic ideas. Ultimately, my use of examples aims at showing that our practical methods of language use stand in no need of theoretical explanation, that giving a theoretical account of these practices is putting the cart before the horse. My investigations demonstrate a new method for treating problems about the way our language works; a method where the aim is to find the *solution* in what seemed to be the *problem* – that is, in a more careful and common-or-garden description of examples of our everyday linguistic practices which, from certain perspectives, may appear to be problematic, and to stand in need of explanation.

I will use many examples in which children play a role, or in which a person is learning some part of our language. By using such kinds of examples, it is easier to focus on practical features of language to which we otherwise have a tendency to become blind. The choice of such examples serves the same end as the use of the notion of a language game. Looking more closely at the details of children's language learning also helps us to avoid a questionable tendency in many theories of language, namely, the tendency to conceive of a language in general as though it were one of the second languages we learn. Reminding ourselves of the details of original language learning helps us to see the enormous difference between learning one's native language and learning a new language on the basis of the language one already possesses.

My approach is inspired by the works of Ludwig Wittgenstein and the Swedish philosopher Sören Stenlund. What I have learnt from them is not this or that standpoint, or idea, or theory – but *a way of thinking*: a way of treating philosophical problems. As regards the work of Wittgenstein, I make no exegetic claims except where explicitly stated, and in those cases only as a digression from the main subject of the investigation.

The investigation is philosophical rather than linguistic. The results of the investigation are solutions to philosophical problems. While the results should be highly relevant to pragmatics, the investigation is not a contribution to pragmatics. My critical discussion of pragmatic notions should not be confused with the discussion that is going on *within* pragmatics as a normal manifestation of a living discipline of research. My discussion is not committed to the scientific loyalties to established notions, methods and results which characterize the discussion within pragmatics. Rather, my effort has been that of being loyal to the ordinary facts upon which we all agree in our practices of language use.

Part I

Deixis

1
Language and Context

1.1 DEIXIS AND THE NOTION OF LANGUAGE AS AN AUTONOMOUS SYSTEM

In contrast to formal languages such as the language of the predicate calculus, natural languages contain deictic expressions, that is, expressions of the following kind: 'I, you, this, that, here, there, now, yesterday.'

This feature of natural language becomes problematic for a certain conception of language which underlies the current discussion in semantics and pragmatics. This conception is that language is some sort of a *system* that can be conceptually isolated from the contexts of its use. The problem posed by deictic expressions is that their meanings seem to be closely related to features of the context of use, as observed by Stephen Levinson:

> ... aspects of linguistic structure sometimes directly encode (or otherwise interact with) features of the context. It then becomes impossible to draw a neat boundary between context-independent grammar (competence) and context-dependent interpretation (performance). (Levinson 1983: 8)

Levinson's remark might be viewed as a possible threat to the idea of language as an autonomous system. But consider John Lyons's observation about deixis:

> There is much in the structure of languages that can only be explained on the assumption that they have developed for communication in face-to-face interaction. This is clearly so as far as deixis is concerned. (Lyons 1977: 637–638)

Here, Lyons expresses himself as though the facts of deixis not only can, but *should* be reconciled with the idea that language is a structure which is conceptually separate from the contexts of its use. As a matter of fact, Levinson describes deixis in a similar manner:

> The single most obvious way in which the relationship between language and context is reflected in the structures of languages themselves, is through the phenomenon of *deixis*. (Levinson 1983: 54)

In the latter two quotations we see how the underlying picture of language as an autonomous system *incorporates* the facts of deixis, despite the opposite suggestion of Levinson's first statement above. Language is conceived of as an autonomous, linguistic structure. When people use bits of this structure – when they produce sentences – certain structural elements are designed for the purpose of relating the utterance to aspects of the immediate surroundings of the interlocutors: 'Natural language utterances are thus "anchored" directly to aspects of the context' (Levinson 1983: 55). When Levinson says:

> The facts of deixis should act as a constant reminder to theoretical linguists of the simple but immensely important fact that natural languages are primarily designed, so to speak, for use in face-to-face interaction, and thus there are limits to the extent to which they can be analysed without taking this into account. (Levinson 1983: 54)

he is not therefore questioning the concept of an autonomous linguistic structure. He is only saying that since this structure is designed for a specific purpose of use, many of its features can be understood only by considering their uses. However, these features still belong to an autonomous linguistic structure. If he did not think so, it would not make sense to talk about *reminding* theoretical linguists about the use of language. *The separation of language from contexts of use is an important feature of the established notion of language in linguistics.*

What pragmatics has found regarding the indexicals of natural language, then, seems to be this: indexicals are irreducible parts of language structure, designed for the function of anchoring utterances to aspects of the context. Consequently, linguists have to investigate the indexicals as they are given in natural language without trying to reduce or translate them to non-indexical expressions, as has been common in philosophy.[1] Yet precisely because the pragmatist stresses the close relationship between language and the context of use, it is clear that he *separates* language, with its indexical expressions, from the situations of use where these expressions have their function. Our investigation into deixis will focus on this conception of the relation between language and use.

1.2 THE LINGUISTIC PERSPECTIVE IN PRAGMATICS

Compare the following two sentences:

(A): Those two cars crashed here yesterday morning.

(B): Car K851 SGR and car H596 YTM crashed at King's Cross, London, at 9:45 a.m. on 24 May 1990.

When compared in this way, written on paper, the two sentences appear to be utterly different. The meaning of sentence (B) seems complete in a way that does not seem to be the case with the indexical sentence (A). In sentence (B), it appears that a state of affairs is completely described, and the only remaining question is whether this crash did or did not happen; that is, the remaining question is whether the sentence is true or false. In contrast, the meaning of sentence (A) appears to be only generally suggested. It has something to do with two cars crashing at a particular place and on a certain day: but what cars, at which place and on what day?

The pragmatic explanation of the fact that even sentence (A) can be used to describe a specific state of affairs is that the indexicals in (A), i.e. 'those', 'here' and 'yesterday', are designed to interact with the context of utterance. A speaker of (A) does not rely on the linguistic structure of the sentence exclusively. He also draws on features of the context in which he utters the sentence, for example, the fact that the two cars are located within view and that he and his hearer are standing at King's Cross.

Thus it now appears as though there existed *two* dimensions in which the meaning of an utterance is determined: a *semantic* dimension of meaning drawing on linguistic structure, most salient in case (B), and a *pragmatic* dimension of meaning drawing on features of the context of use, most salient in case (A). Yehoshua Bar-Hillel makes the same kind of observation in connection with three other sentences:

> Whereas, for instance, the sentence
>   (1) Ice floats on water
> will be understood by almost every grown-up normal English-speaking person to refer to the same state of affairs..., what the sentence
>   (2) It's raining
> is intended to refer to will be fully grasped only by those people who know the place and time of its production, and the identification of the intended reference of the sentence
>   (3) I am hungry
> will require the knowledge of its producer and the time of its production. (Bar-Hillel 1970: 69)

What motivates this procedure of starting out from written sentences isolated from their concrete uses, in order to investigate what information they carry? If pragmatics is a study of the use of language, why does the identification of the problem start with an observation of written sentences in isolation from their uses? Of course, this is motivated by the underlying notion of language as an autonomous structure: if the speech situation contains sentences as autonomous, linguistic objects, then pragmatics is justified in asking about the meaning they contribute. However, the idea of sentences carrying meaning into the situation of use is not an established fact. Rather it is a manifestation of the notion of language that I am here questioning. In questioning this notion, I am therewith also questioning this procedure of identifying the problem of deixis.

1.3 THE MASTERY OF LANGUAGE INVOLVES THE MASTERY OF ACTIVITIES OF LIFE: AN EXAMPLE

Is it not possible to react in other ways to the fact that language contains indexical expressions? Is it not possible to view the use of indexicals as something that shows how the underlying picture of language as an autonomous system might be a mistake altogether? I even want to ask: does not the meaning of *every* sentence disturb this picture of language in a way that is similar to the way in which deixis *clearly* disturbs it? Let us investigate that part of sentence (B) which reports the time of the crash, that is, let us investigate sentence (C):

(C): Incident P happened at 9:45 a.m.

What is needed for an understanding of this sentence? The mastery of language, of course, but what does this mastery involve? Is there a structural or semantical part of this mastery sufficient for an understanding of the sentence, for example, a tacit knowledge of the meanings and references of the individual words, together with semantical rules for combination?

What is it that we teach children when we instruct them in how to tell time? Where does the difficulty lie for children when they are beginning to understand this kind of sentences? Is it to interpret the meaning of the phrase 'it is nine forty-five'? If children have a problem here, it essentially involves the difficulty of mastering the face of the clock. To understand sentence (C), or the meaning of the phrase 'it is nine forty-five', *involves mastering the use of ordinary clocks*.

The understanding of language *involves* the mastery of activities of life. For what would it mean to understand sentence (C) without mastering any kind of time-measuring activity where those words are used? A child who learns to tell time is not only learning a system of signs. Above all, he is learning what we might call a system of contexts: the system of the clock face. A child cannot understand the words 'it is nine forty-five' if he does not master this system of contexts.

To begin to master language, a child has to acquire familiarity with the circumstances where language has a use, that is, the circumstances of life; clock faces belong to these circumstances. When we teach children to understand new *words*, we are teaching them to master new *circumstances*. One might say that these circumstances *belong* to language. *They are part of language as a human activity and are not merely 'contexts.'*

It seems as though we were so familiar with the everyday use of phrases such as 'it is nine forty-five' that we no longer have eyes for all the various facts that are involved in their having meaning (but maybe we get a feeling for these complexities when we teach children how to handle clocks to tell time). We have a tendency to oversimplify the matter by saying, for instance, that the understanding of sentence (C) is 'only a matter of understanding words.' But to understand words involves a great deal!

1.4 HOW TIME-EXPRESSIONS HAVE MEANING

In order to understand what is involved in what we simplify as 'understanding words' or 'interpreting sentences,' imagine a new way of reporting time: imagine a new vocabulary together with a new kind of clock. We will gradually introduce facts about the system of signs and about the machine that is to be used as a clock and ask ourselves if we have now described all the facts that are involved when these signs express time.

How could the sign-system:

$$A, A1, A2, A3, \ldots, G8, G9, H, \ldots, Y8, Y9, Z$$

express time? What would it involve, if these signs did express time?

Imagine that I construct a machine that slowly pulls a marble along a stick. On the stick, there are marks: A, B, C, ..., Z. Between these marks, we find smaller marks: 1, 2, 3, ..., 9. As soon as the marble reaches the mark Z, it is quickly pulled back to A where it resumes its slow movement. To 'read the machine' means to observe at what mark the marble is situated: A, A1, A2, ..., Y8, Y9, Z.

Is a reading of the machine a reading of time? Do the signs express time? Is the machine a clock? If someone answers, 'At least we can imagine that the machine *could* be a clock and that its signs *could* express time,' what possibility is it that this person imagines?

Imagine that I produce a number of machines such as this one, and in such a way that they are all synchronized in some way (and perhaps even correlated with the rotation of the earth). People begin to use the machines in the following manner: they carry them around in small suitcases and use them, for example, to arrange meetings. 'See you the next time the marbles are at G9,' they say, and meet at the moment the marbles of both machines reach the mark 'G9'. In this case, the machines obviously function as kinds of clocks and the signs express time in some sense.

Language and Context   21

Yet in what sense can we say that *words* express time in a sentence such as 'The marble is at G9'? What would it mean to talk about a sentence-meaning in this case?

Where do we find the semantics of the signs of these machines? Is it the mathematical structure of the series 'A, A1, A2, . . ., Z=A' that constitutes this semantics? Obviously not. In that case, we would immediately be able to understand these signs as expressions of time. It is clearly not the fact that '9:45' belongs to a mathematical series of expressions that makes it an expression of time. Still, we *can* imagine the possibility of 'G9' expressing time, just as '9:45' actually does. But what is the nature of this possibility? What is essential for this possibility?

What is it that makes the machine a clock and what is it that makes the signs expressions of time? It is not the mathematical structure of the series. What then is it? Perhaps we have to add to the stick with its series of signs, the marble *with its movement*? What expresses time, then, is not the marks in themselves, but how the marble through its movement passes successively from mark to mark.

We said that one could read the machine by observing where the marble was situated. If such a reading were 'The marble has reached G9,' has time then been expressed? Certainly not. The only thing that has been expressed is what mark the marble has reached through its movement along the stick. Still, the corresponding report on the position of the hands on an ordinary clock face functions as an expression of time. We know too that it must be *possible* for the expression 'The marble has reached G9' to function in a similar way. What facts have we forgotten in our description of the machine with its series of signs and its moving marble, since we have not yet managed to describe how it can express time?

Perhaps we have to add the fact that there are a number of machines that are all synchronized? No, that will not do; a reading of the machine 'The marble has reached G9' does not become a reading of time simply because there are a number of machines with their marbles simultaneously at G9. We are still missing something in our description.

What is it that separates our synchronized machines from all the synchronized machines with hands that *do* express time? What do these clocks have that our machines, as we have described them up till now, lack? The only thing that is still missing in our description is the way to *use* the machines and their system of signs, for instance, when we arrange meetings. But that is not even similar to a semantic account of sentence-meaning! It is not a description of how signs autonomously express meaning. Our attempt to isolate an autonomous system of sentence-meaning has been forced toward a description of the whole institution of time-measurement, to a description of the concrete use of clocks and time-expressions.

1.5   TO ASCRIBE MEANING IS TO ESTABLISH A PRACTICE

Someone might object: 'But we know what time is, independently of the different ways of using clocks, hourglasses and other devices. And that is the explanation of how clock faces and time-expressions can function as indications of time: we simply *let* them be signs of time (given, of course, that the system of these expressions has the requisite logical structure). What you forgot when you searched for the mechanism that your constructed machine would use for the indication of time, was to *ascribe* temporal meaning to the marks on the stick. For how can people use the machine in the way you propose – to arrange meetings – if they do not first understand the position of the marble as a sign of time?'

Let us try to 'ascribe' a temporal meaning to 'G9'. What do we have to do? Of course we can decide that 'G9' means 9:45 a.m., but that does not solve our problem, since it concerns ordinary clocks and their sign-systems just as much as it concerns our machine and its signs.

At last my machine is finished, and now comes that important moment when I give meaning to 'G9', when I ascribe temporal meaning to the marks on the stick. What can that mean, if not that I determine the use of the machine; that I will use the machine in a certain manner when I boil eggs, for instance? Objection: 'No, first you must decide that the marks have a temporal meaning. *Then* using the machine when you boil eggs comes naturally. How could you arrive at the idea of using the machine in that way, if you had not first understood its marks as indications of time?' What does it mean to decide to use an object, our machine for example, as a clock? The marble is moving slowly along the stick, and now I decide to use this as an indication of time. But what did I do? I *may* have said to myself: 'I will use this mechanism to determine time' – but what does this decision *involve*?

What must the conditions be for us to say that an hourglass indicates time? If our investigation of the clock-machines is correct, this amounts to the following question: how must one *use* an hourglass in order for us to say that the hourglass is measuring time? Suppose that I use the hourglass in the following way: every night when I go to bed, I calm myself down by looking at how smoothly the sand runs down. This hourglass does not indicate time any more than does the rain outside my window. For when we want to say that all physical systems involving movement or change are, in some sense, clocks, we merely have a feeling that it would be possible to *use* these systems as time-measuring devices. In what way must my use of the hourglass change in order for it to constitute a measurement of time? Is it enough that I count the number of times that I turn it? That could be done in basically the same way as one counts sheep.

Whatever it is that will make my use of the hourglass a measurement of time, it is an activity or a group of activities within a way of living. To boil an egg for three turns of the hourglass would be an example of such an activity. We might decide to use the boiling of eggs as a way to measure duration of time: I put a number of eggs in boiling water. Now and then I pick up an egg to check whether it is soft-boiled or hard-boiled. The moment I pick up an egg that is just about to become hard-boiled, the tea is drawn and can be served.

If the machine is to be used to indicate time, there are many concrete arrangements to be made. When I imagine the possibility of using the machine as a clock, it is the possibility of making these particular arrangements that I grasp: one can read the position of the marble the moment the water begins to boil and take the saucepan from the stove when the marble has passed a certain number of marks. One can build a number of machines, synchronize them, distribute them, and arrange meetings by specifying positions of the marble. One can build a reference-machine. One can correlate the system of clocks with the rotation of the earth. These different arrangements are parts of different concrete time-indicating activities. When I understood that the machine could indicate time, *I understood that I could make it a part of activities of this specific kind.*

The decision to let the marks on the stick be expressions of time can be nothing other than the decision to build a certain kind of organization around the machine, to decide to make certain very concrete arrangements, *to introduce certain practices into one's life*.

What we oversimplify as 'ascribing meaning' is, in reality, a making of a number of concrete arrangements. To *let* a sign stand as a name for a point of time is to make a concrete arrangement. The *possibility* for a sign to be a name of a point in time, and for a machine to be a clock, is the possibility of a concrete activity involving the sign and the machine. To understand that 'G9' could express time is to understand that it is possible to *do* certain things.

That the sentence 'It is nine forty-five' expresses time can only mean that it is part of a certain kind of activity. But we are so enormously familiar with the everyday use of this sentence that we do not properly see what it concretely involves, the fact that it has temporal meaning. *Instead, we tend to talk about meaning as a property of linguistic expressions*.

1.6 CONCLUDING REMARKS

A result of this investigation is that the meaning of the *non*-indexical sentence (B) cannot be conceived of as a sentence-meaning that can be studied by semantics in isolation from the context of use. If the part of the sentence reporting the time – 'at 9:45 a.m.' – has a meaning, if it does report time, then this fact involves nothing less than *the concrete use of clocks and time-expressions*: a semantic meaning cannot be abstracted from concrete use.

Why then does pragmatics – which claims to have language use as its subject-matter – not consider sentence (B) to be a proper subject for a pragmatic study of use, as it does in the case of the indexical sentence (A)? Why does pragmatics restrict its subject-matter in this way?[2] The explanation seems to be that pragmatics finds a study of use motivated primarily in those cases where the complete meaning detected in actual use in some way overrides the meaning motivated by traditional semantic techniques. This is clearly the case with indexical sentences.

Pragmatic research, then, seems to work as a helping hand to a misleading and highly technical oversimplification of language and meaning. It is where our use of language clearly exposes the untenability of this semantic oversimplification that pragmatics finds its subject-matter.

2

The Pragmatic Account of Deixis

2.1 THE NOTION OF GRAMMATICALIZATION

Here is how Levinson introduces the notion of deixis in technical terms:

> Essentially, deixis concerns the ways in which languages encode or grammaticalize features of the *context of utterance* or *speech event*, and thus also concerns ways in which the interpretation of utterances depends on the analysis of that context of utterance. Thus the pronoun *this* does not name or refer to any particular entity on all occasions of use; rather it is a variable or place-holder for some particular entity given by the context (e.g. by a gesture). (Levinson 1983: 54)

Let us apply Levinson's conceptual apparatus to an example. Suppose that a surgeon in a critical moment orders one of his assistants to immediately come over to him, and that he does so by uttering the sentence:

(D): You, come here, now!

A pragmatic description of this event employing the notion of codification (or grammaticalization) might be the following: 'The speaker is using (i) the person-deictic, (ii) the place-deictic and (iii) the time-deictic codes:

(i) "you" could be said to codify the *addressee*

(ii) "come" and "here" could be said to codify a *movement toward the speaker* and a *place proximate to the speaker* respectively

(iii) "now" could be said to codify *at the time of utterance* (sometimes called "CT", for coding time).

The speaker is using these codes correctly since he wants the addressee to move toward the place where he is situated as speaker and since he wants this action to be carried out in immediate connection with the time of utterance. As regards the addressee, he seems to have decodified the utterance correctly: he is moving toward the speaker.'

The pragmatic explanation of the fact that the utterance of sentence (D) can have the effect it has on the assistant seems to have two basic ingredients:

1. Contextual parameters are grammaticalized in language structure by indexical expressions or grammatical forms.

2. Indexical sentences are uttered in contexts that supply the values of the parameters for which they contain indexicals.

The indexicals, then, are viewed as variables to be filled in on the occasion of use. As a competent language user, the assistant tacitly knows the deictic codes and has the ability to fill in the unique values that the unique context provides, but which the sentence with its grammaticalized information only abstractly describes. In this way, an abstract and incomplete meaning is supposed to interact with the context and make it possible for the assistant to uncover the surgeon's complete request. As Levinson comments on the subject-matter of his book *Pragmatics*: 'Much of this book is concerned with spelling out these mechanisms which, like other aspects of linguistic knowledge, we use daily in an unconscious way' (Levinson 1983: 18).

The concept of grammaticalization is clearly fundamental in the pragmatic account. It functions as an antipode to the notion of use: in order for the utterance of sentence (D) to express a complete request, the sentence must carry some kind of abstract and invariant meaning into the speech event that can interact with the context of use. General contextual information must be codified in language *prior to use.*

2.2 THE PRAGMATIC ACCOUNT OF DEIXIS PROJECTS THE GENERAL DESCRIPTION OF A SPEECH EVENT ONTO THE ACTUAL EVENT

The assistant heard the request 'You, come here, now!' and went to the surgeon. Pragmatics explains this outcome on the basis of the claim that the assistant, as a competent language user, has the tacit knowledge that this sentence grammaticalizes that *the addressee should move toward the speaker at the time of utterance*. But the latter phrase is obviously a general *description* of the speech event! Why should the actual speech event implicitly contain a description of itself? Are the words 'You, come here, now!' not good enough by themselves? Must the assistant implicitly relate these words with a general description of what is said in order to react as he does?

To immediately go to the one who utters 'You, come here, now!' is part of the ordinary use of these words. That is the language game we teach children. To master this sentence involves mastering this *doing* – a doing which, of course, could be given a general description in terms of 'speaker', 'addressee' and so forth. The pragmatist, on the other hand, represents the sentence 'You, come here, now!' as a piece of linguistic structure that codifies the general description of the doing; a specification of the 'general directions' for the use of the sentence on particular occasions.[1] Thus it now seems as though this information were lying there, firmly based on the structures, or conventions, of language: 'I'-*speaker*, 'you'-*addressee*, 'now' – *at the time of utterance* and so forth. Yet these representations of meanings are in reality nothing other than a different vocabulary; the vocabulary of speech-event description.

Why is it so tempting to explain the meaning of the words 'I' and 'you' in terms of the words 'speaker' and 'addressee'?

Previously I showed that expressions of time have their meaning only as parts of activities involving clocks. The same is true of the vocabulary for describing speech events. To understand the words 'speaker' and 'addressee', for example, is to master the use of these words in connection with actual speech events; it is to master judgements of the type:

> the *speaker* is located by the window
> the *addressee* is my brother
> the *speaker* is my cousin

when confronted with actual speech events. Think of how we would teach a person these concepts, how we would train him in making these judgements, *in connection with actual speech events*.

The words 'speaker' and 'addressee' are as deictic as the words 'I' and 'you' are. There is one difference, however, that is relevant to our investigation: the former vocabulary has a use as applied to speech events of which they are *not parts*, while the latter words have a use as applied to the speech event of which they *are parts*. That is why it is so tempting to explain the meaning of the words 'I' and 'you' in terms of the words 'speaker' and 'addressee': the latter words might seem a little more autonomous, relative to use. *But this is an illusion*: the word 'addressee' may be a word that we use to describe a speech event from the outside – from another speech event – but that does not mean that this word represents an invariant, or abstract meaning. It is part of another speech event and has its meaning determined by the way it is used *there*: it belongs to another language game.

Thus what we find in pragmatics is in reality a paraphrase, a translation similar to the ones of which we find many examples in philosophy. It is a translation that is presented as the representation of an abstract and invariant meaning. Nothing is gained, however, through this paraphrase. It is just another deictic vocabulary,[2] presupposing another concrete use of words, albeit a use that applies to the speech event from the outside, that is, from another speech event.

The purported grammaticalized information involves a doing too, a concrete use, albeit a use of a more formal and impersonal vocabulary. The separation that pragmatics tries to keep between language and language use is impossible to maintain. As soon as we investigate what is involved in the grammaticalized information, we land in concrete ways of using words in actual situations.

2.3 SIMILAR ACCOUNTS OF DEIXIS IN PHILOSOPHY

Since it is the same notion of language that forms the background to both the linguistic and the philosophical reaction to deixis, it is instructive to observe that when philosophers do not react with a paraphrase or a regimentation of natural language, their reaction is similar to the one I have described above. Let me give just one example. David Kaplan notices the following property of deictic sentences:

> What is said in using a given indexical in different contexts may be different. Thus if I say, today,
>
> > I was insulted yesterday
>
> and you utter the same words tomorrow, what is said is different. (Kaplan 1989: 500)

The complete but varying meaning which in this way is 'said' on a concrete occasion of use, Kaplan calls *the content*. In order to explain this varying content, Kaplan introduces another meaning which he calls *the character*:

> The second kind of meaning, most prominent in the case of indexicals, is that which determines the content in varying contexts. The rule
>
> > 'I' refers to the speaker or writer
>
> is a meaning rule of the second kind.
> ...
> Let us call the second kind of meaning, *character*. The character of an expression is set by linguistic conventions and, in turn, determines the content of the expression in every context. Because character is set by linguistic conventions, it is natural to think of it as *meaning* in the sense of what is known by the competent language user. (Kaplan 1989: 505)

It is clear that the concept of character serves a function in this account similar to that of the concept of grammaticalized information. Kaplan treats the word 'I' as a part of the syntactic structure of language and the word 'speaker' as a representation of a conventional linguistic meaning. But both words have a concrete use in our language! On some occasions I use the word 'I', just as I on other occasions use the word 'speaker': *two related moves in two related language games*.

Why is Kaplan tempted to use one ordinary word as a representation of the linguistic meaning of another ordinary word? *Because* of the subtle relationship between the use of 'I' and the use of 'speaker', Kaplan is tempted to treat one ordinary word as part of the explanation of another. Primarily, however, this temptation is caused by the linguistic notion of language that I am calling into question. Only against the background of this notion and its procedures of studying language does the word 'I' seem problematic and the word 'speaker' explanatory.

2.4 CONCLUDING REMARKS

The methods and concepts of pragmatic theory are based on the separation of language from language use. When our language does not fit into the picture of language as a completely self-contained structure, the linguist cannot disregard this: it is the task of linguistics to describe natural languages as they happen to exist. But since pragmatic research is carried out *within* the notion of language that deixis disturbs, pragmatics has to *modify* this notion. It is this modification that we are witnessing in the concept of grammaticalization.

The pragmatic account of deixis is not so much a description of the actual use of indexicals, as it is an attempt to make our ordinary language fit into the picture of language as a system that is conceptually independent of its use. I have shown that this attempt fails: the notion of the grammaticalized meaning of deictic expressions consists of a translation of one form of deictic expressions to another form of deictic expressions, and it presupposes the concrete use of the latter expressions.

In philosophy, many problematical notions are produced through turning oversimplifications into technical concepts. We found this to be true of the notion of sentence-meaning and of the notion of meaning-ascription, and now we find it to be true of the notion of grammaticalization.

3
Context-Dependence

3.1 THE PRAGMATIC NOTION OF THE DIFFERENCE BETWEEN DEICTIC AND NON-DEICTIC EXPRESSIONS

When pragmatists characterize the distinction between deictic and non-deictic expressions, and the corresponding distinction between pragmatics and semantics, they often employ a mathematical notion of functional context-dependence. A deictic sentence such as: 'I am hungry' would be characterized by having a context-dependent meaning in the sense that the complete meaning conveyed by using the sentence varies systematically with the context of use (and requires knowledge of the context). In contrast, a non-deictic sentence such as: 'Ice floats on water' would be characterized by having a context-independent meaning in the sense that the meaning conveyed by using the sentence does *not* vary with the context of use (and does not require knowledge of the context). The study of context-dependent meaning is then said to belong to pragmatics, while the study of context-independent meaning belongs to semantics, which studies meaning in abstraction from the context of use.[1]

I do not deny that there are important differences between the two sentences above, but is the pragmatic characterization a *good* description of the differences? Is the meaning of indexicals context-dependent in the functional sense, and is it possible to describe the meaning of non-indexical sentences in abstraction from the context of use? These and related questions will be investigated in this chapter.

3.2 THE WAY TIME-EXPRESSIONS REFER DEPENDS INTERNALLY ON THE ORGANIZATION OF THE CONTEXT

Consider an utterance made in the system of time-expressions that we imagined in Chapter 1, for instance, the following utterance: 'The marble is at G9'.

Consider how differently this utterance functions, depending on the way the machines are used. First imagine that the machines are used solely as stopwatches. In that case, the utterance would express time only if a particular machine has been started (for the purpose of determining the duration of some process). The utterance refers to the marble of this particular machine, and it reports the time as determined by this machine. When no such machine is given in *some* way in the context, saying 'The marble is at G9' would (normally) be as meaningless as saying 'The man over there is my cousin' when no man is 'over there.' Moreover, if the machines are never stopped and calibrated so that the determination of time requires an initial reading, then the period of time expressed by the utterance varies, depending on the context of use.

Imagine another use of the machines, namely, our most common use of clocks: the machines are synchronized, distributed in society, and used to arrange meetings. In this case, the meaning of the utterance 'The marble is at G9' would no longer vary with the context,[2] and it would make sense to make the utterance even if no particular machine is given in the context. Moreover, the expression 'the marble' would normally not refer to the marble of any particular machine. Wherein does this difference lie? Let us describe these two ways of using the machines more closely.

Case 1: the machines are used as stopwatches

To use a stopwatch is an action that we perform only *sometimes* and for the purpose of determining the duration of distinct processes. If the duration of distinct processes happens to be measured simultaneously with distinct stopwatches, there is no rule of connection between those stopwatches. (However, there is a rule that connects a stopwatch with the particular process that this watch measures: start the stopwatch the moment the process begins, and stop it the moment the process terminates.) To utter 'The marble is at G9' is the way to report time within this activity. Since there is no rule of connection between simultaneously performed activities of this kind, neither is there a connection between the reports made: to report 'The marble is at G9' is to report time as determined by a particular machine within a particular execution of the activity. If no stopwatch is started, then it does not make sense to make a typical report of time, nor even to make an estimation of time; if no particular stopwatch is started, then there is no time measured to report or to estimate.

Case 2: the machines are used as regular clocks

Clocks are distributed in society and are *constantly* in function. Distinct clocks are not part of distinct time-indicating activities; they are part of *one* organization, part of *one* time-indicating system. Within this organized use of clocks, there is a rule of connection between every simultaneously functioning clock: they are designed to be simultaneously in the same state through concrete methods of synchronization. To utter 'The marble is at G9' is the way to report time within this organization. Since there is a rule of connection between the simultaneously functioning clocks, there is a corresponding connection between reports made with the aid of distinct clocks. To report 'The marble is at G9' is to report time as determined by *any* clock within this organization. Finally, since this system of synchronized clocks is *constantly* functioning, it does always make sense to make, for instance, an estimation of time even though no *particular* clock is given in the context.

In Case 1, the utterance 'The marble is at G9' refers to a particular marble of a particular time-indicating machine, and it expresses the time as determined by this particular machine. In Case 2, on the other hand, the utterance does not refer to any particular machine, and it expresses the time in general. Is it correct to claim that this difference consists in the fact that the utterance 'The marble is at G9' has different kinds of meaning in the two cases; a pragmatic context-dependent meaning in the first case, and a semantic context-independent meaning in the last case? Is it not rather the case that the difference consists in the different arrangements made regarding the use of the machines?

The machines are required in the context in the last case too, albeit, not as *particular* machines in *particular* contexts. The requirement is that the machines are synchronized and distributed in society, that they *generally* can be found, and in the same state as *any* machine. We have *arranged the context to be completely general and constant* by using reference clocks and methods of synchronization. An utterance does not refer to any particular clock and does not express time as determined by any particular clock, since *any* clock is in the same state as *any* other clock at *any* occasion of use *within this complex arrangement of the use of clocks in society*.

To say that an utterance in the second case expresses time in general, with no reference to particular clocks, is therefore not to say that it expresses time *independently* of the existence and the use of clocks. It is not to say that the sentence carries an *autonomous* meaning. It is, on the contrary, precisely as an integrated *part* of the particular arrangement of synchronized and constantly working clocks, that the utterance can be said to express time in general.

According to Yehoshua Bar-Hillel, however, the study of constant context-independent reference belongs to semantics which studies language *in abstraction* from the context of its use:

> ... the abstraction from the pragmatic context, which is precisely the step taken from descriptive pragmatics to descriptive semantics, is legitimate only when the pragmatic context is (more or less) irrelevant and defensible as a tentative step only when this context can be assumed to be irrelevant. (Bar-Hillel 1970: 70)

If my description of the two uses of clock-machines is correct, this semantic abstraction from the context is mistaken. To establish that the reference of 'The marble is at G9' is independent of the context in the functional sense is *not* to establish that the context is irrelevant to the way in which the utterance refers. Only if we treat the organization of the context as something *relevant* can we understand why meaning and reference are more or less constant in Case 2, but vary in Case 1.

If the linguistically based procedure of tracking functional independence is employed to justify a conceptual isolation of language from the contexts of use, as it is by Bar-Hillel, then this procedure is a way of generating systematically misleading semantic accounts of the ways in which expressions refer.

Consider also how Quine describes the difference between context-independent and context-dependent reference:

A notable trait of 'this', 'this river', 'this water', and similar terms is their transiency of reference, in contrast to tenacious singular terms like 'mama', 'water', 'Nile', 'Nadejda'. Such is the effect not only of the two demonstrative particles, but of the *indicator words* generally: 'this', 'that', 'I', 'you', 'he', 'now', 'here', 'then', 'there', 'today', 'tomorrow'. The child's learning of 'mama' and 'water' depended on fixity of reference; he was trained, by reinforcement and extinction on multiple occasions of utterance, to adjust to norms or boundaries of reference which were held fast for him. In learning the indicator words he learns a higher-level technique how to switch the reference of a term according to systematic cues of context or environment. (Quine 1960: 101)

Quine's talk about a 'transiency of reference' of indexicals and about 'tenacious' non-deictic singular terms is contingent on his fixing upon words as autonomous, isolated parts of language structure through the different occasions of use. It is an impressionist description of something that technically would be expressed with the mathematical notion of a function. But does a child really learn how to *switch* the reference when he learns to use the word 'this'?

Quine's poetical description brings out the fact that linguistically based methods of observation *affect our conception* of, for example, the nature of reference. My description of the concrete differences between two ways of using the clock-machines is an attempt to show that these effects of linguistic methods of observation can be deeply misleading. In the following sections I will give more examples of these effects, and of their role for certain philosophical conceptions of features of our language.

3.3 EFFECTS OF LINGUISTICALLY BASED METHODS OF OBSERVATION: THE CASE OF DISAMBIGUATION

Compare the following three systems of time-expressions:

System 1. In English, the time-expression '9:45' can refer to a point of time in the morning *or* to a point of time in the evening. The expressions 'a.m.' and 'p.m.' are often used to discriminate between these two possibilities. The first system of time-expressions does *not* contain the latter expressions.

System 2. The second way of reporting time that I will investigate is the one that *does* use the expressions 'a.m.' and 'p.m.'.

System 3. In Swedish, for instance, there is a system of time-expressions which contains two distinct numeral constructions for the two points of time: '9:45' refers to a point of time in the morning, while the expression '21:45' is used to refer to a point of time in the evening.

Concerning System 2, it is tempting to conceive of the meaning of the expression '9:45__' as being functionally dependent on whether the expression is followed by the sign 'a.m.' or by the sign 'p.m.' According to such a conception, these two signs are treated as *discriminators* of ambiguous time-expressions. The idea of this discourse-dependent meaning is contingent on conceiving the sign '9:45' as a well-defined linguistic structure that can be identified in two different discourses: '__a.m.' and '__p.m.'

What kind of thinking is involved in the claim that '9:45 a.m.' is the same time-expression as '9:45 p.m.', but with another discriminator added to it?

We are misled by the fact that there is a possibility of using the expression '9:45' with *or* without the two signs 'a.m.' and 'p.m.' That fact tempts us to make a false comparison. It makes us identify one and the same expression of time in two different discourses:

'__a.m.' and '__p.m.',

instead of identifying two different expressions of time:

'9:45 a.m.' and '9:45 p.m.':

which is similar to:

'9:45' and '21:45'

in the third system of time-expressions. How can the signs 'a.m.' and 'p.m.' disambiguate the expression '9:45'? The answer, it seems to me, can only be that the two signs belong to a system of time-expressions where '9:45 a.m.' and '9:45 p.m.' are *distinct expressions of time*, just as '9:45' and '21:45' are distinct within the third system. That is why the addition of one of the two signs functions as a disambiguation.

The sole expression '9:45' belongs to a different system of time-expressions than the expression '9:45 a.m.' does. To add 'a.m.' to the expression '9:45' is to *go from the first system of time-expressions to the second system.* If this addition disambiguates the expression, it means that the latter system contains '9:45 a.m.' and '9:45 p.m.' as distinct expressions of time, in precisely the same sense that '9:45' and '21:45' are distinct within the third system. It is the system with its internal multiplicity and concrete interrelation with an organization of clocks that is essential.

In other words, the act of disambiguation that we sometimes perform regarding the expression '9:45' consists in moving over to another system of time-expressions *where no disambiguation takes place*. The notion of 'a.m.' as a discriminator rests on a *comparison* between distinct systems of expressions. (To use the second system is not constantly to disambiguate expressions of time.)

I am not trying to revise the talk about disambiguation as the addition of a discriminating sign to an ambiguous expression. I do, however, want to draw attention to the fact that disambiguation *consists in using another system of expressions*.

We can indeed observe that a possible ambiguity in the expression '9:45' is removed by the addition of the sign 'a.m.'. But that is not an insight into a *process* going on in language. It is an observation of an effect of comparing expressions that belong to distinct systems of use; '9:45' belongs to System 1, while '9:45 a.m.' belongs to System 2.

3.4 EFFECTS OF LINGUISTICALLY BASED METHODS OF OBSERVATION: THE CASE OF THE COMPOSITIONAL NATURE OF MEANING

A typical semantical account of the meaning of the expressions of the third system would be to describe the meaning of the expression '21:_5' as a six-valued function of the omitted component, to describe the meaning of the expression '21:__' as a sixty-valued function of the way the latter half of the expression is composed, and so forth. This account is an example of the idea that the semantic meaning of an expression is a function of the way the expression is composed.

It is an uncontroversial linguistic observation that there are sixty ways of composing time-expressions of the form '21:__', and that these sixty distinct expressions refer to sixty distinct points of time. It is also a fact that this linguistically based observation can be described mathematically as a function of the composition of the expression.

Why does the reference vary in this way? Is it because the meaning of the expression '21:__' *is* a function of its composition? That function is just the description of our *observation*! It is not possible to explain this effect by projecting the mathematical description of the effect onto the expression itself. So, once again, *why* does the reference vary like this?

The explanation is, I think, as simple as this: it is a fundamental fact that there exists a use of clocks and time-expressions (in Sweden, for instance), where sixty succeeding time-expressions of the form '21:__' are used in connection with sixty succeeding states of clocks. This fact explains why a semanticist who fills the empty space with numbers from the series:

00, 01, 02, ..., 58, 59,

will compose sixty expressions of time that can be observed to refer to sixty points of time. *His method of observation draws on the actual use of these expressions.*

The semantic method of observation consists in *comparing* the meaning of (well-known) sentences from a formally defined point of view, the point of view of their linguistic analysis. Of course, one *will* observe systematic variations in meaning! Explanation: the differently composed expressions that one studies have different uses in our language. That is the basic fact that this method of observation draws on.

If substitution of a word in a sentence has an effect on meaning, that merely means that we have built up a different expression that has a different use in language. The process of substitution does not determine the new meaning of the new sentence. The new sentence simply has another use, and the process of substitution belongs to the linguistic method of comparing the meaning of expressions that belong to different forms of use.

The idea of the compositional nature of meaning is a mistaken projection of this method of observation onto language itself. It is an idea that presupposes a blindness to the fact that the semantic method of investigation draws on meaning as determined by use.

3.5 EXPLANATION OF THE PHENOMENON OF CONTEXT-DEPENDENCE AND OTHER FORMS OF FUNCTIONAL DEPENDENCE

According to a pragmatic way of thinking, the expression '9:45' has a context-dependent meaning that can take one of two values. This idea presupposes an identification of one and the same expression, '9:45', in two different contexts:

9:45 (*morning*)

and

9:45 (*evening*)

Linguistic identity criteria are applied as a basis for comparison between different uses of words: that is what Quine does in an earlier quotation, when he applies the linguistic notions of demonstrative particles, singular terms and indicator words to identify parts of language structure in different surroundings.

The notion of functional dependence is contingent on the way that expressions are identified linguistically. Identifying '9:45' as an identical element in the two discourses '__a.m.' and '__p.m.' is a prerequisite for the notion of a two-valued functional *discourse*-dependence. Identifying '21:__' as an identical element of a segment of the third system of time-expressions is a prerequisite for the notion of a sixty-valued functional *composition*-dependence. Similarly, identifying '9:45' as an identical linguistic element in the two contexts *morning* and *evening* is a prerequisite for the notion of a two-valued functional *context*-dependence.

A linguistic element is held constant while the discourse or the composition or the context is varied. If the meaning or the reference connected with this identical linguistic element varies systematically with the parameter with which one works, then one accounts for this variation with the mathematical notion of a function. As has already been remarked, however, this functional account is just a description of an *effect* of this particular way of observing language and, as such, it cannot *explain* the variation.

The true explanation of this variation, then, does not consist in an account of how *language* functions, but in an account of the linguistic methods of *observing* language.

3.6 A NOTION OF CONTEXT-DEPENDENCE CONTINGENT ON A MISUSE OF LINGUISTIC TERMINOLOGY

The appearance that a user of the expression '9:45' switches the reference depending on the context is, as we have seen, an effect of holding a linguistically identified element constant. But is the use of '9:45' in the morning and the use of '9:45' in the evening really two uses of the same expression of time?

Imagine that for some reason we never measured time between 12:00 p.m. and 12:00 a.m. so that the expression '9:45' was used to refer only to a point of time in the evening. An internal mechanism stops all clocks at 12:00 p.m. and starts them up again at 12:00 a.m. Now imagine that there arises a need for measuring time between 12:00 p.m. and 12:00 a.m. It is decided that the internal stop-mechanisms should be removed in order to make it possible to use the same clocks and the same series of time-expressions to measure time constantly. Does this change have an effect on the meaning of the expression '9:45' *as it is used in the evening*?

Concentrate on the concrete activity of using '9:45' in the evening as a way to read the time. Is this use changed by the fact that the clocks are turned into constantly working clocks? Has the way the expression refers to a point of time in the evening turned into the result of a *switching* of the reference? Is it not rather the case that the expression, *as part of this evening-use*, functions in basically the same way as it did before the change?

We might say that it is not the same expression that is starting to be used in the morning too, but a twin-expression of the evening-expression. No matter how identical the expressions actually are from a linguistic perspective, they are as distinct as twins are: *they fulfil different functions in different parts of language*. Their being linguistically identical is purely accidental and has no effect on their respective uses. Of course, problems of ambiguity may appear in certain cases, just as similar problems appear in connection with twins. That does not, however, alter the fact that the expressions, and the twins, are distinct. It just requires a consciousness of the concrete possibilities for misunderstanding that comes with being twins.

According to this investigation, the context-dependence of '9:45' is an effect of letting linguistic terminology decide what is identical and what is distinct. I am not claiming that these criteria are false: '9:45' used in the morning *is* linguistically identical to '9:45' used in the evening. My point is that if the same linguistic expression has two distinct uses, then the linguistic identity is accidental: the expression has meaning and refers in exactly the same way as it would if the other use consisted in using a linguistically distinct expression, such as '21:45'. The idea that a user of the expression '9:45' switches the reference presupposes that a purely accidental identity is treated as an essential identity.

3.7 USING ORDINARY THINGS IN COMMUNICATION

We have found it instructive to talk about two established uses of '9:45', namely, one morning-use and one evening-use. None the less, it is only misleading to talk about an unlimited number of uses of the indexical 'this', corresponding to each distinct utterance of it. We must investigate the use of 'this' from another perspective.

A unique feature of the use of many indexicals is that we use the entity that the indexical indicates in order to refer to this very entity. When I utter 'This book is amusing', I am referring to a particular book, but instead of giving the title of the book, I *show* the book to my addressee. This showing of the book is a part of my use of symbols. The indexical expression 'this book' indicates the book as being a *part* of my utterance. It indicates that I am not only using *linguistic* symbols in saying what I say. The expression 'this book' is used to build up a complex symbol which *contains* the book.

The entity that the indexical 'this' indicates seems to fulfil a 'linguistic' function: the entity fulfils a function *in* language.

The pragmatic problem might be posed in the following way: 'How does a competent language user uncover the complete meaning of an utterance of the sentence "This book is amusing"? How does he come to know *which* book is amusing?' This problem is contingent on the simple fact that the employed linguistic method of representing the used symbol by writing down a sentence, excludes the thing-showing component. The speaker *shows* which book is amusing, just as he *says* that it is amusing.

If anything determines the reference of my utterance 'This book is amusing,' it is the particular book that I hold in my hands (and which I *show*). Objection: 'But how does the listener know which book it is that has this property? How does he know that it is not the book that *he* might be holding that determines which book it is that you are describing as amusing?' Maybe because I use the word 'this', or because I move the hand in which I hold the book, or because I look at the book, or because I point at the book, or because it is evident that I have not seen the listener's book, or because the listener just saw me finish reading the book and smiling....

I will not investigate all the ways in which it can be clear which book I am using in order to establish which book it is that I find so amusing. All that matters to me is the fact that there *are* typical ways in which such things can be clear. That there are such ways means that it is possible to *use* the book that I am holding, to establish which book it is that is amusing: the book in my hands can be used to say things about itself. These remarks should not be confused with Howard K. Wettstein's idea that:

> pointing gestures not only provide cues as to the reference, they actually determine the reference.... There are a host of such contextual features that provide cues to the auditor and, at the same time, enter into the determination of reference. (Wettstein 1991: 165)

Wettstein is trying to *solve* a problem that I am trying to show is a misconception, namely, the following problem:

> 'That' can be used to refer to anything at all. Its lexical meaning does not vary, however, from use to use. The reference of an utterance of 'that' is thus not determined solely by its meager lexical meaning. What exactly bridges the gap between the *meager* lexical meaning of such an indexical expression and its *determinate* reference? (Wettstein 1991: 161)

The very idea of a 'gap between the meager lexical meaning of an indexical expression and its determinate reference' has its origin in the method of paraphrasing indexicals that I questioned in §§2.2–2.3, and in the linguistic methods of observation that were investigated in §§3.3–3.6. In this section I am trying to show that there are these *two* aspects of the use of the indexical 'this': (i) the indexical indicates a particular entity, and (ii) the indicated entity is *used* to fulfil a function in language.

Generally, only the first aspect is observed. The basic reason seems to be the widespread use of linguistic terminology as a normative delimitation of language. This use of linguistic terminology has two effects:

(i') it makes the indication of a particular entity with the indexical seem problematic, since this indication presents itself as a step from language – identified by notions of linguistics – to an entity in an external context,

(ii') it makes the use of the entity *invisible* since language use, according to this terminology, must be conceived of as a use of linguistic elements. (Wettstein seems to be prepared to supplement these elements with, e.g., pointing gestures, but his aim is to solve the alleged problem in (i').)

It is as if the indexical 'this' were like a name with the paradoxical feature of naming different bearers on different occasions of use. The point I am trying to make is the following: 'What can be compared with a name is not the word "this" but, if you like, the symbol consisting of the word, the gesture, and the sample' (Wittgenstein 1969: 109).

To use an indexical is not to constantly shift the reference. It is to use an indicated entity as a *part* of a certain kind of linguistic practice – and not merely as a 'contextual feature.' My use of the word 'this' is inseparable from the book that I hold in my hands and that I show. Ordinary things *belong to* the language games played with the word 'this'.

3.8 CONCLUDING REMARKS

We must distinguish between three ways of using the notions of linguistics:

1. *As a grammatical calculus.*
Notions of linguistics are applied in the definition and in the solution of strictly grammatical problems (e.g., the problem of analysing the syntax of questions in Swedish). This work of solving grammatical problems is performed *within* the system of linguistic concepts. This is how grammarians use linguistic notions.

2. As a terminology.

Notions of linguistics are employed merely to facilitate communication between people who are working with different practical problems connected with language in one way or another. The work is not performed within the system of linguistic concepts, but rather *utilizes* this system. Sociolinguists, descriptive pragmatists, speech therapists, teachers of language and others who deal with language in some practical way, often use linguistic notions in this way in order to facilitate communication with colleagues, patients, students, readers etc.

3. As a conception of language.

The third way of using linguistic notions can be viewed as a confusion of the first two. The grammatical calculi of the grammarians are instinctively taken for *realities*, or at least for hypothetical realities – namely *languages* – that are spread by teachers of language, adjusted by speech therapists, and studied in a wider context by sociolinguists and pragmatists. It is instinctively taken for granted that the notions of linguistics define the limits of language. It is this employment of linguistic notions that forms the basis for theoretical pragmatics, semantics, cognitive science and psycholinguistics.

I have tried to show that the alleged context-dependent meaning of indexical expressions is an illusory phenomenon, caused by the third way of applying the notions of linguistics.

4
Ironical Use of Indexical Expressions

4.1 THE PRAGMATIC CONCEPTION OF IRONY

I have questioned the pragmatic distinction between language and use, a distinction for which Levinson gives the following argument: '... the possibility of regular ironic usages of, for example, honorifics to children, argues for the existence of prior and well-established meanings independent of rules of usage' (Levinson 1983: 93).

Although Levinson does not give any examples of what he means, I suppose that he is thinking of how we sometimes address children as 'Sir,' 'my Lady,' 'my Lord' or 'Your Majesty' with an ironical effect. Levinson probably means that if this ironical effect is to arise, the honorifics must codify some kind of social information that can clash with the fact that the addressee is just a child. If there were not such a distinction, if there were only use and rules of use, Levinson seems to think, then this particular use of honorifics would be as straightforward as any, and no ironical effect would arise. There would simply not be anything that could clash with the fact that the addressee is a child, and the word 'Sir' would, in this use, have the same meaning as the word 'buster'. According to Levinson, then, irony arises in the collision between an autonomous meaning, codified in language, and aspects of the context.

In Levinson's argument, I think we find an oversimplified picture of what it means to use a word in addressing someone. When a child is addressed as 'my Lord,' the act of addressing is not simply an event where an honorific is uttered in the presence of the child. The act of addressing the child belongs to a whole way of behaving with many subtle features. These features are different from those that characterize the normal use of the word 'buster'.

We can imagine a situation in which a parent asks his child most *humbly* 'Shall I tidy up my Lord's bedroom?' The child might reply with an *aristocratic* 'By all means, please do.' By intentionally *acting* as a lord and *treating* the parent as a servant, the child turns the irony back against the parent. This use of honorifics contains not exactly a codified meaning, but ways of behaving which differ from the normal use of the word 'buster'.

The irony does not arise simply because the addressee is a child and not a lord. The irony presupposes that the situation is such that there is some *truth* expressed in addessing the child as 'my Lord.' The child will perceive the irony only if he perceives the truth in being addressed as a lord. It is an embarrassing truth, and the parent will probably perceive the truth in being addressed as a servant.

4.2 THE UTTERANCE OF A WORD IS A PART OF A WAY OF ACTING

The ironical use of honorifics is related to the games of pretending. Children master these games. A child may address a doll as 'Sir,' that is, not only *utter* the word in the *presence* of the doll, but actually *treat* the doll as one treats a Sir. The child does not bring a mere *word* 'Sir' to the doll: he brings the *language activities* with the word 'Sir' to the doll. Through these language games, the child learns much about the use of words such as 'Sir', 'my Lord', or 'my Lady'. It is not an implicit meaning of the word 'Sir' that clashes with the fact that the addressee is a child or a doll; it is the ordinary way of *using* the word 'Sir'.

What I want to show is that irony and the games of pretending are forms of use that happen to presuppose other forms of use, namely, the *normal* uses of, for example, honorifics. It is the latter forms of use that Levinson confuses with 'prior and well-established meanings.' (We might instead talk about prior and well-established *uses*.) We can *show* a child that a lord is something different from what he is, by addressing the child very humbly and very politely with 'How are you today, my Lord?' How could this be possible, if what we try to teach the child about lords were something implicit or *concealed* in every polite expression, every gesture and every utterance of the word 'Lord'?

The meaning of the word 'Lord' is not something implicit. It consists, for instance, in the particular questions we ask a lord, in the unique tone of voice that we employ; it consists in the way we use the word.

4.3 MEANING AND ESTABLISHED USES OF WORDS

Imagine that a parent addresses his child as 'my little Lord' with a loving and perhaps a slightly childish tone of voice. Imagine that he asks his child, 'Does my little Lord want to come to daddy?' What is the meaning of the word 'Lord' in this use? Is it ironical? Is it not a meaning that is clearly similar to the meaning of the word 'buster'?

In a way, then, the meaning of the word 'Lord', in some uses, *can* be identical with, or at least similar to, the meaning of the word 'buster', namely, if we *use* the two words in a similar way. In order for a use of an honorific to be an ironical use, it is not sufficient that we simply confront the word with a particular context. We must *use* the word *in a way* that is similar to its basic use. We must concretely apply some 'prior and well-established rules of *use*.'

The loving use of honorifics to children is an example which conflicts with the idea of 'well-established meanings, independent of rules of usage.'

Someone might object: 'If you address a child with an honorific such as "Sir", or "my Lord", the honorific codifies that the addressee is valuable in some way, and this is important if you are to accomplish the loving effect. If the word were only an empty label, carrying no meaning, how could you achieve *anything* by using it? And it would be very difficult to accomplish this loving effect with the word "pig", no matter how much you try to use it in the manner of "buster". Use, and the effects of use, must be contingent on the different meanings that are associated with words. The word used must bring certain information into the situation of use.'

This objection already presupposes the separation of language from language use which it defends. When I say that the idea of an autonomous meaning is a misleading oversimplification, and that the fact that a word has meaning can be understood only in terms of the concrete use of the word, it is tempting once again to apply grammatical notions to this statement, and to think that

I am talking about the use of a *syntactic object*, as though the use of language consisted in moving around the empty formulas of a syntactic calculus. Such a view would be even more susceptible to our criticism, since it contains an even more radical distinction between language (as a bare syntactic structure) and use.

Obviously the words 'It is nine forty-five' must have a meaning if the use of them is to accomplish anything *on a particular occasion*; but that means nothing more than the following. There must be an established and mastered use of the words in connection with clocks and activities involving clocks; a practical method.

When a parent ironically asks his child, 'Shall I tidy up my Lord's bedroom?', it is indeed important that the parent uses the word 'Lord' or some similar word. We might even say that the irony depends on the meaning of the word 'Lord'. But recall once again what is *involved* in a word having a meaning.

When the parent ironically uses the word 'Lord', many features of the normal use of this word are manifest in his use. Many features of the child's behaviour made it possible to use the word in this way. I have expressed this fact by saying that the ironical use of 'Lord' expresses a truth about the child's behaviour. A pragmatist who postulates an implicit social meaning for the honorific 'my Lord' is blind to the *overt* subtleties involved in this *doing*. What he does not perceive in this concrete activity, he postulates as a concealed meaning following the word into the speech event.

4.4 IRONY IS A MODIFIED LANGUAGE GAME

In the games of pretending, the child finds it amusing to play a lord and to be addressed as something that he is not. It might be a part of this game to leave the bedroom untidy and to be asked 'Shall I tidy up my Lord's bedroom?' When the child is addressed 'my Lord' *outside* the games of pretending, this might be something unpleasant and ironical. The child is in a way behaving as a lord, although no longer as part of a game of pretending. His leaving the bedroom untidy is no longer a game.

Here we see how close the relationship is between the games of pretending and irony. The answer 'By all means, please do,' which the child could give playfully in the game of pretending would, in the case of irony, be a way of turning the irony back against the parent.

In pretending, the child *acts* in a particular way. The child talks and behaves as a lord, and his parents treat him as a lord. Something similar is true in the case of irony. The ironical use of honorifics to children can be characterized as a modified way of acting based on the normal use of honorifics. To say something in an ironical way is to make concrete moves within certain modified language games. The concept of 'meaning the opposite,' which often occurs in pragmatic accounts of irony, is the concept of a particular kind of linguistic practice, not a concept of some advanced, cognitive ability that we exercise in these practices.[1] Our 'ability' to mean the opposite is the *fact* that we have these language games in which features of normal use are exaggerated to make a certain contrast more obvious and embarrassing. This contrast is salient in the situation in which the ironical utterance is made: a person is tired and absent-minded *when* he ought to be alert, 'How alert you are today'; a *child* acts as if his parents were his servants, 'Shall I tidy up my Lord's bedroom?'. The truth expressed by an ironical utterance, then, is not only the opposite of what is literally said, but this *contrast* in the situation; a contrast which the ironical utterance highlights.

4.5 CONCLUDING REMARKS

The ironical use of honorifics to children does not support the existence of 'prior and well-established meanings independent of rules of usage.' On the contrary, this use shows that the pragmatic notion of language oversimplifies and misrepresents facts of language use.

(ii) The reading of formal logic has consequences for the notion of semantic well-formedness. If the formal paraphrase is a well-formed formula of the applied logical calculus, then the paraphrased sentence is considered to be semantically well-formed too (at least as far as the formal aspect of semantic reading is concerned). Examples of nonsensical sentences that become treated as semantically well-formed sentences in this way are:

The lone ranger rode into the sunset and jumped on his horse
He wanted coffee but got coffee
Charles' children live in Torquay and he has no children
It is raining but I do not believe it is raining

(iii) A further consequence of the formal reading is that the sentence 'Some of Bob's marbles are green' is read as being compatible with the possibility that *all* of Bob's marbles are green (*all* implies *there exists* in predicate logic). In a similar manner, Levinson reads the sentence 'Nigel has fourteen children' as being compatible with Nigel's having *twenty* children (1983: 106), and the sentence 'The flag is white' as being compatible with the flag's being white, red and blue (1983: 99, 106).

2. The lexical reading

When we consider sentences taken in isolation from the ordinary situations in which they might be used, many sentences for which we cannot imagine a use still have a ring of meaningfulness. It *sounds* as though left-handedness were predicated of someone in the sentence 'He was left-handed for two minutes'. For is not the sentence *formulated* so as to express that someone was left-handed? But is it *conceptually* possible to be left-handed for two minutes? Would that be left-handedness? One aspect of the semantic reading is the distinction between linguistically codified meaning (lexical meaning) and background assumptions about the world. That distinction is applied in these types of queries. The semanticist's reading of the sentence will depend upon what he is inclined to view as codified in the lexical element 'left-handed' and what he is inclined to conceive of as mere background assumptions about left-handed persons.

The lexical reading consists in abstracting from many features of the use of an expression, features which, for some reason, are considered not to belong to the meaning of the expression or to the concept expressed by it. According to one way of carrying through the distinction between linguistically encoded meaning and background assumptions about the world, the following sentences must be assessed as semantically well-formed (as expressing a literal meaning):

> I was left-handed for two minutes
> At 11:54 he could suddenly speak Spanish
> My mother is younger than I am
> He is pregnant
> The horse miaowed
> His typewriter has bad intentions
> After Sue died, she finished her thesis

According to the lexical reading, then, these sentences are perfectly meaningful. It is just that they express extremely *rare* events, events that probably have never occurred but, who knows, perhaps one day may occur. The lexical reading of the problematic sentences above implicitly contains analogies to sentences with unproblematic, clear uses. The sentence 'He is pregnant', for example, is read in analogy with 'She is pregnant'. Similarly, the sentence 'I was left-handed for two minutes' is read in analogy with 'I was numb for two minutes'. The sentence 'My mother is younger that I am' is read in analogy with 'My brother is younger than I am', and the sentence 'My typewriter has bad intentions' is read in analogy with 'My cousin has bad intentions'.

The lexical reading is a technique of paraphrase in the sense that the question 'What does the sentence "The horse miaows" mean?' is answered by treating the sentence as though it expressed meaning in basically the same way as the sentence 'The cat miaows' does.[1] That is, the word 'miaows' in 'The horse miaows' is read as it is in 'The cat miaows'. Similarly, the expression 'older than' in 'I am older than my mother' is read as it is in 'I am older than my brother'. Paraphrases containing variables, such as 'X miaows', or 'X is younger than Y is', are sometimes given as expressions of common, lexical elements of meaning in different sentences.

It is this aspect of the semantic reading that varies the most among different semanticists, and the variation depends upon which aspects of concepts the individual semanticist is inclined to view as linguistically codified, and which aspects he is inclined to view as mere background assumptions about the world. Lyons (1977:

420), for instance, reads the sentence 'His typewriter has bad intentions' as semantically well-formed, while Manfred Bierwisch (1970: 167) reads it as semantically anomalous.

I suppose that an additional feature of the lexical reading is this: although the sentence 'Pass the salt' normally is used to express that the speaker wants salt immediately, the lexical reading of the sentence does not contain an indication that this passing of salt should be done immediately, since the lexical item 'immediately' is not a component of the sentence.

3. The reading which disregards situation

The third aspect of the semantic reading is the cultivation of a standardized type of paraphrase that abstracts from the different possible interpretations of sentences in different situations. Some problematic consequences of this aspect of the semantic reading are expressed in the following examples:

(i) Although the sentence 'I heard sounds coming from the kitchen' might occur as a reply to the question 'Where is Sarah?', and in that conversation communicate that Sarah might be in the kitchen, it is paraphrased as meaning only that *the speaker heard sounds coming from the kitchen*. Semantically read, the sentence has nothing to do with the possibility of Sarah being in the kitchen.

(ii) Although the sentence 'I have to work tonight' is sometimes used as a refusal to proposals such as 'Let's go to the movies tonight', the sentence is semantically paraphrased not as a refusal, but as a *description of the speaker's activities during the night*.

(iii) Although the sentence 'You do work fast' is sometimes uttered ironically to a person who is working incredibly slowly, its semantic paraphrase is that *the addressee works fast*.

This aspect of semantic reading consists in abstracting from the possibilities of different interpretations that exist in different situations of use. This is often accomplished through more or less *repeating* the sentence, thereby detaching it from the situation that suggests a certain interpretation.

To sum up: the semantic reading is a technique of paraphrasing linguistic expressions which prevails within the community of semanticists and pragmatists. Semanticists and pragmatists instinctively take their employment of this reading as an expression of the literal content of sentences. I will investigate this employment of the semantic reading in Chapter 6, which deals with the notion of literal meaning. First I will sketch the pragmatic notion of conversational implicature.

5.3 THE PRAGMATIC NOTION OF CONVERSATIONAL IMPLICATURE

The notion of conversational implicature was originally designed by Paul Grice (1975) in order to deal with the problem of the divergences in meaning between the connectives, quantifiers and operators of formal logic, and certain natural language expressions:

> It is a commonplace of philosophical logic that there are, or appear to be, divergences in meaning between, on the one hand, at least some of what I shall call the *formal* devices – $\sim$, $\wedge$, $\vee$, $\supset$, (x), $\exists(x)$, $\int x$ (when these are given a standard two-valued interpretation) – and, on the other, what are taken to be their analogs or counterparts in natural language – such expressions as *not, and, or, if, all, some* (or *at least one*), *the*. (Grice 1975: 41)

Expressed in terms of the three aspects of semantic reading, Grice's primary aim with the notion of implicature, was that of justifying the first aspect of the technique of semantic reading, that is, the reading of formal logic:

> ... Professor H. P. Grice drew the attention of the philosophical public to a most intriguing hypothesis about the familiar logical particles of natural language 'not', 'and', 'if ... then ...', and 'either ... or ...'. I shall henceforth call this the Conversationalist Hypothesis. What it asserts is that those particles do not diverge in meaning, or linguistic function, from the formal-logical symbols, '$\sim$', '&', '$\rightarrow$', and '$\vee$' respectively, as standardly interpreted by two-valued truth tables, and that wherever they appear to diverge from truth-functionality the appearance is due to the various standing presumptions with which natural language utterances are understood. (Cohen 1971: 50)

The Semantic Reading

However, the notion of conversational implicature can just as well be employed to justify the lexical reading and the abstraction from the situation of use which are characteristic of traditional semantic conceptions of literal meaning. The notion of conversational implicature interacts with all three aspects of the semantic reading, and that makes the notion a perfect companion to semantics and its conception of what is 'actually said' by speakers. Grice's ideas have been employed in, for example, John R. Searle's (1979) theory of indirect speech acts, and in various attempts to explain irony and metaphor (see, for example, Martinich (1984)). According to Levinson, one of the main contributions made by the pragmatic notion of implicature is that it:

> provides some explicit account of how it is possible to mean (in some general sense) more than what is actually 'said' (i.e. more than is literally expressed by the conventional sense of the linguistic expressions uttered). (Levinson 1983: 97)

The observation of the general phenomenon that it is possible to mean more than what is 'actually said' presupposes a delimitation of what is said, a delimitation of literal meaning. This delimitation is, as I have remarked, accomplished by the semantic reading. Applying the semantic reading in the way that pragmatists generally do, we can produce the following examples of the phenomenon. Observe how the literal meanings are determined by different aspects of the semantic reading:

(i) The sentence 'Charles opened his eyes and saw a lion' is normally used to express that Charles *first* opened his eyes and *then* saw a lion. We often use the word 'and' to express an order of events, but this order is not part of the literal meaning of 'and'. (The reading of formal logic.)

(ii) A student may use the sentence 'I was left-handed for two minutes' to express that for two minutes he succeeded to fool his teacher into thinking that he was left-handed, but that is not what the sentence literally says. (The lexical reading and the reading that disregards situation.)

(iii) Uttering the sentence 'I heard sounds coming from the kitchen' as a reply to the question 'Where is Sarah?,' is a way of expressing that Sarah might be in the kitchen. Literally, however, the sentence does not say anything about someone named Sarah, nor about the location of any person. (The reading that disregards situation.)

(iv) An utterance of the sentence 'Some of Bob's marbles are green' is normally understood as conveying that *not all* of Bob's marbles are green. Still, that fact is not expressed by the literal meaning of the sentence. (The reading of formal logic.)

(v) A strange consequence of the semantic reading is the following. The two sentences 'The lone ranger rode into the sunset and jumped on his horse' and 'It is raining but I do not believe that it is raining' are nonsensical and do not have normal uses. Still, the two sentences do have literal meanings – that is, they have semantic readings. (The reading of formal logic.)

Notice the similarity to the problem of deixis. In the examples above, the idea of language as an autonomous system is threatened by elements of meaning conveyed in the use of language. Since traditional semantic techniques cannot account for these elements, the phenomenon is conceived of as a pragmatic phenomenon, that is, as a phenomenon that arises only in the *use* of language in conversation. Grice's theory of conversational implicature demonstrates how the limitations and the oversimplifications of semantics may give birth to stimulating problems of a new kind.

According to Grice's theory, communication is organized around a general agreement of cooperation in the community of language users. Grice expresses this agreement in the form of a cooperative principle, which in turn is explained by a number of maxims that specify what participants in a conversation have to do in order to converse in a rational, cooperative way. This is how Levinson presents Grice's maxims of conversation:

The co-operative principle
make your contribution such as is required, at the stage at which it occurs, by the accepted purpose or direction of the talk exchange in which you are engaged

The maxim of Quality
try to make your contribution one that is true, specifically:

(i) do not say what you believe to be false
(ii) do not say that for which you lack adequate evidence

The maxim of Quantity
(i) make your contribution as informative as is required for the current purposes of the exchange
(ii) do not make your contribution more informative than is required

The maxim of Relevance
make your contributions relevant

The maxim of Manner
be perspicuous, and specifically:
(i) avoid obscurity   (iii) be brief
(ii) avoid ambiguity   (iv) be orderly

In short, these maxims specify what participants have to do in order to converse in a maximally efficient, rational, cooperative way: they should speak sincerely, relevantly and clearly, while providing sufficient information. (Levinson 1983: 101–102)

These maxims are meant to form the basis for a pragmatic explanation of the discrepancy between semantic meaning and the complete meaning conveyed in the use of language. In the following passage, Levinson applies Grice's theory in an explanation of the fact that the sentence 'There's a yellow VW outside Sue's house' can be used in a conversation to communicate that, if Bill has a yellow VW, he might be in Sue's house:

> ... in most ordinary kinds of talk these principles are oriented to, such that when talk does not proceed according to their specifications, hearers assume that, contrary to appearances, the principles are nevertheless being adhered to at some deeper level. An example should make this clear:
>
> A: Where's Bill?
> B: There's a yellow VW outside Sue's house
>
> Here B's contribution, taken literally, fails to answer A's question, and thus seems to violate at least the maxims of Quantity and Relevance.... Yet it is clear that despite this *apparent* failure of co-operation, we try to interpret B's utterance as nevertheless

co-operative at some deeper (non-superficial) level. We do this by assuming that it is in fact co-operative, and then asking ourselves what possible connection there could be between the location of Bill and the location of a yellow VW, and thus arrive at the suggestion (which B effectively conveys) that, if Bill has a yellow VW, he may be in Sue's house. (Levinson 1983: 102)

So by *apparently* violating the maxims, a speaker is able to mean more than he literally says. Many implicatures arise, however, when the speaker demonstratively and drastically flouts some of the maxims, but in such cases it must be assumed that the speaker still is being cooperative: it must be assumed that the speaker intends to convey some meaning by blatantly flouting, for instance, the maxim of Quality. Levinson exemplifies this kind of implicature in the following way:

This maxim [Quality] might be flouted in the following exchange:
A: What if the USSR blockades the Gulf and all the oil?
B: Oh come now, Britain rules the seas!

Any reasonably informed participant will know that B's utterance is blatantly false.... The only way in which the assumption that B is co-operating can be maintained is if we take B to mean something rather different from what he has actually said. Searching around for a related but co-operative proposition that B might be intending to convey, we arrive at the opposite, or negation, of what B stated – namely that Britain doesn't rule the seas, and thus by way of Relevance to the prior utterance, the suggestion that there is nothing that Britain could do. (Levinson 1983: 109)

Thus another way of meaning more than we literally say is that of demonstratively flouting some of the maxims. The result may be, for example, irony or a metaphor.

5.4 SOME EXAMPLES OF HOW THE THEORY OF IMPLICATURE WORKS

Through the notion of implicature, pragmatics supplements the semantic conception of what is literally said. The element of temporal order that is conveyed in many uses of 'and', for instance, is added to the semantic content as an implicature arising from the assumption that the speaker is observing the sub-maxim 'be orderly'. Moreover, implicatures are sensitive to background assumptions about left-handedness, mortals, type-writers, pregnancy, horses, ageing and so on. They are also sensitive to the situation in which the conversation takes place. Without going into any details, I will sketch four examples of how the notion of implicature works in this respect:

(i) A speaker uttering

   Charles opened his eyes and saw a lion

communicates that Charles *first* opened his eyes and *then* saw a lion. This *and then*-sense is not part of what is literally said, but is added within the pragmatic dimension of speaker-implicated meaning. This is done in the following way. We assume that the speaker observes the maxims and, in this case, we specifically assume that he observes the sub-maxim 'be orderly', which states that events should be recounted in the order in which they happened. Since the speaker recounts the events in a particular order, we infer that he intends to implicate that the events happened in that particular order. (The anomalous character of 'The lone ranger rode into the sunset and jumped on his horse' can be explained on the basis of the sub-maxim 'be orderly' together with our background knowledge about riding: you jump on the horse before you ride.)

(ii) A speaker uttering

   I was left-handed for two minutes

says something that (literally) must be false. Left-handedness is not something that you get into for short periods of time. Let us assume, nevertheless, that the speaker is cooperative, and that he observes the maxim of Quality at a deeper level, meaning something different from what he literally says. Suppose that the speaker's friends know that he often invents practical jokes, and that he is talking to a friend about his first day in a new school. If this is the situation, then the speaker can be assumed to implicate (to his friend) that he *acted* left-handed for two minutes.

(iii) In a conversation about where Sarah might be, someone utters

> I heard sounds coming from the kitchen.

Semantically read, this sentence seems both irrelevant and uninformative. The question is, assuming that the speaker is speaking relevantly and informatively, what meaning can he intend to communicate? What can he *mean* (since he does not *say* such a thing) that is both relevant and informative? He probably intends to implicate the following: 'I do not know where Sarah is, but since I heard sounds coming from the kitchen and since kids tend to make a lot of noise, it is probable that she is there.'

(iv) The utterance

> Some of Bob's marbles are green

does not literally deny that perhaps all of Bob's marbles are green. How can it be explained, then, that this utterance normally communicates that not all of the marbles are green? The theory of implicature explains this fact on the basis of an ordering of the degree of informativeness of interchangeable linguistic expressions. The expression 'all' is estimated as being more informative than the expression 'most', which in turn is estimated as being more informative than 'many' and 'some'. Among these interchangeable expressions, the speaker decided to use the relatively uninformative expression 'some'. Now if the speaker was in a position to use the stronger expression 'all', then his choice of 'some' would be in breach of the first maxim of Quantity. Assuming that the speaker is observing the maxim of Quantity, we infer that the speaker wishes to communicate that he is not in a position to use the stronger expression 'all', and that he knows that it does not apply.

5.5 DEFEASIBILITY OF IMPLICATURES

An important property of implicatures is that they are cancellable, or defeasible. I leave it to Levinson to explain this property:

> ... implicatures are more like inductive inferences than they are like deductive ones, for implicatures too are inferences easily defeasible.... Consider for example (51) and its straightforward Quantity implicature (52):

(51) John has three cows
(52) John has only three cows and no more

Notice too that (51) entails (53):

(53) John has two cows

Now we can immediately see that implicatures are suspendable by mention in an *if* clause:

(54) Johns has three cows, if not more

which does not have the implicature (52). Note here that entailments, being non-defeasible, cannot be suspended in this way:

(55) John has three cows, if not two

(Levinson 1983: 115)

Implicatures can also disappear in contexts where it is clear that such an inference could not have been intended by the speaker. Suppose that a university course will be postponed if the number of students is below five. As an answer to the question 'Do you have the requisite number of students?', the utterance 'Yes, I have five students all right' will not implicate that the number of students is *exactly* five.

5.6 CONCLUDING REMARKS

The notion of conversational implicature is an attempt to justify the traditional conception of literal meaning as determined by the semantic reading. Facts of use that might threaten this conception of meaning are interpreted positively as a pragmatic phenomenon of conversation, as the phenomenon of 'meaning more than we actually say.' However, since the notion of this pragmatic phenomenon is contingent upon the very conception of literal meaning that it justifies, the justification is circular. Therefore the investigation of the notion of conversational implicature will be preceded by an inquiry into the notion of literal meaning.

6
Literal Meaning

6.1 LITERAL MEANING: AN INSTINCTIVE ATTITUDE TOWARD THE SEMANTIC READING

The semantic reading is a technique of paraphrase that anyone can learn independently of his philosophical views on the nature of meaning. Students of logic and students of linguistics acquire the fundamentals of semantic reading already during their first term. In semantics and pragmatics the system of semantic paraphrases is instinctively employed as a way of giving a direct and ideal expression to the meaning of expressions. The system of semantic paraphrases is treated as being almost the meanings themselves (or at least as being the ideal representations of the meanings).

This attitude toward the semantic reading is manifest in the fact that the reading often is employed as the *final criterion* of the meaningfulness of sentences. For example, when an informant does not accept a sentence with a semantic reading as one that makes sense, his response is often explained away as depending on such factors as, for instance, the informant's inability to imagine circumstances where the sentence has a use: 'When our informants tell us that a particular utterance is deviant, anomalous, bizarre, etc., they may simply mean that they cannot immediately imagine the circumstances under which they would produce it' (Lyons 1977: 420).

I have no objections to this general remark. It is not uncommon that we judge sentences as senseless, just because we fail to recall the situations in which they are used. What I do object to, however, is the normative role played by the semantic reading in these troublesome cases. A sentence might in fact be senseless; its having a semantic reading does not alter that fact. The risk is that the semanticist, due to the normative role played by the semantic reading, *invents* either a nonsensical description of an alleged situation of use, or a new and specialized use of the sentence. Consider, for example, John Lyons's argument for the meaningfulness of the sentence 'My mother is younger than I am':

> ... although most native speakers would probably say that *My mother is younger than I am* is anomalous (on the assumption that 'my mother' refers to the speaker's genetic or uterine parent) they might be persuaded to agree, upon reflection, that there are imaginable, if biologically impossible, situations which could be correctly described by the proposition 'My mother is younger than I am'. All we have to do is to envisage the possibility of arresting or reversing the biological process of ageing; and many works of science-fiction take this possibility for granted. (Lyons 1977: 419)

In this chapter I will inquire into the presuppositions of this argument, that is, into the semantic notion of literal meaning.

6.2 DISTINCT USES OF ONE SENTENCE

In the last quotation above, Lyons talks about the possibility of a person being older than his own mother. 'All we have to do,' he claims, 'is to envisage the possibility of arresting or reversing the biological process of ageing.' Lyons even takes the fictitious description of this 'state of affairs' in science-fiction as a further support for its possibility. The point of Lyons's argument is to establish that the sentence 'My mother is younger than I am' is meaningful, that it has a literal meaning. According to Lyons, it is merely false background assumptions about the biological process of ageing that cause us to perceive this sentence as being anomalous. But what is the literal meaning of this sentence? What kind of situation does it describe?

Lyons talks about 'the biological process of ageing' as though the *biological* sense of ageing was somehow the self-evidently literal one. He takes for granted a particular concept that presupposes an application of biological or medical methods of measurement. Given that Lyons considers such a biological notion of age, it comes as no surprise that a mother can be younger than her own child. In fact, we need not call upon science-fiction to argue for this possibility: we know it as a fact that some persons grow old more quickly than others do in the sense that they look old sooner, or in the sense that their bodily functions grow weak faster. We can find many examples of mothers who are younger than their own children *in this sense*. But there are other, and more common, criteria of age according to which it would be *nonsense* to say 'My mother is younger than I am.' Think, for instance, of a person who, while comparing his mother's medical record with his own, says the following: 'Damned! My *own* mother is younger than I am. Well, not *younger* of course. Or, yes! she *is* younger than I am – look at these medical records.' The person begins with using the expression 'younger than' in the medical sense. Then he remembers the more common use of the expression within which it is nonsense to say what he says, so he hesitates for a moment. Finally, he accepts his use of words as *distinct* from the common use, and adds 'look at these medical records' in order to establish how he is using the expression 'younger than', that is, to establish which criteria he is applying.

Perhaps Lyons would claim that what this person is doing is ultimately separating literal meaning from his background assumptions about ageing. That is not true. He can still maintain that his mother is older than he is since that is in fact the case, given that we use the expression 'older than' in the common way: the mother has turned sixty-five, which the son, if he is lucky, will do twenty years later. Our imagined speaker separates a specialized use of the word 'age' from our more common use of the same word.

6.3 THE NOTION OF LITERAL MEANING CONDENSES DISTINCT USES INTO ONE PARAPHRASE

Lyons treats a specialized use of the expression 'younger than' as an argument for the existence of a completely *general* literal meaning of the expression. What we encounter here is the manner in which semanticists sometimes use a combination of two tricks to persuade us that there is such a literal meaning:

(i) *The semantic reading*: one gives a conventional, completely general reading of the expression 'younger than' as this expression occurs in distinct sentences. The paraphrase, *X is younger than Y is*, is used to express a common element of meaning in distinct sentences.

(ii) *The suggestion of a particular use*: in a case such as 'My mother is younger than I am', where the paraphrase seems unsatisfactory, one suggests a particular use of words where it *is* meaningful to substitute 'my mother' for '*X*' and 'I am' for '*Y is*'.

Taken together, these two tricks give us the impression that there is a common element of meaning in the sentences:

>Charles is younger than Bill is
>My mother is younger than Bill is
>Richard is younger than I am
>My mother is younger than I am

and this common element is that *someone is younger than someone else is*:

>*X is younger than Y is.*

If we feel reluctant to perceive this element in the last sentence, thinking that the idea of a mother being younger than her own child is nonsensical, the semanticist suggests a *particular use* of this sentence, but presents this use as an instance of the common element *X is younger than Y is*. As soon as we perceive in what particular sense it is possible for a mother to be younger than her child is, the semanticist takes us back to the semantic reading: 'So you see that *X is younger than Y* in the last case too. It makes no difference how you substitute. You just had a preconceived belief about the biological process of ageing.' Of course it makes no difference how we substitute, *given a use where it makes no difference*! Within the common use of words, however, it does not make sense to say that *X* is younger than *Y* is, if *X* is the mother of *Y*.

Let us distinguish between the following three facts:

(i) Given the common criteria of age, the last sentence does not express how *X is younger than Y is*, as the other sentences do: it is nonsensical.

(ii) Given medical criteria of age, there is a common element of meaning in the sentences: all the sentences express how *X is younger than Y is* in the sense given by some medical method of measurement.

(iii) Given the semantic reading, the sentences share a common paraphrase: *X is younger than Y is*.

Here we have three distinct facts which Lyons confuses in his notion of semantic meaning. The root of this confusion is the tendency to *trust* a semantic paraphrase while *shutting one's eyes* to the different techniques of use – including the one which is implicitly taken for granted.

6.4 DOES USE FOLLOW FROM MEANING?

Consider the phrase 'to open a book'. Why do we call a certain action an *opening* of a book? Is it because the word 'open' has a literal meaning which applies to that action, besides applying to actions such as the openings of, wounds, doors, boxes, hands, taps, bottles and eyes?[1]

Suppose that I witness the blasting of a road tunnel through a mountain: is there a literal meaning of the word 'open' which determines whether this activity constitutes an opening? Does the sentence 'The road builders are opening the mountain' *describe* the activity that I witness? Of course, it is a tempting description and one which we may find appropriate.

Suppose that I walk up to one of the workers because I want to know when the mountain will be opened, but when I ask 'When will this mountain be opened?', he surprises me by saying 'It is already opened. Don't you see that we have already done the first blast over here, beneath the ledge!' It turns out that these workers actually use the expression 'to open a mountain', but use it to refer to the first blast and not to the last one, which was the sense that had struck me: opening a mountain, in their sense, is akin to a surgeon opening a wound.

It is important to notice that their use of the word *may* strike me as completely incomprehensible: 'How can you call this mountain opened? You have hardly *started* to open it! If it's open, it's open, and then I can walk right through it. You have merely done a blast.' The question is: what can make me accept the worker's use of the word? Some alleged literal meaning of the word 'open'? What helps me is likening the first blast with a surgeon's opening of a wound. It is the concrete similarity to a particular *use* of the word that can make me prepared to apply it to the first blast.

Similarly, the first use of the word that struck me (in which the mountain is opened through the last blast) has a certain likeness to the activity that we describe as opening a door.

The meaning of the word 'open' does not *determine its applications in advance*. We have *learnt to apply it* to particular activities. Its meaning is this determinate application, this use. If this use is expanded to include the blasting of tunnels as well, that is not because the extended use is concealed in the meaning of the word. It is because *we actually* determine a new way of using the word in connection with this activity – a new use that might be *caused* by the fact that it resembles, in certain respects, other already established uses. Thus if the use of a word expands, it is because we determine a way of expanding it. The actual application of the word, not some postulated previous (potential) applicability, is what is fundamental.

Why did I not accept the worker's use of the word, according to which the mountain was already opened by the first blast? Why did I object: 'If it's open, it's open, and then I can walk right through it'? The answer is that I used the word according to *other* rules, that is, I applied criteria according to which the mountain was not yet opened. Why did I accept his use later on? Because I was taught to apply the word as the worker did. Comparing the first blast with the opening of a wound was a way to *preparing myself* for using the word as the worker did.

It may seem a bit odd to imagine that the tunnel builders use the word 'open' to refer to the first blast, since the purpose of blasting a tunnel is to make it possible to pass through the mountain. But perhaps this use was established by geologists, and was only later extended to the blasting of tunnels. This application of the word 'open' is clearly a contingent fact: we have to *learn* that it is in this way that one *happens* to talk about opening mountains.

A third way of talking about opened mountains can be imagined in connection with mining. Within this use, a mountain is said to be opened by the blast that takes the miners to the metalliferous vein. This use of the word 'open' is clearly similar to its use in the sentence 'The jar is open'.

Why do we not say that we open a *teapot* when we lift off the lid, but say that we open a *jar* when we perform a very similar action? First of all, there are no logical *reasons* why we do not speak of opening teapots, just as there are no reasons why we actually do not use the expression 'to open a mountain' in the ways we have imagined here. It is simply a *fact* concerning our present use of the word 'open'. Secondly, this fact may have *causes*. One such cause could be that when we talk about opening things containing foodstuffs, the fact that this opening makes the foodstuff accessible is a central feature, and this is not the point of lifting the lid off of a teapot.

The central feature in the use of the expression 'to open a door', on the other hand, is in many cases the possibility of *passing through* the doorway. But to open a door means different things when the opening is done for the purpose of letting in fresh air and when it is done for the purpose of letting in a person.

I offer these examples in order to show that there are no general rules by which the use of words is determined in advance. I am trying to show that the various uses of a word do not follow from a common literal meaning. There are no general criteria for 'opening things' which apply to the opening of books, doors, wounds, eyes and mountains. Each one of these uses consists in the application of *particular* criteria. When I applied the word to the activity of tunnel-building, I did not apply some *general* criteria for the expression 'to open *something*' to find that these criteria were met. I invented *new* criteria on the basis of a likeness to the opening of doors, but I found that these were not the criteria which were applied by the workers. Comparing certain aspects of the activity of tunnel-building with the opening of wounds, prepared me for the particular criteria applied by the workers.

Am I saying, then, that there is *a multitude* of criteria that make us use the word 'open' in a multitude of ways? No, the diversified uses of a word do not follow from a diversified set of rules. There are no criteria *independent* of the action of opening a door that can make me say about that action, that it constitutes an opening. To know what it is to open a door so as to let someone in or so as to let fresh air in, is a prerequisite to understanding the meaning of the word in these two senses. There are not two autonomous meanings that *will make me* apply the word to these two actions if I happen to encounter them. In order to apply the word to these actions, I must *already* be familiar with the application of the word to them or to similar actions. The word is not applicable 'in advance.' To learn the meaning of the word 'open' as it occurs in the sentence 'The door is open' is to learn how to *actually* apply the word to the action of opening doors.

If this is the case, how can we explain the use of a word? *Ulti-*

mately, the use of a word is not an explainable phenomenon.[2] The use of a word, as a practice, is a logically fundamental fact. If, by the word 'criteria' (or 'rules'), we mean something that is *independent* of, or *prior* to, the actual use of the word 'open', then this use has no criteria. My way of speaking about criteria here is just a way of *focusing* on features of different uses of the word 'open'.

6.5 MEANING IS NOT GROUNDED IN LINGUISTIC STRUCTURE

The idea that the application of a word is determined in advance by its literal meaning, as discussed above, reappears in connection with sentences. The intuitive idea seems to be that there are general linguistic mechanisms of literal meaning in the form of rules of sentence composition. The sentence 'My mother is younger than I am', for instance, is supposed to express the literal meaning that the speaker's mother is younger than the speaker is – *because the sentence is formulated or composed such as it is.*

> It is an assumption standard in linguistic semantics that semantic theory must give an account of the compositional nature of sentence meaning, of the way in which the interpretation of a sentence is dependent on the interpretation of the words of that sentence and the structural relations which hold between those words. (Kempson 1977: 28)

This much is true: we are sometimes tempted to say that we *hear* that the sentence 'My mother is younger than I am' is formulated so as to express the meaning that *the speaker's mother is younger than the speaker is*, and that the sentence 'The mountain is open' is formulated so as to express the meaning that *the mountain is open*. In these cases we are somehow *satisfied* with the repetitions and the paraphrases of the semantic reading.

To claim that the composition of words expresses that *the speaker's mother is younger than the speaker is*, is simply to repeat the sentence, however seductively. What we must ask is this: according to which criteria is the mother said to be younger than her child, according to which use of the expression 'age'? Someone might suggest that Donald Davidson's (1967) attempt, for example, to apply Alfred Tarski's theory of truth on natural language solves this problem, since such a theory seems to *specify* the conditions in the world that I am asking about.

In truth-conditional semantics, the meaning of the sentence 'John's mother is younger than John is' might be explained by specifying that the sentence is true if and only if *there exists an individual X and an individual Y, such that X is the mother of Y, and Y is John, and X is younger than Y*. But that specification is just the paraphrase of the semantic reading that we have found problematic!

The truth-conditions are expressed by precisely those paraphrases of the semantic reading which I have tried to show are problematic. *Truth-conditional semantics is just the idea of a formalized semantic reading.*

One and the same sentence 'Bill is younger than John is' can mean a variety of things; it can, if you like, have a variety of truth-conditions. What determines these different truth-conditions is a variety of techniques for establishing age. One notion of age is determined by the number of years that have passed since birth. Other notions can be determined by facts about the liver, facts about the heart, or the brain, or the teeth, or by all of these medical facts taken together. The truth, and even the meaningfulness, of a sentence of this form will depend on which one of these techniques for establishing age that is being employed.

It might be objected that it was never Davidson's intention to *clarify* the conditions under which an individual sentence is true, but merely to account for the *systematic effects* of words on the meaning of sentences in a language as a whole.

I do not deny the observation that meaning varies systematically with the words that build up sentences and with the syntactic structure of sentences. But notice that when a semanticist varies the composition of sentences, he produces sentences that have different uses in our language. Are these different uses explainable as *consequences* of the different compositions of sentences? It is the other way around. The *impression* of a compositional nature of meaning is a consequence of the method of comparing sentences with distinct uses from the point of view of their linguistic analysis. Truth-conditional semantics treats *effects* of linguistically based methods of observation as the *inherent nature* of literal meaning.[3]

6.6 CONCLUDING REMARKS

The notion of conversational implicature presupposes an identification of literal meaning. This identification is accomplished in practice through the semantic reading, which is a method of paraphrasing sentences. In truth-conditional semantics one assumes the possibility of deriving these semantic paraphrases in a formal manner as a theory of meaning for natural languages.

I have tried to show that these means of specifying literal meaning, or truth-conditions, are *just* standardized paraphrases which, if they are themselves meaningful, have their meanings determined within particular uses. A paraphrase such as *snow is white* is not only *used* to specify meaning according to Quine's (1951) distinction between use and mention. The meaning of a semantic paraphrase is above all *determined* within an actual use of the paraphrase; a practical method. But the idea behind the semantic employment of paraphrases is that meaning is determined by *general formal rules* within a linguistic system. Thus one result of this investigation is that the semantic project *contains* and *conceals* precisely that from which it claims detachment and, finally, which it would like to see explained in collaboration with other disciplines such as pragmatics and psychology: the uses of language.

The pragmatic observation that language users often 'mean more than what they actually say' is contingent upon the employment of the semantic reading that I have questioned above. I will now enter into an investigation of this alleged pragmatic phenomenon as it is explained by the theory of conversational implicature.

7
The Pragmatic Notion of Order

7.1 THE CONCEPTUAL POSSIBILITY OF A REVERSED ORDER OF EVENTS

Grice's fourth sub-maxim of Manner – be orderly – states that participants of a conversation should recount events in the order in which they happened. We should not say 'Charles saw a lion and opened his eyes' but 'Charles opened his eyes and saw a lion.' It seems to me, however, that this maxim contains an oversimplified notion of the order of events.

Does the statement 'A boy went to the bus terminal and bought a ticket' describe *two* events? Did the boy perform two actions when he went to the bus terminal and bought a ticket? It is true that the action of going to a bus terminal, *in general*, is not the same action as the action of buying a ticket. But it is also true that someone who goes to the bus terminal and buys a ticket, does not first go to the terminal as someone who is *not* going to buy a ticket, and then buys a ticket as someone who has *not* gone to the terminal to buy a ticket.

The problem here is of course whether we should read the word 'and' as the conjunction of propositional logic. A careful logician such as Quine, for example, would perhaps claim that such a reading would be a mistaken formalization of 'and' as it occurs in sentences such as 'Bill went to the library and borrowed a book'. Pragmatists, on the other hand, find the sub-maxim 'be orderly' motivated by the fact that it *allows* semantics to treat 'and' formally as a conjunction, even in sentences of the kind exemplified:

> He [the semanticist] need not claim that there are two words *and* in English, one meaning simply that both conjuncts are true, the other having the same meaning plus a notion of sequentiality.

> For the sequentiality, the 'and then' sense of *and* in sentences like [*Alfred went to the store and bought some whisky*], is simply a standard implicature due to the fourth sub-maxim of Manner, which provides a pragmatic overlay on the semantic content of *and* wherever descriptions of two events, which might be sequentially ordered, are conjoined. (Levinson 1983: 108)

The possibility of applying the sub-maxim 'be orderly' on sentences like 'Alfred went to the store and bought some whisky' presupposes an external and sequential order of separate events. Let us look more closely at this presupposition.

If someone orders me to 'Wash the dishes first and then vacuum the living room,' I can easily disobey this command in the sense that I can reverse the order of execution and begin by vacuuming the living room. The reversed order of execution is possible and counts as a specific violation of the command. But what is the reverse order of execution in connection with the command 'Go to the bus terminal and buy a ticket'? To buy a ticket from a friend and then go to the bus terminal? But that is not the reverse order of execution: I was not commanded to go to the bus terminal first and then buy a ticket in any way I see fit, for instance from a friend. I was commanded to buy the ticket at the bus terminal.

Suppose that I go to the bus terminal, that I buy a ticket there, and then go to the terminal again without buying a ticket. Can we not conceive of that as being a reversed execution of the command? No, this action consists in obeying the command exactly as it was described. My going to the terminal after having obeyed the command has nothing to do with the command and cannot be thought of as a transgression of it.

In the cases where the sub-maxim 'be orderly' is supposed to apply, it seems clear that there is no sequential order of separate events. The action that we describe as 'to go the bus terminal and buy a ticket' does not consist of two externally related actions: *it is one unique action* even though, of course, we might discern two essential *aspects* of the action. In these cases, the word 'and' is not used to relate two distinct actions in a sequential order: it is used to express a *third* type of action which is *not* built up by the other two and their sequential order.

What these facts show is that the meaning of a sentence such as 'A boy went to the bus terminal and bought a ticket' is not a function of its composition. The application of the sentence is not determined by the meaning of its constituents, the compositional structure 'p&q', and the sub-maxim 'be orderly'.

The state of affairs in which a boy went to the bus terminal and bought a ticket is not built up from the state of affairs in which a boy went to the bus terminal and the state of affairs in which a (this) boy bought a ticket. Yet the idea that meaning is a function of the way sentences are composed presupposes such a combinatorial architecture of states of affairs. In such cases as these, it is evident that the alleged combinatorial structure of states of affairs is a projection of the structure of the propositional calculus onto reality.

That the reversed order of execution is inconceivable shows that the action of going to the bus terminal and buying a ticket does not consist of the sum of two externally related actions. Hence we can talk about *one* action with an *internal* order of before and after.

7.2 HOW ORDER IN LANGUAGE IS DETERMINED

Let us continue the investigation of the sub-maxim 'be orderly'. In the foregoing section I questioned the idea of an external order of events that is presupposed in the sub-maxim. But it is evident that the sub-maxim also presupposes a notion of an order *in language*: it would otherwise not make sense to talk about an ordered *recounting* of events. Yet it seems to me that it is precisely this order in language that the maxim of order is supposed to *introduce*! Observe how Levinson comments on this matter:

> ... perhaps the most important of the sub-maxims of Manner is the fourth, 'be orderly'. For this can be used to explain the oddity of . . .:
>
> The lone ranger rode into the sunset and jumped on his horse
>
> This violates our expectation that events are recounted in the order in which they happened. But it is just because participants in conversation may be expected to observe the sub-maxim 'be orderly' that we have that expectation. (Levinson 1983: 108)

This is a paradox. If we find the sentence that Levinson exemplifies odd because of an *expectation* that events are recounted in the order in which they happened, that presupposes that we know what it *means* to recount events in the order in which they happened, which in turn presupposes that we already know the 'and then' sense of 'and' that is meant to be *introduced* by the sub-maxim 'be orderly'.

It is probably assumed that there is an independent physical (or formal and sequential) order in language, and that it is this order that the sub-maxim presupposes. But the maxims are supposed to specify rational conduct, and how can it be more rational to place the description of the first event before the description of the latter event (in some alleged self-evident sense of *before*)? There is no reason why we should not express the action of going to the bus terminal and buying a ticket by saying 'To buy a ticket and go to the bus terminal.' It all depends on what we might call *the rule of use* of the expression 'to buy a ticket and go to the bus terminal'.

We could imagine a language that was different from ours in this respect. Would it be correct to maintain that the users of this language report events in a reversed order? As I see it, this claim presupposes the rule of use of *our* language, the order in our language. These persons could just as well claim that *we* report events in a reversed order. So the question is: what does the sub-maxim 'be orderly' prescribe?

Distinguish between three facts: (i) the temporal order of events; (ii) the temporal (or spatial) order of sub-sentences; (iii) the rules of use. Given these distinctions we can perhaps say that the language we have imagined expresses the temporal order of events through the reversed temporal (or spatial) order of sub-sentences – *and that this is due to the rules of use of that language*. What represents or expresses the temporal order of events in that language, then, is not the temporal (or spatial) order of sub-sentences *by itself*. What is essential is the rules of use.

Compare the state of affairs of a boy going to the bus terminal and buying a ticket with a written text. How should you represent this state of affairs orderly in speech? (There are systems of writing in which one reads from right to left.) Which aspect of the state of affairs should you represent first in speech if someone told you to report it orderly? Of course it is true that the boy *began* by walking to the terminal and *thereafter* bought the ticket (this is the internal order of the action of going to the bus terminal to buy a ticket). But *you* are not going to buy a ticket; you are going to represent the state of affairs in speech. As long as the rule of use is undetermined, it does not make sense to require an ordered reading of the state of affairs. Of course it might be tempting to describe the first part of the activity first, but that way of describing the action does not express an 'and then' sense if this way of reporting is not established as *the way* of expressing that order within the action.

Is the maxim 'be orderly' what I am calling 'a rule of use'? It cannot be: since it is the rule of use that determines the notion of order in language, such a rule cannot consist of the statement that we should report events in an orderly fashion. That it is impossible for the rule of use to have such a form is shown by the possibility of different forms of ordered recountings of events. What tempts the pragmatist to perceive a recounting of events that starts with the first event as being *the* ordered recounting of events, is probably the fact that this happens to be the form of expression in our language, together with the simple iconic character of this form.

It is not the fact that the temporal order of events is reflected in the corresponding temporal order in the recounting that expresses the order of events. What is essential is the *rule* that this is how we (happen to) recount events. The recounting is orderly if it is an instance of the established way of recounting events. Only against the background of the established way of using 'and' does it make sense to say that someone describes an action in an orderly fashion, or in a reversed order (and here, 'in a reversed order' means *in a nonsensical way!*) *The sub-maxim 'be orderly' presupposes that use of the word 'and' which the maxim is presumed to determine.*

7.3 CAN THERE BE AN INDEPENDENTLY DEFINED NOTION OF THE ORDER IN LANGUAGE?

Perhaps someone might think that a way out of this circularity would be to restate the sub-maxim with the aid of an independently defined notion of order.[1]

Imagine a kind of nonsense poetry that one reads in both directions. The instruction 'Read orderly' or 'Read in a reversed order' could be given to a reader of this poetry, where the notion of order is defined in terms of the left-right distinction. Does this mean that the two ways of reading poems of this kind are based on, or specified by, an independently defined notion of order? Is the applied notion of order *really* independent of the practice of reading this kind of poetry in both directions? Let us distinguish between two kinds of facts:

(i) On a *particular occasion* a person reads poems from right to left. The explanation of this fact can be that he has been instructed to 'Read from right to left' (perhaps this instruction is printed together with the poem).

(ii) There exists a *practice* of reading from right to left.

We are tempted to think that since the fact that a person reads from right to left on a particular occasion can be explained by the fact that he has been instructed to do so, it is also possible to explain the reading from right to left *in general* as a following of such an instruction: in each case where someone reads poetry from right to left, this fact is explainable by the fact that he is following the rule 'Read from right to left' (explicitly or implicitly given). I want to question this generalized explanation.

Is the reversed reading of this kind of imagined nonsense poetry *based* on, or *specified* by, the rule 'Read from right to left'? It is, of course, true that if someone commands me to read according to this rule, I will read from right to left. But what is it that makes it possible for me to follow the rule? Is it my knowing the general distinction between right and left? The application of this general distinction might be undetermined in this particular case: should I read from right to left in the sense of pronouncing words backwards, or in the sense of reading the last word of a sentence first, though pronouncing it normally? And note that someone who has learnt to read only in the sense of recognizing words as we recognize faces would not understand what it means to read a word from right to left (nor from left to right). The technique of reading a word in a particular direction presupposes the technique of pronouncing parts of words. But even in this case, given the technique of pronouncing words from left to right, it is not clear how words should be pronounced from right to left. How should the sequence of letters 'ng', or 'th', be read from right to left, and how should the letter 'a' in the word 'same' be pronounced? The general distinction between right and left does not contain an answer to these questions; they must be settled through the establishing of a particular way of reading from right to left. We must make a *decision* in connection with the invention of a particular technique of reading.

The instruction 'Read from right to left' gives us a problem: what does it mean to read from right to left? We can imagine all kinds of solutions to this problem: the general distinction between left and right can only function as a *general guideline* to the invention of different techniques of reading.

What makes it possible for me to follow the rule 'Read from right to left,' then, is the particular technique of reading from right to left that I have learnt and that I have learnt as *the way* of reading from right to left. So when we explain a *particular instance* of reading from right to left by reference to the rule, the determination of this rule by this technique of reading is already taken for granted. Consequently, the technique of reading cannot be explained or reconstructed on the basis of the rule, since the rule is determined in connection with that particular technique of reading.[2]

7.4 THE DIFFERENCE BETWEEN EXPLAINING PARTICULAR ACTS OF LANGUAGE USE AND EXPLAINING THE PHENOMENON OF LANGUAGE USE IN GENERAL

The aim of Grice's maxims is, of course, to ground the use of language in general in pragmatic principles, playing an explanatory role:

> Grice's suggestion is that there is a set of over-arching assumptions guiding the conduct of conversation. These arise, it seems, from basic rational considerations and may be formulated as guidelines for the efficient and effective use of language in conversations to further co-operative ends. (Levinson 1983: 101)

I have tried to show that the rule 'Read from right to left' cannot guide or specify a way of reading in general, since the distinction between left and right does not determine the nature of this reading in advance. Unless the rule is explained in terms of a particular technique of reading, in terms of a particular practice of following the rule, the rule cannot guide a reader of our imagined kind of poetry on a particular occasion. There is an essential circularity between the rule and the following of the rule, an internal relation that must be established, normally through a training or a decision.

We can indeed explain a *particular case* of a certain kind of action (e.g. reading a nonsense poem from right to left), by saying that the subject is following a certain rule. But the rule cannot explain this kind of action *in general*, because the attempt at such an explanation would leave the rule undetermined. If rules presuppose the following of rules for their determination, then rules cannot explain activities in general, since the activity is essentially involved in the determination of the rule.

7.5 CONCLUDING REMARKS

A pragmatic justification of the sub-maxim 'be orderly' is that it allows semantics to give a uniform, formal interpretation of the word 'and' of natural language. The fact that 'and' often is used in a way that clearly deviates from the conjunction of propositional logic is explained by adding the pragmatic maxim as a kind of supplement to the semantic rules of sentence-meaning.

The application of the sub-maxim 'be orderly' to the ordinary use of 'Charles opened his eyes and saw a lion' is a simple and clear example of the way in which pragmatic theory works. Pragmatics is an attempt to save semantic approaches to language from facts of language use which conspicuously expose the untenability of these approaches. Pragmatic theory thus makes it possible to continue traditional theorizing by placing the language-system in a hidden zone beneath an overlay of pragmatic principles: pragmatics protects semantics.

8

General Principles of Rationality as a Basis for Language Use

8.1 THE SEMANTIC READING IS RESPONSIBLE FOR THE PHENOMENON OF 'MEANING MORE THAN WE ACTUALLY SAY'

That general principles of rationality cannot function as a basis for the practices of language use remains to be shown through an investigation of the more important maxims of Quantity, Quality and Relevance. Let us begin by considering an example from Levinson, quoted in a previous section:

A: Where's Bill?
B: There's a yellow VW outside Sue's house

According to Levinson, '*B*'s contribution, taken literally, fails to answer *A*'s question, and thus seems to violate at least the maxims of Quantity and Relevance.' It is evident that the semantic reading is applied as a first step in the identification of this feature of the exemplified conversation. The idea that *B*'s contribution fails to answer *A*'s question at the level of literal meaning is caused by thinking that when *A* apprehends *B*'s answer, *he primarily apprehends it as the semanticist reads it*, as though *A* were not *primarily* in the situation of wondering where Bill might be, and asking *B* to assist him! I consider this a most remarkable way of perceiving the conversation; it shows how deeply rooted the semantic reading is in linguistic theorizing.

Here, as in the case of deixis, we encounter a typical pragmatic problem: we know that *B*'s contribution is a perfect answer to

A's question, but this fact cannot be accounted for with traditional semantic techniques.

How does pragmatics solve the problem of how we nevertheless understand B's contribution as a satisfactory answer to A's question? Levinson claims that we *interpret* B's contribution 'by assuming that it is in fact cooperative, and then asking ourselves what possible connection there could be between the location of Bill and the location of a yellow VW, and thus arrive at the suggestion (which B effectively conveys) that, if Bill has a yellow VW, he may be in Sue's house.'

Observe that B's contribution to the conversation contains *evidence* for the location of Bill. According to Levinson, we arrive at that fact as a pragmatic inference that is based on the assumption that B's contribution is in fact relevant and informative. But suppose that A and B know that Bill does not know Sue, that Bill does not have a yellow VW, nor even a driver's licence: in that case, B's contribution would not be easily interpretable as a satisfactory answer to A's question. Why not? Because in such a situation, B's contribution does not contain evidence for the location of Bill.

But wait! According to Levinson, that B's contribution contains evidence for the location of Bill was an *inference* at which we arrived by *assuming* that his contribution was in fact cooperative: we asked ourselves for a possible connection between the location of Bill and the location of a yellow VW, and thus arrived at the suggestion that, if Bill has a yellow VW, he may be in Sue's house. But clearly, that connection is *not* arrived at as a result of a reasoning. Either the situation *is* such that a yellow VW outside Sue's house constitutes evidence for Bill's being there, or the situation *is not* such.

We can imagine a situation in which a yellow VW outside Sue's house constitutes *conclusive* evidence for Bill's being there. In that situation, B could answer A's question simply by saying: 'Bill is at Sue's house.' This would be a literally relevant answer to A's question, since it contains 'Bill' as a subject and since it straightforwardly describes the location of Bill. Yet what possible connection is there between the location of a yellow VW and the location of Bill? How is it possible for B to *say* more than the state of affairs that he *sees*? (It is Bill's *VW* he sees, not *Bill*.)

There is a relation of *being evidence for*, but that relation immediately vanishes if we paraphrase the situation in the way in which the semantic reading paraphrases *B*'s contribution to the conversation. Furthermore, if the presence of a yellow VW outside Sue's house constitutes evidence for Bill's being there, why should *B*'s utterance not be *immediately* recognizable as a statement of that evidence? It is not difficult to see that the semantic reading is the factor which makes pragmatics blind to the fact that *B is straightforwardly answering A's question by stating the evidence.*

Let us sum up: that a yellow VW outside Sue's house constitutes evidence for Bill's being there *is a fact of the situation*. If it is a fact of the situation that the yellow VW outside Sue's house constitutes this kind of evidence, then it is also *a fact of A's and B's conversation* that *B* states this evidence.

Levinson treats the conversation about the location of Bill as a novel sequence of utterances, the underlying connection of which must be inferred through pragmatic reasoning. He does not treat the conversation as a *typical example* of the familiar language game of answering someone by informing him of the evidence. The semantic reading dissolves the language game into unconnected utterances, thereby necessitating the theory of implicatures: '... if the implicatures were not constructed on the basis of the assumption of relevance, many adjacent utterances in conversation would appear quite unconnected' (Levinson 1983: 107).

I would like to make the reverse claim: if the semantic reading were not applied to typical examples of language use, conversations would not *appear* as sequences of quite unconnected utterances.

8.2 THE MAXIMS OF QUANTITY AND RELEVANCE, AND THE LANGUAGE GAME OF EVIDENCE

It is significant that Levinson does not use the notion of evidence in his reconstruction of the pragmatic inference, but instead speaks loosely of 'asking ourselves what possible connection there could be between the location of Bill and the location of a yellow VW.' It is significant because it is the exclusion of this notion that makes it seem necessary to *infer* the status of *B*'s contribution. Given the notion of evidence, it is *an immediate fact* that *B* states the evidence for Bill's being at Sue's house. And the exclusion of the notion of evidence is caused by the semantic reading, which favours the notion of states of affairs.

That we have a notion of evidence means that we have language games where we answer questions by stating the evidence for the state of affairs that the question concerns. We master these language games. Compare the following two language games:

1. *The language game of states of affairs*
A: Where is Sarah?
B: Sarah is in the kitchen. (B *has heard sounds from the kitchen*)

2. *The language game of evidence*
A: Where is Sarah?
B: I heard sounds from the kitchen.

The difference between the two language games is this: in the first game, the evidence is conclusive (depending upon further facts of the situation which we can imagine), and is used by B to verify and state that Sarah is in the kitchen. In the second game, the evidence is not conclusive, and is expressed by B. In the first game, B answers by giving A the location of Sarah. In the second game, B answers by giving A the evidence for the location of Sarah.

Very young children may master the first language game, but not the second one. It is important to note that such a child cannot answer questions about the evidence. Think about how a small child can turn completely silent when we ask: 'How do you know that?'. We tend to think that the child suddenly turns contrary since he just recently told us 'Sarah is in the kitchen' with such certainty.

Suppose that a young child asks, 'Where is Sarah?', and that an adult answers, 'I heard sounds from the kitchen.' If the child does not master the language game of evidence, then he will probably not run into the kitchen (unless he does so simply because he heard the word 'kitchen' being uttered). If the child himself had heard the sounds from the kitchen, he would most probably have run there: in *this* way, he does master the evidence. Still, the child does not find anything 'relevant' in our verbally informing him that we have heard sounds from the kitchen. What is it that changes when the child grows older and reacts differently to this kind of answer?

The child we are imagining does not understand the point of our talk about sounds from the kitchen: he does not react. We must *make* him react: 'Come, let's see if she is there' (said while leading the child to the kitchen). We teach the child a reaction, not only to sounds from the kitchen, but also to the *information* that sounds come from the kitchen – and, in this way, we teach the child the use of evidence. We teach the child the nature of our answer (a statement of the evidence) by training him to react in a particular way to the answer. We teach the child to *use* the answer as evidence for the location of Sarah. And of course, we teach the child not only a reaction, but also the normal *result* of this reaction: that of finding Sarah on the basis of the evidence.

So what is it that makes it possible for the child to understand the answer given in the language game of evidence? It is our training him in the mastery of this language game. Consequently, before the child can apprehend the answer as relevant and informative, he must master the language game. *The relevance of the answer is contingent on the fact that it belongs to a mastered language game.*

In order to apprehend 'I heard sounds from the kitchen' as a relevant and informative answer, one must perceive that answer as a move in the language game of evidence. Observe that I did not say 'as a *relevant and informative* move in the language game.' That the answer can be described as relevant and informative is contingent on the fact that it is a move in the language game. But then language game (2) is logically more basic than the notions of relevance and information. Therefore, the maxims of Relevance and Quantity cannot ground language game (2).

8.3 THE MAXIM OF RELEVANCE AND THE USE OF A SIMPLE IMPERATIVE

Let us investigate a simpler example. According to Levinson (who symbolizes the implicature '+>'), the maxim of Relevance is

> responsible for producing a large range of standard implicatures. For example, where possible imperatives will be interpreted as relevant to the present interaction, and thus as requests to implement some action at the present time. Hence:
>
> Pass the salt
> +> pass the salt now
>
> (Levinson 1983: 107)

Semantically read, the sentence 'Pass the salt' does not indicate *when* the passing of salt should be done. Nevertheless, it is a fact that we understand an utterance of the sentence as communicating the speaker's wish that the passing should be done immediately. This takes the form of a typical pragmatic problem, and the solution which Levinson proposes is based on the maxim of Relevance: assuming that the utterance is in fact relevant, it must have some connection with the present interaction. Since we are sitting at the dinner table where it is not uncommon that someone would like some salt, we infer that the speaker wants salt now, and that he implicates that the passing of salt should be done immediately.

So now it seems as though we have explained or rationally based a procedure which we can witness almost daily: we immediately pass the salt to someone who says 'Pass the salt, please.' It seems to me, however, that this account presents things in a *logically reversed order*. For why is it relevant to utter 'Pass the salt' only if we want the salt immediately, and why is the salt actually passed immediately? Is it not for the obvious reason that this is the use that we have been taught? A pragmatist would have to object: 'No, the use of the imperative is not logically primary; it is rationally *based*. To ask for salt long before you (perhaps will) need it is irrational, just as it is irrational to ask for salt long after you needed it. Any intelligent being can calculate the only rational use of the imperative: that of requesting salt *the moment you want it passed*.'

Let us imagine that our values change: our lives become more and more directed toward maximizing our pleasure of, for instance, food. Together with this new way of living, the following language game develops: we pass salt about a minute after the request 'Pass the salt' is made. During this minute, the speaker is preoccupied with building up an even stronger need for salt (this is a part of the game) and, when the salt finally is passed, the pleasure is *total*! A pragmatist who considers language use to be based on general, rational principles, must describe the imagined situation like this: 'In the case described above, the new values must be incorporated in our rational considerations concerning cooperative conduct. In this case, it is obviously cooperative to wait a minute before passing the salt, in order to make it possible for the speaker to intensify his desire. The speaker must assume that we can infer that this is what he intends in making the utterance.'

I think that we can make the following objection to the pragmatist's description. A person who is not familiar with the (imagined) practice of passing salt after a minute will be irritated and confused if the salt is not passed to him immediately – *regardless* of (or perhaps *because* of!) his hedonistic tendencies. Only a person who is familiar with the practice will wait for the salt, confident that it will be passed, while intensifying his desire. That is the rule, the pattern of acting for which he is trained.

The fact that a group of people develops hedonistic values, and habits of intensifying desires before satisfying them, does not make it rational to pass the salt after a minute. If this way of acting does not belong to a well-known practice, then it will be treated as an irrational and contrary kind of behaviour. Particular activities must be established 'one by one': they do not follow from a system of values or from a system of general principles of rationality. The children within the imagined group must be trained to wait for *certain* requested things, trained to intensify *certain* needs – as a rule, as something completely natural after *certain* requests. They must be trained to appreciate *certain* things by being trained in *certain* practices.

The use of imperatives such as 'Pass the salt' cannot be explained or reconstructed on the basis of general maxims of rationality. The use that *happens* to belong to our practices in language is *fundamental*.

8.4 THE MAXIM OF QUALITY AND THE IDEA OF A GENERAL NOTION OF TRUTH

I have tried to show that the maxims of Relevance and of Quantity cannot function as a basis for language use, since the notion of the relevance and of the informativeness of utterances rests on those familiar uses of language that pragmatics purports to explain. We now turn to the maxim of Quality, the maxim which says: 'try to make your contribution one that is true.' This maxim obviously presupposes a notion of the *truth* of utterances. Can the maxim of Quality form a basis for language use, or does the notion of truth too rest on the practices of language use?

The problem is: how can I *try* to make my contribution one that is true? How do I know whether an utterance is true or not? Suppose that someone asks me what time it is, or asks me if a certain friend of mine is younger than I am, or suppose that he asks me if the door to my flat is open. How am I able to judge the truth of possible answers such as:

> It is 9:45 a.m.
> He is older than I am
> The door is closed

In order to *be able* to try to make utterances that are true, I must, of course, already know under what conditions it is true to say that 'the time is 9:45 a.m.,' or to say that 'someone is older than I am,' or to say that 'the door to my flat is closed.' Pragmatics assumes that the explanation of that ability offered by semantics is not based on facts concerning language use. According to pragmatics, I can try to make my contribution to verbal exchanges true because the language that I know contains a general notion of the truth of sentences. But these ideas have already been dealt with in the investigation of literal meaning, and in the investigation of time in Part I. By investigating the *concepts* of time, age and openness, I showed that:

(i) The notion of the truth of the sentence 'The sun rose at 5:50 a.m.' cannot be conceived of as a property of language as a system isolated from the concrete use of clocks and time-expressions.

(ii) The notion of the truth of sentences containing the expression 'younger than' cannot be abstracted from the techniques of establishing age. What it means to say that someone is younger than someone else is, is determined within a use, within an employed practice of determining age.

(iii) The notion of the truth of the imagined sentence 'The mountain is open' is not a calculable property of the sentence; it does not follow from the way the sentence is linguistically built up from meaningful components. The meaning of the sentence is determined by the way in which we in fact decide to use it. (I imagined three uses of the sentence.)

(iv) The compositional nature of the meaning of the time-expression '21:45' is an effect that arises in a linguistic procedure of observation that takes meaning – *as determined by use* – for granted.

The result of these investigations, then, is that *the distinction between truth and falsity exists only against the background of the practices of language use*. And if the notion of truth rests on the various uses of language, then these forms of use cannot be explained or reconstructed on the basis of the maxim of Quality.

How, then, does the command 'Speak truthfully!' work? Are my investigations in opposition to the obvious fact that we sometimes *do* command people to speak truthfully? What my investigations are intended to show is that such a command cannot be conceived of as a tacit basis for language use in general. The command is used only in certain *exceptional* situations, for instance, when someone can be suspected of lying. But in order to be *able* to give a truthful time-report, for example, the speaker must already master the normal way in which we report time by means of clocks.[1]

The fact that we can command a person to be relevant, informative or truthful *on certain particular occasions* (and thereby actually affect his conduct) cannot be generalized to form a basis for the practices of language use. On the contrary, such commands work only against the background of the mastered practices of language use.

8.5 THE NOTIONS OF RATIONALITY AND COOPERATION CANNOT GROUND OUR CONDUCT

Let us finally investigate the most general notions that occur in Grice's theory; the notions of rationality and cooperation. Concerning the rational basis for the conversational implicatures, Levinson claims the following: 'The sources of this species of pragmatic inference can be shown to lie outside the organization of language, in some general principles for co-operative interaction...' (Levinson 1983: 97).

A little later, he elucidates what he means by an example of garage work:

> But what is the source of these maxims of conversational behaviour? Are they conventional rules that we learn as we learn, say, table manners? Grice suggests that the maxims are in fact not arbitrary conventions, but rather describe rational means for conducting co-operative exchanges. If this is so, we could

expect them to govern aspects of non-linguistic behaviour too, and indeed they seem to do so. Consider, for example, a situation in which A and B are fixing a car. If the maxim of Quality is interpreted as the injunction to produce non-spurious or sincere acts . . ., B would fail to comply with this if, when asked for brake fluid, he knowingly passes A the oil, or when asked to tighten up the bolts on the steering column he merely pretends to do so. Similarly, A would fail to observe the maxim of Quantity, the injunction to make one's contribution in the right proportion, if, when B needs three bolts, he purposely passes him only one, or alternatively passes him 300. Likewise with Relevance: if B wants three bolts, he wants them *now* not half an hour later. . . . In each of these cases the behaviour falls short of some natural notion of full co-operation, because it violates one or another of the non-verbal analogues of the maxims of conversation. This suggests that the maxims do indeed derive from general considerations of rationality applicable to all kinds of co-operative exchanges, and if so they ought in addition to have universal application . . . (Levinson 1983: 103)

I agree with Levinson that *B*'s behaviour is irrational and uncooperative. But on the basis of what do we say that his behaviour is uncooperative? On the basis of the fact that it violates general maxims of cooperation? That is evidently what Levinson claims, and also what the theory of conversational implicature demands in order to avoid the kind of circularity that I have tried to disclose.

Levinson seems to argue like this: since *B*'s behaviour can be described as a *violation* of the general principle 'Be cooperative,' the conduct that we expect from *B* can analogously be described as a *following* of that principle. But how is it possible to follow such a principle? Would not the most helpful, cooperative and rational person in the world fail to follow this principle if he did not know anything about the fixing of cars, about the use of bolts, about brake fluid, about oil, or about the tightening of bolts?

I suppose that someone might object: 'In order for a person to be cooperative in a garage, he must of course know what a bolt is, what oil is, and he must know how to tighten bolts. But it is equally clear that a person does not become cooperative just because of his having this knowledge. So it seems necessary to add something to his knowledge of garage work in order to account for the cooperative way of applying that knowledge. What we have to add is evidently the maxims specifying cooperative conduct.'

To a certain extent, I can agree with what this objection states. A person who masters an activity need not perform this activity as one generally does, and when he does not, we do claim that his behaviour is irrational and uncooperative: a child refuses to pass the salt, or passes the salt incredibly slowly; a mechanic pretends to do what his superior asks him to do. What I do *not* agree with, however, is the idea that this conduct is irrational and uncooperative in some *general* sense of rationality and cooperation. Neither do I agree with the view that the *normal* way of interacting in a garage 'derives from general considerations of rationality applicable to all kinds of co-operative exchanges.'

Imagine that a mechanic decides to be uncooperative, perhaps because of his low salary. His superior notes this and starts to supervise his conduct as much as possible. Whenever the mechanic behaves uncooperatively, his superior exclaims, 'Try to be a little cooperative!', which immediately affects the mechanic's work: he actually begins to tighten up the bolts. How can the exclamation affect his conduct? How does the mechanic know what his superior demands of him?

That is no problem: as a trained mechanic, he knows exactly what he ought to do, exactly what his superior demands of him. If the mechanic has a problem, it is rather that of being *uncooperative*. The possibility of being uncooperative is not a *general* possibility of violating or simply not caring about abstract principles. It is a *concrete* possibility of distorting details of an extremely well-known activity. To be uncooperative requires – this is a logical remark – *ingenuity* together with a *mastery* of the normal way of performing the particular activity that is being distorted.

If the superior's command 'Be cooperative' has any function, it cannot be that of reminding the mechanic about a general principle that should *guide* his conduct. Its function is rather that of *preventing* the mechanic from doing something most particular, namely, inventing actions that, in a subtle way, differ from those of normal garage work and that cause problems in the garage. *The cooperative–uncooperative distinction thus centres around an established way of doing things.*

As a commentary on the objection stated above, I would like to say the following: in order for *this* mechanic to apply his knowledge in a cooperative manner, it is true that his superior must be in the vicinity, commanding him to work cooperatively. But this command, 'Be cooperative,' is not tacitly followed in the practice of collaborating in a garage *in general*. The command merely explains why *this* particular mechanic actually tightens up the bolts on *this* particular occasion.

It is possible to command the mechanic to 'Be cooperative' only because he is a trained mechanic, only because he is closely familiar with the activity that he deliberately distorts. *It is the established practice that gives content to the notion of cooperation.*

Let us discuss a related idea; the idea of a rational and efficient way of reaching a goal. Given a way of doing things, a way of repairing cars, for example, certain actions work in an obstructive way, while some are simply unrelated to repairing the car. Other actions, on the other hand, work in an efficient way and are clearly connected with the repairing of the car. This fact makes it tempting to try to explicate rationally this overall way of repairing cars as being that way of combining elementary mechanical actions which most efficiently leads to the goal of having the car repaired. That idea seems to be a basic intuition behind Grice's theory:

> Our talk exchanges do not normally consist of a succession of disconnected remarks, and would not be rational if they did. They are characteristically, to some degree at least, cooperative efforts; and each participant recognizes in them, to some extent, a common purpose or set of purposes, or at least a mutually accepted direction.... We might then formulate a rough general principle which participants will be expected (ceteris paribus) to observe, namely: Make your conversational contribution such as is required, at the stage at which it occurs, by the accepted purpose or direction of the talk exchange in which you are engaged. One might label this the *Cooperative Principle*. (Grice 1975: 45)

Grice's way of thinking consists in abstracting components of activities (to make an utterance in a conversation, to tighten up a bolt in a garage, etc.) from the overall activities to which these component activities belong. He then tries to *reconstruct* the overall activity (to discuss where Sarah might be, to repair a car, etc.) as the result of tacit goal-oriented considerations.

Consider a young and inexperienced mechanic: he might have a fantastic talent for tightening bolts without therewith having any idea of how to repair a car. He might be useful in a garage, but only to a very limited extent. As soon as he attempts to perform some 'goal-oriented' action, the result is criticized: 'No, not now!,' 'Do only what you are told to do!'. We might say that his superiors' reactions show that they have the ability to judge that the young mechanic's actions will not lead to the goal in an efficient and rational way. But how can they have such an ability? Would it not be possible to invent a new way of repairing cars in which the young mechanic's actions are steps toward the goal? And what is the content of the superiors' reaction? Is it to rule out the efficiency of the mechanic's actions *in general*? They might be most efficient actions within a hitherto unknown way of repairing cars. Think of the different methods of assembling cars that are employed by different manufacturers!

The young mechanic's superiors criticize his attempts as obstructions to an *established* way of repairing cars. That is the only way that it makes sense to criticize him. The superiors' ability to criticize the young mechanic's conduct is not based on general notions of rationality and cooperation. It is based on their mastery of the particular method of repairing cars that is employed in that particular garage. Given that particular way of repairing cars, certain actions can be judged as obstructive, others as effective.

The content of the word 'rational' is determined by the particular way of doing things that we (at that moment of judgement) use as a norm: the word 'rational' is merely a way of bringing out the normative role played by a particular way of doing things. The notions of rationality and cooperation *cannot* – and the reason for this is logical – have the *basic* conduct-grounding function imagined for them in Grice's theory.

I am not denying that there are cases where a person *can* be said to consider the most efficient and rational way of reaching a certain goal *without* using an already existing method as a norm. Perhaps he is developing a new method of assembling cars. But even here the idea of 'a rational and efficient way of reaching the goal' is determined by very particular standards, namely, certain other goals that can often be defined quite exactly. Normally, the method must be tried out in practice, modified, tested again, and finally a decision must be made. This is *not* the kind of case to which Grice's theory is applied. Recall the language game of evidence, or the case of asking for some salt at the dinner table, or the case of passing the brake fluid to a co-worker who needs it: established practices that give content to the notions of rationality and cooperation that figure in Grice's attempt to provide these practices with a rational foundation.

8.6 MEANING-INFERENCES

My investigation might seem to be in opposition to the obvious fact that we sometimes do ponder the meaning of utterances. What we succeed in hearing, remembering, or understanding of an utterance might present itself as absurd, false, irrelevant or trivial. In cases such as these – where the meaning of utterances *actually* troubles us – we do indeed reason in a way that bears similarities to the pragmatically postulated process of interpretation: 'No, he couldn't have meant that, he must know that to be false'; 'He couldn't have meant to express such a trivial observation,' etc. If we succeed, these reasonings lead to results which are very similar to the pragmatically postulated implicature: 'Of course, he must have meant the opposite'; 'He must have meant it as an expression of evidence'; 'He must have meant it as a refusal,' etc.

What I have tried to show is that these judgements rest on forms of language use. But that result does not contain a claim that problems of meaning never occur in the practice of language use. Contained in that result, however, is the logical insight that these problems of meaning can only be *exceptions*; more or less trivial cases of obscure speech, misunderstandings, mishearings or misrememberings; cases which Grice's theory does not treat.

Language users do, at times, infer what a speaker means by a particular utterance, but only in those exceptional cases where the utterance *actually* happens to be, in one way or another, unclear, strange, not understood. If these reasonings lead to clarity, then what becomes clear is which familiar move the speaker made (or tried to make) in which familiar language game.

From a logical point of view, a problem of meaning cannot be a basic problem implicit in the use of language in general: it can only be an exceptional problem that an individual has and perhaps solves on a particular and exceptional occasion. *It is the instinctive application of the semantic reading that makes problems of meaning seem inherent in the forms of language use.* Therefore, I conclude: there are no informal considerations of meaning implicit in the use of language. Considerations of what meaning a speaker intends to communicate are explicit and exceptional.

8.7 CONCLUDING REMARKS

The idea that the basic examples of language use that pragmatics studies should be examples of a general phenomenon of 'meaning more than what is actually said' is, according to this investigation, an *illusion* caused by the employment of the semantic reading. The theory of conversational implicature is better described as an attempt to *save* the idea of literal meaning from facts of language use that clearly disclose the untenability of that idea.

Grice's theory of conversational implicature takes for granted that general maxims of rationality and cooperation can be conduct-grounding. My investigation has been concentrated on this concept of human action. The results can be summed up in the following proposition: the general notions of relevance, information, truth, cooperation and rationality are contingent upon the particular forms of language use that the theory attempts to explain or reconstruct in terms of those notions. Grice's theory suffers from a circularity that is concealed by the general philosophical readiness to accept oversimplifications as fundamental notions.

9
Formal Pragmatics

9.1 ON SOME PREVAILING MOTIVES FOR FORMALIZATION

In order to defend the attempt to formalize pragmatic theory, Gerald Gazdar invokes, in his introduction to *Pragmatics: Implicature, Presupposition and Logical Form*, a quotation from Kleene:

> Anyone who doubts the advantages of symbols (in their proper place) is invited to solve the equation $x^2 + 3x - 2 = 0$ by completing the square (as taught in high school), *but* doing all the work in words. We start him off by stating the equation in words: The square of the unknown, increased by three times the unknown, and diminished by two, is equal to zero.
> Anyone who doubts that *apt* choices of mathematical symbolism have played a major role in the modern development of mathematics and science is invited to multiply 416 by 144, *but* doing all the manipulations in Roman numerals. His problem is thus to multiply CDXVI by CXLIV. (Kleene as quoted by Gazdar 1979: 5)

Gazdar's reference to this statement of Kleene's is highly questionable as a defence of applying formal techniques in pragmatic theory, and what makes it questionable is that Kleene is talking about *mathematics* which, from the very outset, *is* a use of symbols. The content of the mathematical concepts square, sum, times, equal to, etc., is *determined* within the calculi of mathematics. So if there is any content in Kleene's verbal expression of the equation above, that content is given by the mathematical practice of solving equations in the symbolism. The symbolic expression of the equation not only has *advantages* over the verbal one: the invention of the symbolism *is* the invention of that mathematical content which the words 'The square of the unknown, increased by three times the unknown, and diminished by two, is equal to zero' hint at *to those who are already familiar with the use of the mathematical symbolism*.

Gazdar seems to view mathematical-logical symbolisms as an ideal of precision and rigour:

> Formalization both allows and demands standards of rigour and exactitude in the expression of theories, standards which are beyond the scope of informal statements... Formalization of theoretical claims allows their properties to be critically studied by the powerful techniques made available by mathematical logic. (Gazdar 1979: 8–9)

This enthusiasm over formal methods is based on a very simple picture of mathematics:

1. There exist mathematical notions or intuitions.

2. The invention of a mathematical symbolism is the invention of a system of notation that expresses these notions *with precision*.

When mathematics is conceived of through this picture, it might seem justified to invent formalisms in other areas too, as a way of making 'informal intuitions' precise. But if mathematical notions are determined within the technique of use of the mathematical symbolism,[1] then it cannot be said that mathematical symbolisms have certain advantages over words in expressing these notions. To invent a mathematical symbolism (which is not just an alternative notation) is to invent new mathematical concepts, and not to define exactly prior ideas about, for example, the way our language works. Thus the widespread tendency to formalize linguistic theories in an attempt to give an exact formulation to prior informal intuitions is better described as a tendency to *invent mathematical calculi* that are *inspired* by certain formal features of the linguistic perspective on language.

9.2 THE CALCULUS CONCEPTION OF THE PROCESS OF LANGUAGE USE

Hans Kamp expresses the view that we cannot claim that contemporary, formal linguistic theories describe psychologically real processes. His reason for this view seems to be that we do not as yet know enough about the workings of the human mind to interpret and answer questions about the psychological truthfulness of the proposed theories:

> ... at the present time it isn't even possible to make an educated guess at how long it will be before we acquire the degree of understanding of the workings of the human mind necessary to give these questions a coherent interpretation that will render them at least in principle amenable to definite answers. Yet, until then nothing much can be said about the psychological adequacy of linguistic theories. (Kamp 1979: 283)

A claim that Kamp *does* attach to formal theories, however, is that those theories that in a distant future turn out to be 'psychologically true,' will be theories of computational processes:

> It is my conjecture that if we ever reach this level of sophistication we will find there to be not just one computation procedure for each (unambiguous) expression, but in general a multiplicity of such procedures – different computations being used by different speakers of the same language and perhaps even by the same speaker on different occasions. (Kamp 1979: 283–284)

Even though Kamp modestly denies having formulated *the true* linguistic theory, he is still having most definite pretensions regarding the *general formal methodology* typical of modern linguistics. This is evident from the way in which Kamp talks about 'different computations being used by different speakers,' thus taking for granted that speakers perform calculations. This general claim will be the concern of this chapter.

9.3 ON THE FORMAL TREATMENT OF SCALAR IMPLICATURES

Certain implicatures, so-called generalized Quantity implicatures, are easily formalized, as is their defeasibility[2] in various contexts. I will discuss a formal treatment of scalar implicatures, a subclass of generalized Quantity implicatures, and try to show that the *applicability* of the formal theory does not justify taking it as an *hypothesis* of the way language works, or of the way language users 'process language.'

To get an idea of the phenomenon of scalar implicatures, consider the following pragmatically framed observations, contingent on the semantic reading:[3]

(i) The semantic content of the sentence 'Charles has three children' is that Charles has three children in a sense that is compatible with his having four or more children. But the sentence is generally used to implicate that Charles does not have more than three children.

(ii) The semantic content of the sentence 'Some of the boys went to the party' does not contradict that perhaps all of the boys went to the party. But the sentence is generally used to implicate that *not all* (nor most or many) of the boys went to the party (as far as the speaker knows).

(iii) The semantic content of the sentence 'Charles often bicycles to work' does not contradict that Charles perhaps always bicycles to work, but the sentence is generally used to implicate that Charles does *not always* bicycle to work.

The above seem to be observations of a quite general phenomenon: by choosing a certain expression – 'some' in example (ii) – among an ordered set of linguistic alternates – all, most, many, some, few – the speaker implicates pragmatically that the informatively stronger expressions of this set do not hold (as far as the speaker knows). Implicatures that arise in this way are called scalar implicatures.

Now let us look at the defeasibility of scalar implicatures. Although scalar implicatures are regularly tied to linguistic items such as 'some', 'three', or 'often', they can be suspended in certain surroundings, as the following observations show:

(i) In the utterance: 'Some, if not all, of the boys went to the party,' the scalar implicature due to 'some' is suspended by the *if*-clause.

(ii) The scalar implicature is similarly suspended by the last clause in the following utterance: 'Some of the boys went to the party, in fact probably all.'

(iii) Scalar (and other) implicatures also disappear when the context of utterance is such that the implicature could not have been intended by the speaker. Suppose that a university course will be postponed if the number of students is below five. As an answer to the question 'Do you have the requisite number of students?', the utterance 'Yes, I have five students all right' will not implicate that the number of students is *exactly* five.

Let us finally look at the attempt to formalize the scalar implicatures and their defeasibility. The formalization I will discuss is basically that of Gazdar (1979) as presented by Levinson (1983). The idea behind the formalization is simple. It consists in laying down ordered sets of linguistic alternates, such as the scale:

<all, most, many, some, few>

together with a rule which states that if a speaker uses one of these alternates in an assertion, then he implicates the negations of the informatively stronger assertions containing the stronger items in the scale. (Example: if I assert that *some* of the boys went to the party, I implicate that *not all* of the boys went to the party.)

Since scalar implicatures are defeasible, this rule will sometimes make wrong predictions. Therefore, Gazdar makes a distinction between *potential* implicatures and *actual* implicatures, and he identifies the implicatures generated by the above rule with the potential implicatures. This distinction requires a rule that specifies the way in which potential implicatures become actual implicatures. The rule that Gazdar suggests introduces a sequential order according to which:

(i) the entailments,
(ii) the clausal implicatures,[4]
(iii) the scalar implicatures, and
(iv) the presuppositions

of an utterance are added to the context (the context being interpreted in a way that we need not go into). The essential constraint imposed on this process of incrementation is consistency with previously added elements of meaning. I leave it to Levinson to summarize and exemplify Gazdar's rule:

> Thus on Gazdar's account *defeasibility* is captured by making implicatures acceptable only if they are consistent with entailments and other implicatures that have priority. Note that this mechanism also explains why implicatures may be overtly denied as in (156):
>
>> (156) Some of my best friends are drug-addicts, in fact probably all
>
> for the entailments of the second clause, being added to the context first, will cancel the implicature due to *some*. (Levinson 1983: 143)

9.4 REMARKS ON THE APPLICABILITY OF THE FORMAL THEORY

What I have sketched above is a quite successful formalization of scalar implicatures. We may of course expect that counter-examples will be found requiring more or less radical modifications of the theory. Finding those counter-examples is a task of formal pragmatics, not of this investigation. What I will do is to look more closely at the *relation* between the formal theory and simple facts of our actual language use. Let us discuss an utterance of:

Some, if not all, of the boys went to the party.

Applying the above calculus, 'some' gives rise to the scalar implicature that *not all* of the boys went to the party. The clause 'if not all', on the other hand, gives rise to the clausal implicature that *possibly all* of the boys went to the party. This results in a contradiction which is resolved by the incrementation rule: the clausal implicature is added to the context first, and the scalar implicature is cancelled. *This is all performed in the applied calculus.*

My question is: is it possible *in principle* to conceive of actual language use as the tacit application of such a calculus? A pragmatist might reply: 'If I use the expression "some" in asserting that some of the boys went to the party, it is a fact that I mean that *not all* of the boys went to the party. That fact is captured in the formal calculus. If I add to this assertion the clause "if not all", the content of my utterance is changed in a certain manner. That fact too is captured in the calculus. It is quite obvious that expressions such as "all", "some" and "if not all" in our actual language function in a way that is reflected in the applied calculus. You cannot deny that the clause "if not all" of actual language works in a way that is at least *roughly* captured in the formalization.'

What the pragmatist forgets in making this objection is that he is *already* applying formal points of view in the description of the 'actual' use of 'some' and 'if not all'. He applies the way of conceiving language that a formal pragmatist applies when he *sets out* to formalize some part of language use, or when he *evaluates* a particular formalization in the light of new cases. *The pragmatist treats the formal perspective as the universal perspective on language use.*

As I have pointed out a number of times, this perspective is a linguistically based method of observing language. What the formalization above captures is not some actual effect of the clause 'if not all' on the meaning of the utterance 'Some, if not all, of the boys went to the party.' The formalization captures an effect which is contingent upon the imposed method of comparing the meaning of the pair of sentences:

Some of the boys went to the party
Some, if not all, of the boys went to the party,

from the point of view of their linguistic analysis. It is indeed a fact that the two sentences differ in meaning in a way that can be linked to certain linguistically identified parts of them (i.e., to 'some' and 'if not all'). The observed difference in meaning *can* be captured in a formal calculus, *since the observation, from the very outset, is an application of formal points of view.*

Formal methods are applied already in the 'informal' preparatory work of *observing* the facts that are to be formalized, and also in the subsequent work of *testing* the formalization against new cases. The formalized features are features that are already determined by the formal techniques applied to language – formally *or* informally. The idea that expressions such as 'all', 'some' and 'if not all' have a function in our actual language which is basically similar to their function in a formal calculus is therefore an illusion.

Consider a simple non-linguistic example. Suppose that two chess players decide that if one of them moves his queen to a certain square, say F4, then they will exchange certain rules that govern the moves of the pieces: they will switch to another game. The leading chess player might get a most unfortunate position in the new game, although the pieces are distributed as they were before the game-changing move was made. As I see it, the new roles that the pieces get, and the new sense of the distribution of pieces on the chessboard, are determined by the new rules, that is, by the new game.

Now suppose that someone claims that the normal sense of the distribution of pieces is *cancelled* or *modified* by moving the queen to F4. Suppose that he claims that that particular move constitutes an *operation* on the sense of the distribution.

To describe the game-changing move in this way is to *compare* distinct games, and to *focus* on the move which makes the players switch games (or rules). I am not opposed to the expression 'sense-modifying move,' but I want to draw attention to the fact this move is not an operation that determines the new sense of the distribution. The new sense is determined by the new use of the chess pieces, by the new game played with them after the imagined move. The move we imagine is nothing other than the visible signpost at which the players change games.

Let us apply this to the formalization of scalar implicatures. I am not questioning the utility of Gazdar's theory as a formal calculus: it might have important applications in, for example, expert systems. But the theory is systematically erroneous and misleading *if taken as an explication of the way in which meaning is determined in language*. The addition of a clause such as 'if not all' to a sentence such as 'Some of the boys went to the party' is not associated with an operation that determines a new meaning. *The clause is simply what linguistically distinguishes two sentences with distinct uses*. No active role can be ascribed to this clause in the actual process of determining meaning.[5]

9.5 CONCLUDING REMARKS

Our language and its formal representation in linguistics are two distinct phenomena. A formal representation of language does not have to resemble language in order to be applicable on language. The applicability of formal calculi to language does not demonstrate that actual language use is based on tacit calculations.

Part III

Speech Acts

10
The Speaker–Hearer Scheme of Communication

10.1 TWO APPROACHES TO MEANING AND COMMUNICATION

In Part I and II, I have dealt with a conception of meaning and communication in which semantics is taken to be a description of the *core* of meaning in language, a core that is assumed to have a logically primary function in relation to the use of language in communication. The parameters one varies in the study of meaning are determined by linguistic techniques of analysis, and meaning is constructed as a property of sentences. In this way of thinking, the interest in communication stems from the fact that semantic methods have certain conspicuous limitations when applied to ordinary language. The most prominent feature of language that exhibits these limitations is, of course, indexicality. The path one takes out of this dilemma, the path that leads to a particular notion of language use and a particular notion of pragmatics, is to claim that the semantic techniques have a perfectly general application *to a limited dimension of meaning*: the semantic dimension of sentence-meaning. Pragmatics becomes a supplementary discipline which studies language use as an *external* property of language. Pragmatics becomes a study of language in a wider setting, involving speakers, hearers, contexts, and so forth. In this wider setting, sentence-meaning is conceived of as one component within a logically secondary dimension of meaning, the dimension of speaker-meaning.

This view of the core of meaning as firmly based within a semantic system and in logical priority to use has been questioned by philosophers and linguists who would rather see the notion of meaning explained in terms of the communication-intentions of speakers. This conflict is described by P. F. Strawson (1990: 91) as a conflict between 'theorists of formal semantics' and 'theorists of communication-intention.'[1]

I suppose that many readers are inclined to object to my previous investigations of the notions of deixis and conversational implicature, on the grounds that my results are valid only for a conception of pragmatics based on the formal semantics approach to meaning. Perhaps these readers would refer to the following statement from John R. Searle:

> The unit of linguistic communication is not, as has generally been supposed, the symbol, word or sentence, or even the token of the symbol, word or sentence, but rather the production or issuance of the symbol or word or sentence in the performance of the speech act... More precisely, the production or issuance of a sentence token under certain conditions is a speech act, and speech acts... are the basic or minimal units of linguistic communication. (Searle 1969: 16)

Here it seems as though speech–act theorists actually are doing what I so far have criticized pragmatists for *not* doing: namely, examining language use in its own right. In Part I, for instance, I questioned pragmatists' tendency to define the problems of indexicality by comparing sentences that were isolated from their uses by being represented in writing. Speech–act theorists do not seem to follow this procedure. They rather study linguistic expressions as they are used by speakers in communication with hearers.

Still, from the point of view of this investigation, the speech–act approach to language use does not seem essentially different from the approach I have examined in Part I and II. Whether one claims that 'addressee' represents a semantic meaning of 'you', or attempts to explain conventional meaning as a regularity in speaker-meanings, my remarks about the notion of deixis are valid. Why? Because theorists of communication-intention, such as Paul Grice and Stephen Schiffer, *do make a distinction* between a constant, conventional meaning of the word 'you', and a varying speaker-meaning communicated on particular occasions of use.[2] Furthermore, no matter whether one claims that the conventional meaning of sentences is grounded in a linguistic system, or should be explained ultimately in terms of speaker-meanings, my remarks about literal meaning and conversational implicature are valid.

Why? Because theorists of communication-intention *do make a distinction* between a constant conventional meaning of the sentence 'I heard sounds coming from the kitchen', and a varying speaker-meaning communicated on particular occasions of use. The technique of semantic reading is basic to both approaches, as is the conception of how literal meaning, in interaction with maxims of conversation, contributes to the complete message communicated in a situation of use.

The difference between the two approaches concerns the way in which the notion of meaning ultimately should be defined; but my investigation concerns what these two approaches have in common, namely, the following way of schematizing meaning and communication:

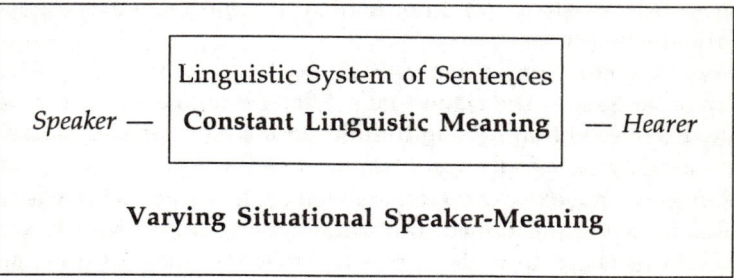

My investigation of pragmatics concerns the *structure* of this scheme, especially the distinction between a constant linguistic meaning and a varying situational speaker-meaning. This structure of the scheme reflects a dogmatic attitude to the techniques and notions of logic and linguistics – an attitude that is common to theorists of formal semantics and theorists of communication-intention.

Paul Grice may not be a formal semanticist, yet one of his aims in 'Logic and Conversation' is to make it possible to conceive of the meanings of 'and', 'or', 'not', 'if . . . then' and 'all' in natural language according to their formal-logical readings. Stephen Schiffer may take Grice's analysis of meaning in terms of communication-intentions as a point of departure in his book *Meaning*. Still, one of his aims in that book is to give a justification for the idea that there exists conventional meanings of linguistic expressions.

Theorists of communication-intention seem to me to be even more concerned with formal semantic notions and techniques than formal semanticists are themselves! They seem even more concerned with preparing safe theoretical grounds for the application of formal techniques and notions onto natural language. It is this concern for semantics that gives rise to pragmatics. So we must not overestimate the difference between the two approaches to meaning and communication.

Another important similarity between the two approaches is the attitude toward syntactic structure as a *discovery* about human language made by linguistics. It is not uncommon that philosophers of language start their inquiries by stating that they find the notion of syntactic structure relatively unproblematic and that they can safely presuppose such a notion in their inquiries. See, for instance, how John R. Searle begins his analysis of promises: 'As our inquiry is semantical rather than syntactical, I shall simply assume the existence of grammatically well-formed sentences' (Searle 1969: 56).

This is a most pervasive attitude to linguistics in the philosophy of language. The claim that artificial intelligence researchers have discovered that human thinking has a computational nature is currently discussed in philosophy, but the corresponding idea that linguists have discovered that language has a syntactic structure is almost never questioned. But to talk about grammatically well-formed sentences, and about the syntactic structure of these sentences, is to talk about features of certain formal systems, namely, the syntactic *representations* of languages in linguistics.

The notion of syntax, in its modern formal sense, belongs to the linguistic method of representing languages within formal systems. Syntactic structure is not an abstract property of a human utterance: it is the structure of a corresponding formula in a formal system (and this structure is determined by the derivation of the formula according to the syntactic rules). One reason why it is so tempting to confuse language with its formal syntactic representation in linguistics is that words in written texts are typographically identical with the primitive symbols of the formal system of syntax. The sentences in a newspaper, for instance, can be treated as formulas in a syntactic calculus *as they stand*. This fact creates the illusion that syntactic structure can be directly *observed* in human languages.[3]

Theorists of formal semantics and theorists of communication-intention, then, do not differ essentially in their reliance on linguistic and formal-logical notions and techniques. This reliance is reflected in the common distinction between a constant linguistic meaning, and a varying situational speaker-meaning. So before beginning the investigation of speech–act theory, let it be established that my previous investigations concern features *common* to both approaches to the notions of meaning and communication.

10.2   THE SPEAKER-HEARER SCHEME

What constitutes an act of communication? It seems that such an act requires at least two persons where one person has the function of being a *speaker* and the other person has the function of being a *hearer*. Consider how this simple scheme of the situation of communicating with someone is developed in John R. Searle's attempt at formulating the basic problems of the philosophy of language:

> How is it possible that when a speaker stands before a hearer and emits an acoustic blast such remarkable things occur as: the speaker means something; the sounds he emits mean something; the hearer understands what is meant; the speaker makes a statement, asks a question, or gives an order? (Searle 1969: 3)

The speaker–hearer scheme is employed by Searle to represent basic, indisputable facts of language use:

> ... we do know that people communicate, that they do say things and sometimes mean what they say, that they are, on occasion at least, understood, that they ask questions, issue orders, make promises, and give apologies, that people's utterances do relate to the world in ways we can describe by characterizing the utterances as being true or false or meaningless, stupid, exaggerated or what-not. (Searle 1969: 3)

However, his employment of the scheme makes certain philosophical problems look not only natural, but even incontestable:

> And if these things do happen it follows that it is possible for them to happen, and if it is possible for them to happen it ought to be possible to pose and answer the questions which examine that possibility. (Searle 1969: 3)

At first sight, it appears as pure stupidity to question this scheme and the philosophical questions to which it gives rise. As Searle himself says, we *do know* that people communicate, that they say things, that they mean things, that they are understood, that they ask questions and make promises. But these facts are not only known to everybody, but also *reported* daily:

> We communicate more often now
> He said something very important
> What he meant was that...
> I understood him perfectly this time
> I think he referred to your mother
> He promised to come tomorrow

But if we *communicate* these facts daily, why do we not normally feel tempted to ask those philosophical questions about language that seem so obvious when we *contemplate* the facts in the philosophy of language? That question too might appear silly, since it is obvious that not every person has philosophical inclinations, and those who do do not pursue them at every moment.

I agree that apprehending philosophical problems is dependent on having philosophical inclinations, but wherein do these inclinations consist? Is it just a question of having a tendency to spend time considering facts that most people usually overlook? I agree that philosophers spend time considering facts that most people usually overlook, but what is it the philosopher does when he is considering these facts? Is the answer that he is *scrutinizing* the facts seriously, or intellectually, as seems to be the view of Noam Chomsky?

> One difficulty in the psychological sciences lies in the familiarity of the phenomena with which they deal. A certain intellectual effort is required to see how such phenomena can pose serious problems or call for intricate explanatory theories. (Chomsky 1972: 24)

I still agree, but that answer simply prompts one more question: what *kind* of intellectual effort is required to see how familiar phenomena can pose serious problems or call for intricate explanatory theories?

In this investigation, we have actually seen some examples of how philosophical problems might arise, and it is clearly not simply a matter of paying attention to familiar phenomena, or of scrutinizing obvious facts. We are dealing with a *particular way of thinking about linguistic phenomena*: remember how the problems of context-dependence and of features of conversation arose precisely because pragmatists *failed* to scrutinize facts of ordinary language use. The important thing to see is how the problems arise as a consequence of the way linguistic notions and techniques of paraphrase are applied within the activity of theorizing.

It seems to me that when Searle states the basic facts of communication, he is using the words 'speaker', 'hearer', 'say', 'mean', 'refer', 'understand' and 'promise' in a peculiar way that does not correspond to their ordinary uses. To see this, imagine that a person decides to use these words to report the speech events that he encounters during one day. We may suppose that this person will make reports of the following kind:

> At 12:45 the speaker said that...
> The speaker probably meant...
> The hearer failed to understand
> The speaker referred to the hearer's mother
> The speaker promised the hearer that...

This systematic employment of a small number of ordinary words could be described as the employment of a scheme for reporting features of occurring speech situations, 'scheme' here being understood as 'a limited number of closely related words.' Political debates might be reported in this scheme by journalists.

An important feature of the scheme in *this* sense is that the words 'speaker', 'hearer', 'say', 'mean', 'refer', 'understand' and 'promise' are used to report features of actually *occurring* speech events. When the person reports: 'The speaker congratulated the hearer,' he reports that a *particular* speaker (e.g., the person's brother) congratulated a *particular* hearer (e.g., their grandfather) on a *particular* occasion (e.g., on the grandfather's eighty-sixth birthday).

In speech–act theory, however, these words are not employed to report, for instance, that I talked to my grandfather this morning and congratulated him on his eighty-sixth birthday. Instead, the speaker–hearer scheme is employed to re-describe such events as instances of general phenomena of communication. The scheme is employed, *not* to report the event that happened this morning, but to go from that event to a general description of the event, that is, to the scheme itself. *The scheme is employed to represent the event as an instance of the scheme.*

A better way of looking at this philosophical use of 'speaker', 'hearer', 'say', 'mean', 'refer' or 'congratulate', is to see it as a *grammatically twisted* mode of use of these words: who is it that congratulates? Common answers are 'John' or 'I myself,' but in this grammatically twisted mode of use, the answer is: 'The *speaker* congratulates' (*not* the hearer). And who is it that is congratulated? Ordinary answers are 'Peter' or 'my grandfather,' but in the grammatical mode of use, the answer is: 'The *hearer* is congratulated.' In this way, my congratulating my grandfather is redescribed in the grammatical mode as an instance of the scheme, '*speakers* congratulate *hearers*.'

The speaker–hearer scheme employed in speech–act theory can, in a sense, be described as a grammatical calculus, with the words 'speaker', 'hearer', 'say', 'mean', 'refer', 'understand', 'promise', 'congratulate' and so forth, as the primitive symbols of the calculus. The philosophical problem about whether it is speakers or expressions that refer to something can be seen as a problem concerning how to design and develop this grammatical calculus.

The grammatically twisted mode of use can be of great value in philosophical investigations, since it can be employed to display facts about the use of words. Wittgenstein's 'grammatical remarks' (as he calls them himself) are good examples of such an employment of this mode of use. But in order not to deceive oneself, this mode must of course be employed *as* a grammatical mode, *as* a way of displaying facts about our use of words. However, that is *not* how this mode is employed by communication theorists. *The grammatical mode of use is employed as if it were a way of stating general empirical facts of communication.*

Searle presents as basic empirical facts 'that people communicate, that they do say things and sometimes mean what they say, that they are, on occasion at least, understood, that they ask questions, issue orders, make promises and give apologies.' Rather than formulating the basic facts of communication, however, such sentences *display* logical connections between notions of communication. 'People make promises' is a grammatical remark, as is 'Physical objects have extension.' This becomes clearer if we consider a negative grammatical remark, for example, 'Stones do not make promises.'

Having represented a series of grammatical remarks as empirical facts of communication, Searle goes on to develop the latter aspect: 'And if these things do happen, it follows that it is possible for them to happen, and if it is possible for them to happen, it ought to be possible to pose and answer the questions which examine that possibility.' By treating grammatical remarks as empirical facts of communication, Searle *constructs* the basic problems in the philosophy of language. But the problems are only grammatical constructions!

10.3 THE METHOD OF PHILOSOPHICAL ANALYSIS EMPLOYED IN SPEECH–ACT THEORY DEFINES THE NOTIONS OF COMMUNICATION IN A LOGICALLY REVERSED ORDER

In Searle's statement of the basic problems of speech–act theory, the notions of communication – 'statement', 'request', 'promise' etc. – are used as though they made sense independently of the actual *practices* of language use to which we have learnt to apply them. Speech-act theory aims at an analysis of the notions of communication which can serve as a basis for a theoretical *explanation* of the possibility of making statements, requests and promises. That explanation must not rest on, for example, actual promising as a familiar practice; a theory cannot rest on the fact which it is constructed to explain.

It is as though the speech–act theorist could know what promising is independently of his acquaintance with promising, and then use this independent notion to establish that he and other people *do* make promises, as a matter of empirical fact. I do not say that it is logically impossible for people *not* to make promises. Of course, there could be societies in which people did not make promises. But if we were to establish that as a fact of some society, the notion of promising which we would employ would rest upon our acquaintance with the actual practice of promising someone something. And if there were such societies, we could use this notion of promising to establish which societies, as a matter of empirical fact, do have the institution of making promises, and which societies do not.

The general remark that 'people make promises,' then, *presupposes* the practice which it seems to *state* as an empirical fact. That is to say, the remark can only be a way of displaying conceptual relations between the uses of words.

The making of promises is not a *realization* of an *underlying* notion of promises, to use the jargon of Searle's speech–act theory. This is, as I see it, perhaps the most essential aspect of Ludwig Wittgenstein's notion of family resemblance. It is an insight that not only sets limits to the applicability of traditional philosophical analysis, but also shows that *any* such analysis will present the analysed notion in a logically reversed order. Searle, on the other hand, gives the notion of family resemblance a less radical interpretation:

> One of the most important insights of recent work in the philosophy of language is that most non-technical concepts in ordinary language lack absolutely strict rules. The concepts of *game*, or *chair*, or *promise* do not have absolutely knockdown necessary and sufficient conditions ... But this insight into the looseness of our concepts, and its attendant jargon of 'family resemblance' should not lead us into a rejection of the very enterprise of philosophical analysis; rather the conclusion to be drawn is that certain forms of analysis, especially analysis into necessary and sufficient conditions, are likely to involve (in varying degrees) idealization of the concepts analyzed. (Searle 1969: 55)

The most important aspect of the notion of family resemblance, as I understand it, is not that the alleged necessary and sufficient conditions for a notion are loose, or vary to some degree from case to case. The point is that we do not call something a promise, or a game, or a chair, *because* this thing has certain features (no matter how loosely we specify these features). The fundamental thing is the fact that we call *this* a promise, and *this* a chair. This is a chair, but not *because* it is so and so.[4]

The method of philosophical analysis, as employed by Searle, Strawson and Grice, is the method of treating examples of use as *evidence* for a satisfactory analysis of a notion. These analyses are meant to reconstruct a *ground* for the application of a word – 'this is a promise *because* it is so and so' – although the demand for exact conformity with actual use may vary; the analysis may be conceived of as being more or less an idealization.[5] However, if the meaning of a word is its concrete use, then this meaning cannot be analysed in terms of necessary and sufficient conditions. Even conceived of as an idealization, such an analysis would represent the meaning of a word (e.g. 'promise') in a logically reversed order, since the meaning of the word is represented as being logically prior to the examples of its use; since the examples are treated merely as *data* for the analysis. The philosophical method of family resemblance, on the other hand, is the method of letting examples of actual use speak *for themselves*.

10.4 CONCLUDING REMARKS

In this investigation I disregard the differences between the 'formal semantics' approach and the 'communication-intention' approach to meaning and communication. Instead, I concentrate on what the two have in common: the distinction between a constant linguistic meaning and a varying situational speaker-meaning, a distinction which reflects a dogmatic attitude to the techniques and notions of logic and linguistics. This distinction is developed within a grammatically twisted mode of use of the notions of communication; a mode of use which is employed as if it were a way of stating the 'basic facts' about meaning and communication. I referred to the resulting philosophical notion of communication as the 'speaker-hearer scheme of communication.'

Philosophical analysis of the notions of communication, as performed by Searle, is an attempt to define certain words (e.g., 'statement', 'promise' and 'request') independently of the practices of language use to which these words belong. It would otherwise not make sense to *test* the analysis, to *search* for counter-examples to it. In Chapter 11, I will demonstrate a different kind of philosophical inquiry. Instead of seeking complicated counter-examples (which would only suggest further, modified analyses), I will investigate simple examples of linguistic practices; examples which speech-act theorists might use to illustrate their basic conceptual framework. My investigations are aimed at showing that the speech-act theoretical schematization of these examples is in conflict with concrete features of our everyday linguistic practices.

11
Speech Acts versus Language Games

11.1 JOHN R. SEARLE'S CONCEPTION OF THE PROBLEM OF COMMUNICATION AND ITS SOLUTION

The following investigation will deal only with one speech–act theory, namely, John R. Searle's theory which has become almost a standard theory of speech acts in pragmatics. I will not discuss J. L. Austin's (1962) pioneer work on speech acts, since Austin did not develop his analyses into a *theory* of meaning and language use in the sense pertinent to this investigation.

The investigation will be concerned with a feature that Searle's theory shares with most current theories of language use: actual use is conceived of as a phenomenon that supplies the theorist with *data*. Language use is conceived of as a phenomenon to *explain* or *account for* within a theory. What I wish to investigate, in other words, is the *theorizing approach* to language use; Searle's theory will be addressed insofar as it is a typical example of this approach.

As is evident from the quotations in Chapter 10, Searle's problem *is* language use conceived of as a general empirical fact. Facts such as '*this* is a promise' and '*that* is a request' are not treated by Searle as fundamental. On the contrary, such facts constitute Searle's problem. Searle's problem is to explain the possibility of communication, the possibility of the linguistic acts that constitute our talking and writing to one another.

I remarked that Searle's statement of this basic problem is a grammatical construction, a grammatically twisted mode of use, treated as though it were a way of stating general empirical facts about the use of language. However, this grammatical construction is not sufficient, I think, to make someone feel tempted to consider the problem important and real, and it is only one aspect of the way the problem arises.

The most seductive element in Searle's formulation of the problem is this: he starts out from a description of communication that represents communication as *something other* than communication:

> How is it possible that when a speaker stands before a hearer and emits an acoustic blast such remarkable things occur as: the speaker means something; the sounds he emits mean something; the hearer understands what is meant; the speaker makes a statement, asks a question, or gives an order? (Searle 1969: 3)

The problem, then, seems to be how an act of communication can occur when we perform *another* act: the act of emitting mere sounds. Searle's problem arises out of a physico-linguistic perspective: '... sentences – the sounds that come out of one's mouth or the marks that one makes on paper – are, considered in one way, just objects in the world like any other objects...' (Searle 1983: vii).

From this perspective, there is something that presents itself as a philosophical problem, namely, the fact that these physico-linguistic objects have meaning and can be used by human beings to do such remarkable things as stating facts, giving apologies, making promises, or asking questions: '... what must be added to these noises, marks, etc., in order that they should be statements, orders, etc.? What, so to speak, must be added to the physics to get the semantics?' (Searle 1986: 209).

In Searle's way of thinking, the fact that '*this* is a promise' becomes a dizzying problem, since '*this*' is interpreted, not as referring to a promise, but as referring to a physical event. The central idea behind Searle's attempt to *solve* the problem can be gathered from the following passage:

> It is only given the institution of marriage that certain forms of behaviour constitute Mr Smith's marrying Miss Jones. Similarly, it is only given the institution of baseball that certain movements by certain men constitute the Dodgers' beating the Giants 3 to 2 in eleven innings. And, at an even simpler level, it is only given the institution of money that I now have a five dollar bill in my hand. Take away the institution and all I have is a piece of paper with various gray and green markings.
>
> These 'institutions' are systems of constitutive rules. Every institutional fact is underlain by a (system of) rule(s) of the

form 'X counts as Y in context C'. Our hypothesis that speaking a language is performing acts according to constitutive rules involves us in the hypothesis that the fact that a man performed a certain speech act, e.g., made a promise, is an institutional fact. We are not, therefore, attempting to give an analysis of such facts in terms of brute facts. (Searle 1969: 51–52)

The physico-linguistic 'brute facts' with which Searle begins in the formulation of the problem are here, in the outline of the solution, embedded within what Searle calls 'institutions.' According to Searle, noises and marks on paper can be seen as instances of communication only within such institutions. The task for speech-act theory is to construct a theoretical analysis of facts embedded within institutions, an analysis of what Searle calls 'institutional facts.' The aim is to construct an hypothesis about the underlying constitutive rules of speech acts which specify how the utterance of linguistic expressions under certain conditions *counts as* performing different speech acts.

11.2 THE NOTION OF A REQUEST IS THE NOTION OF ONE MOVE WITHIN A LANGUAGE GAME

Imagine a simple language game. A parent plays with a child. The parent requests that the child pass various toys with which the child is familiar and which are present when the game is played. The basic moves within the game are these: the parent utters 'Give me the doll,' or 'Give me the green ball,' or 'Give me the tractor,' and the child reacts by passing the doll, the green ball, or the tractor. I could go on describing details about the way this game is played and about the training that is presupposed, but for the moment I leave the description as it is.

Now let us imagine how Searle's conception of the problem and its solution fits with this example. According to Searle's conception, my description of the game is the description of a philosophical problem. The game is given for us basically as a regularity among brute facts: the parent utters 'Give me the green ball' only if there is a green ball present, and the child reacts with passing the green ball if and only if the parent has uttered 'Give me the green ball.' How, according to Searle, is this regularity to be explained?

The obvious explanation for the brute regularities of language (certain human made noises tend to occur in certain states of affairs or in the presence of certain stimuli) is that the speakers of a language are engaging in a rule-governed form of intentional behaviour. The rules account for the regularities in exactly the same way that the rules of football account for the regularities in a game of football, and without the rules there seems no accounting for the regularities. (Searle 1969: 53)

Let us concentrate on the fact that when the parent utters a sentence that begins 'Pass me the . . .', the child reacts by passing a toy to the parent. Searle formulates the problem by first describing the parent's request *not* as a request, but as a kind of physico-linguistic event; thus his solution must re-introduce the request by postulating the possibility of a speaker making requests *by* emitting physico-linguistic signals, and also by postulating the possibility of a hearer *understanding* physico-linguistic events *as* the making of requests.

Searle explains this possibility by analysing the parent's utterances as embedded in the institution of requests: within this institution, the parent's utterances *count as* requests in virtue of the rules and conventions that govern the use of the expressions that the parent uses.

Why, according to Searle's explanation, does the child pass different toys to the parent? The basic answer is that the child *understands* that he is requested to do so. The child's reaction is therefore presented as a consequence of an understanding of meaning: the simple language game, with its requests and passings, is re-presented in this way of thinking as an external regularity that can be explained on the basis of a meaning analysis. The simple language game I described *is* Searle's problem, and his theoretical explanation is based on the speech-act analysis of requests.

Searle presents the child's understanding as a 'mental cause' of his passing a toy. But if it is the child's ability to understand that he is requested to pass a toy that explains why he does so, the child must of course be familiar with the notion of a request (although he cannot *say* in what this notion consists). How does a child acquire such a notion?

It is a fact that parents often do play the described game with their children. How do parents introduce children into the game?

How do they instruct the child to play his part in the game? Parents use all kinds of tricks here, but the aim is one: to *get* the child to react in a particular way to what the parent says. The child is introduced into the game by being led actively by the parent to do that which constitutes compliance with the request.

That way of acting which presents itself to Searle as being basically a brute regularity to be explained – the fact that the child reacts with passing a toy – is therefore something that the child is *trained* and *led* to do as a move within the game. If a child reacts to the request 'Give me the green ball' by passing a green ball, then the explanation, which is rather a conclusion, is this: the training has succeeded, the child has now mastered his role within the game.

The child's reaction is not a brute regularity. The child is trained to react in exactly this manner – as a move within the game. It is not a regularity in the child's external behaviour, it is an *action*, a case of following a rule within a game.

It is only when a child masters this basic language game that he can learn the notion of a request. He learns that a request is *one* of the moves within the familiar game. *The notion of a request is based on a familiarity with the complete language game as an existing practice in language.*

Complete language games with expressions such as 'Give me the . . .' or 'Open the . . .' are, in this sense, *more basic* than the use of the expression 'He requested that I . . .', which refers to one of the moves within the basic games. On the other hand, the use of the expression 'I request that you . . .' is once again a move within the basic language games, but now played with an expression which is taken from the secondary one.

The simple language game described functions *independently* of the notion of a request. The notion of a request is the notion of one of the moves within the game. The notion of a request is therefore a notion that relates to the game as an *existing practice*. It is not because the child implicitly has acquired the notion of a request that he reacts by passing toys. On the contrary, it is because the child masters the passing of toys as his move within the game, that he can learn the notion of a request. *Searle's theory presents the game in a logically reversed order.*[1]

Someone may object that Searle actually has achieved a noncircular explanation of the game, since the explanation is based on an *analysis* of the notion of request and, in the analysis, that notion is not used or presupposed. Although the details of Searle's theory will be investigated more closely in another chapter, it seems already necessary to comment on the formulation of what Searle describes as 'the essential rule.' This rule employs not the notion of a request, but the notion of a certain kind of *attempt*; the attempt to get the hearer to perform the described action. The essential rule says that a request is an utterance which, under appropriate conditions: 'counts as an attempt to get [the hearer] *H* to do [future act] *A*' (Searle 1969: 66).

It is easy to understand why Searle uses the word 'attempt' in the analysis. He conceives of the parent's move within the game as being the *complete* language game. The child's reaction is not conceived of as a part of any language game at all, but merely as an *effect* of the language game of making requests (its 'perlocutionary effect'). The child's reaction is conceived of as an effect of his understanding the parent's communicative act. And, of course, you can only *attempt* to get such a distant effect.

But this is a misuse of the word 'attempt'. That word could be used to describe the parent's actions when *training* the child to participate in the game when the parent stretches out his hand as to get something from the child, for example, or places the requested toy in the child's hand and then takes it. *That* is to attempt to get the child to pass toys (for the purpose of teaching him the game).

Once that training is brought to an end and is replaced by simply playing the game, the parent's moves within the game can no longer be described as attempts to get the child to pass toys. A request from the parent might now be described at most (and only occasionally) as an attempt to *play the game* with the child, an attempt that might fail if the child finds the game boring. But if the child actually participates in the game, then it does not make sense to describe the parent's actions as *attempts* to get the child to pass toys. If the child participates in the game, he *will* pass the toy, since that is his part in the game. And if he does not pass the toy, then he is not simply refusing to pass some toy; he is refusing to play the game.

Within the game, there are no attempts, but only the parent's requests and the child's passings. If the child does not pass the toy, then he is no longer playing the game. The notion of an 'attempt to get *H* to do *A*' is therefore not a notion of anything that goes on within the game. The notion of a request, on the other hand, is such a notion: it is a notion of one move within the complete game *as an existing practice*.

11.3   REMARKS ON THE INVESTIGATION OF THE GAME OF REQUESTING AND PASSING TOYS

I am not trying to *argue* against Searle's conception of the simple language game, the reason being that I am questioning *an entire way of thinking*: I am addressing Searle's inclination to represent facts of language use within a certain philosophical scheme. I am not presenting any new, remarkable cases which Searle has never considered before and which contradict his theory. I am dealing with exactly those simple cases that Searle himself has gone through again and again, in order to rest assured that his analysis is correct according to the traditional standards of philosophical analysis (i.e., the analysis must not be too weak or too strong, and it must not be circular). The method employed in this investigation is not the traditional method of inventing counter-examples, but that of looking more closely at the very facts about which Searle already has an elaborated conception, and looking at them in such a way that it will be possible to compare the facts of language use themselves with Searle's way of schematizing them.

When I started this section by describing a simple language game, my description of the game was not particularly detailed. But I would not say that the description was therefore incomplete: the purpose of the description was to *remind* the reader of an activity with which he is, I think, familiar from his own experience. Were I not writing a book on these problems, but discussing them with a friend, I could just as well have said: 'Remember the game you and your son played yesterday,' and then continue the investigation.

In Searle's writings too, there is a point when the reader is supposed to recall certain familiar facts, but that point is reached only after Searle has described the use of language in naturalistic terms. At that point, Searle wants his reader to remember that there is something *more* to language use: in using language we are not only emitting acoustic blasts and scratching marks on paper – we *mean* something too; we make statements, give orders and make promises. Hearers understand what we mean; they understand that we make statements, that we give orders and that we make promises.

The naturalistic context in which Searle presents these reminders has *alienated* us from our everyday way of relating to the facts to which he wants us to assent. The facts no longer present themselves as simple facts about our use of language, but as astonishing facts that need explanation. The effect is similar to that which we would get from a picture of a desolate moonscape – with two children playing in front of a small cottage.

The dizzying effect of Searle's tendency to give sudden reminders of facts that are alien to the context he has created for them gives Searle's way of thinking a certain atmosphere: we get the feeling that we are confronted with problems of *deep* importance. This atmosphere is created not only in Searle's writings, but in the writings of pragmatists and philosophers of language in general. The description which works as a background for sudden contrapuntal reminders need not employ notions from physics only. Earlier in this inquiry, we saw that notions from linguistics often have a similar function.

Searle's problem concerning the simple language game, then, arises from taking the fact that we call the parent's move a request out of its normal surroundings in the practice of the game, and placing it within a theoretical, physicalistic *representation* of those surroundings.

My investigation of the game, on the other hand, did not present the game in naturalistic terms, not even as a starting point: my remarks were intended as simple reminders of the game as it is familiar to us. I described it *as* a game, as that activity which we know from our daily lives. Parents teach their children the game by using all kinds of tricks in order to *get* the child to pass toys as his move in the game. A child can learn the word 'request' only after he has learnt the simple language game, and he learns to use the word as a name for one of the moves in the now familiar game.

What is important about my investigation is not so much the notion of a language game as the *attitude* with which this notion is employed, namely, that of wanting to remind the reader of ordinary facts that are fruitful to contrast with certain theoretical conceptions of language use.[2] It is not an aim of this investigation to show that we need a *new* theoretical notion to account for language use. We need tools that support our ability to recollect facts in their own actual surroundings in life – for the purpose of treating problematical *conceptions* in philosophy. The notion of a language game is employed here as such a tool.

11.4 THE IDEA THAT SPEECH ACTS ARE EFFECT-INDEPENDENT

My investigation of the notion of requests might seem to be contrary to a simple fact. A request which is not complied with is *still* a request; it would seem, therefore, that a request must be *independent* of the effect it has on the hearer:

> Illocutionary functions must be conceived as effect-independent. Otherwise we cannot do justice to the following fact. Even if an utterance U caused no effect in any hearer, we may adequately say both
>
> (a) that the speaker actually stated something or asked a question or made a request, etc.
>
> and
>
> (b) that U actually was a statement or a question or a request, etc. (Wetterström 1977: 8)

This idea will be investigated in light of another language game: the simple example of a baptism.[3] Imagine that a group of politically active people uses assumed names, since they have to work in secret. Let us furthermore assume that the members of the group change names each month, and that each month begins with a baptism performed by the leader of the group. Later in the month, the members of the group perform various political actions according to instructions from their leader. In the instructions, the members of the group are addressed by their assumed names, and different members are usually given different tasks to perform individually.

Let us say that it is a fact that an instruction from the leader which contains a certain name is always followed by actions performed by the member of the group who was so baptized at the beginning of the month. What kind of fact is this? And why does the leader of the group invent instructions that use precisely the names he used in the baptism?

We might say that this happens *because* of the baptism, that it is in the nature of baptisms that this should be so. But what is the nature of this 'because'? If I understand Searle, he would conceive of the use of names during one month as an *effect* of the baptism performed at the beginning of the month (a perlocutionary effect of the baptism). The members of the group witness the baptism and *understand* their leader's utterances; they understand that he determines their names in uttering what he does. The subsequent use of names is then seen as an effect of this understanding.

Let us now suppose that the baptism is *not* followed by the kind of use of names I have described. Suppose the members of the group choose tasks as they like, so that it becomes impossible to relate their actions to the names used in the instructions; or suppose the leader uses names in the instructions *other* than the names he used in the baptism. Would we still call the baptism an act of determining names? Would we call it a *baptism*? That depends on whether we still treat the group's way of performing political tasks, *as I originally described it*, as a norm; as 'the way the game should be played.'

Only if this rare way of performing the tasks is treated as an *exception* to the pattern of acting that I originally described, can we describe the baptism as a baptism, or as an act of determining names. In that case, we would say that the members of the group for some reason *ignore* the baptism in their performance of political tasks, perhaps because it wearies them to change names every month. If, on the other hand, the members of the group *should* act in this strange, capricious way, then the leader's act in the beginning of the game is *not* what we normally would call a baptism (although it might still be called 'the baptism' in the group's jargon).

But how can the act that begins the group's monthly activities depend on what happens *after* it has been performed? The dependence is not causal. I am offering a reminder of the conceptually necessary *surroundings* for what we call a baptism. I am trying to show that what we call a baptism is just one part of a wider pattern of acting.

Suppose that a member's child witnesses the baptism and is impressed by certain features of it. The child starts playing with the sentence 'I name you . . .' at home, but never *goes on* to use the names he might appear to have determined for the members of his family. What must we teach this child, in order to teach him what a baptism is? We must teach him to *continue* to use the names he has uttered, as the way to continue a first move within a wider pattern of acting. The 'because' we wondered about in the beginning of this section is therefore a logical one. The group's use of names for one month is not *caused* by the baptism at the beginning of the month. In a way, the use of names during the month is a *part of* the baptism. The subsequent use of names is essentially *involved* in what we call the baptism.

But if that is so, why would we say that a baptism has been performed even if the members of the group do not continue their political activities during that month (perhaps because they think they are under surveillance), and consequently do not continue to use the names used in the baptism? Because there is something to continue! Not continuing the political work after the baptism is to depart, at a certain phase, from a normal way of acting. That is, this situation can only be an *exception to a routine*, something that occurs on some particular occasion, but not normally: *it cannot be 'the way to play the game.'*

Now compare this fact with Searle's conception of speech acts. Searle would probably analyse the beginning move, the baptism, as a complete 'language game' in itself. The question of whether an utterance counts as a baptism or not is a question that concerns that move as isolated from the subsequent use of names. The members of the group witness the baptism and understand that their leader (i.e., the speaker) determines their names. This understanding then causes the use of names during one month.

Searle might even claim that this analysis, in a sense, does concern the subsequent use of names, since the speaker's intentions do involve the subsequent political activities, and since the members do understand that their names are determined *for* those activities during the month following the baptism. But still, he would claim that such intentions and understandings *explain* the subsequent use of names. Searle would conceive of the relation between the baptism and the subsequent use of names as being a *problem*. What I have shown is that this relation is rather the *solution*. I find a solution where Searle finds a problem: that is, the problem is a misconception. My solution is not a competing solution to Searle's problem: it *dissolves* Searle's problem.

What we refer to as 'the baptism' may be the *first* move in the group's monthly activities, but the notion of a baptism is still determined only within the *whole* pattern of acting during a month. It is only against the background of that practice that we can say that a baptism has been performed even if the members of the group call off their activities after the baptism, or choose tasks as they like.

Wetterström correctly observes that a request which is not complied with is still a request. But his conclusion that requests must therefore be conceived of as effect-independent is a mistake, since it is only as an *exception to the rule* that a request which is not complied with is still a request.

11.5 INVESTIGATION OF AN INTUITIVE JUSTIFICATION OF THE SPEECH–ACT CONCEPTION OF REQUESTS

It is possible on particular occasions to answer the question 'Why are you sending him those books?' by saying 'He requested that I do so.' Such an answer evidently draws on the notion of a request. The temptation here (the intuitive idea) is to think that we can generalize the question and its answer to cover all particular compliances with requests. In such a manner, the practice of complying with requests would be explainable in terms of the preceding speech act, that is, the request. It would then seem as though the preceding act of making a request was the 'whole' game, and the compliance with the request just an effect of the hearer's understanding of it. A regularity in language use would then seem to have been explained in terms of speech–act rules. But let us look more closely at the way such answers actually work.

In a game of chess, an absent-minded player may wonder why his opponent removes one of his pieces from the chessboard. The opponent may then explain why he does so by describing the move he had made immediately prior to removing the chess piece. Why does this explanation work? Because chess is played in that way: one moves a chess piece to a square where the opponent has one of his pieces and lifts that piece off the board.

So how does the explanation work? It works against the background of the mastered practice of playing chess. The explanation works by informing the absent-minded player of a preceding move of which he was unaware; the explanation presupposes the *practice* of playing chess, according to which the opponent's removing the piece simply belongs to the way that chess is played. The explanation cannot be extended to cover *all* cases where a chess piece is removed from the board: one who is ignorant of this fundamental feature of the playing of chess cannot understand the explanation. To teach him to play chess is, among other things, to teach him when to remove the opponent's chess pieces from the board.

In a similar way, the answer 'He requested that I do so' explains a particular act of sending books to someone, by clarifying the place this particular act has within a wider pattern of acting – a pattern with which we are all familiar. The problem can only concern a particular case, and the explanation presupposes the compliance with requests as a part of a well-known pattern of acting. The explanation removes *momentary ignorance* of the context. It is clear that such an answer cannot be generalized to explain the whole language game, or practice, of making and complying with requests.

Complying with a request can be compared with working out the sum of two numbers. Someone may wonder why I write down '62' on a piece of paper, and I answer him by saying that I am working out the sum of 29 and 33. That is an explanation of why I write down the numeral '62', but it is *not* an explanation of why $29 + 33 = 62$. (But do we not speak of explaining arithmetical rules to children? We do, but here 'explanation' means *teaching* and *training*, *not* giving theoretical explanations.)

There are therefore two mistaken ideas behind the attempt to justify the speech–act conception of the language game of requests, namely, the following:

1. The question 'Why are you doing *A*?' is generalized so as to concern *every* case in which the act *A* is performed as an act of compliance with a request. However, the question presupposes momentary ignorance of the fact that a request has been made and that the act *A*, consequently, is performed as a move within a familiar game or established pattern of acting.

2. One fails to see that the answer 'He requested that I do so' makes sense only against the background of the language game as an existing practice: the answer clarifies the status of the doing of *A* by specifying its place within this language game. The answer informs about the fact that the act in this particular case belongs to a language game where it is simply a basic fact that this is how one acts.

The question 'Why are you sending him those books?' presupposes that he who asks the question is ignorant of the fact that a request has been made. Therefore he can wonder about the cause of, or the reason for, the act. The answer 'He requested that I do so' reports a reason for the act, but this explanation is *not* an explanation of the *move of complying with a request in the game*. It is an explanation of *this particular act of sending books*.

11.6 REMARK ON THE NOTIONS OF MEANING AND UNDERSTANDING

I have already remarked that Searle uses a physicalistic representation of language use as a background for his theorizing about speech acts: 'Illocutionary acts are characteristically performed in the utterance of sounds or the making of marks' (Searle 1969: 42). This way of thinking invites the following question: 'What is the difference between *just* uttering sounds or making marks and performing an illocutionary act?' (Searle 1969: 42).

The difference that suggests itself is that when physical events are involved in the performance of illocutionary acts, they have some kind of additional property – *meaning*:

> One difference is that the sounds or marks one makes in the performance of an illocutionary act are characteristically said to *have meaning*, and a second related difference is that one is characteristically said to *mean something* by the utterance of those sounds or marks. (Searle 1969: 42–43)

And if meaning is a property that characterizes physical phenomena when they are involved in human communication, then there must exist a phenomenon of *apprehending* this additional property – *understanding*: 'The characteristic intended effect of meaning is understanding' (Searle 1969: 47).

I said that Searle's tendency to give reminders of facts that are alien to the context he has prepared for them produces the impression that we are confronted with problems of rare and deep importance. Here, Searle develops the dizzying contrast between the physical representation of language use and the recollection of requests and promises, in the invention of two *philosophical constructions* – 'meaning' and 'understanding': these philosophical notions are *not* used in ordinary circumstances.

In Searle's way of thinking, the simple fact that *this move* within *this game* is what we call a request, or a baptism, or a question, or a promise is transformed into an ethereal property of a physical event, a property that hearers can apprehend only through an equally ethereal process of understanding.

The deep importance one attaches to these two notions in the philosophy of language is an effect of considering statements, questions, requests and promises within a context which is alien to these notions. Since the language-use theorist does not take linguistic phenomena for what they are within the practices of language use, he is forced to explain how language users succeed in *understanding* non-linguistic phenomena *as* linguistic phenomena. This is, essentially, why meaning and understanding have become the two most central notions in the philosophy of language (in the work of Dummett and Davidson, for instance).

It is a result of my previous investigations that meaning and understanding are not involved in language use in the way that speech–act theorists are forced to think. In the first language game we discussed, the child passes toys simply because that is his move within the game. His reaction cannot be explained in terms of an understanding of meaning – an understanding of requests – since the notion of a request, I repeat, is a notion of one move within the complete game as an existing practice.

It must be observed that these remarks on the notions of meaning and understanding are ultimately aimed at the tendency to start out from a syntactic and often naturalistic conception of language. I am not trying to reduce language use to 'futile games with empty strings of sounds.' That the notions of meaning and understanding are so central in semantics and pragmatics is caused by the fact that *these* disciplines employ such a conception of what language use is at bottom as a starting point for theorizing. There is no genuine problem of 'how to get from the physics to the semantics.'

It must also be observed that what I have said here is not opposed to the fact that people do talk about 'understanding what someone means.' We have ordinary notions of meaning and understanding, but these notions are different from the philosophical constructions that bear the same names, and the use of these ordinary notions is limited to those exceptional cases where more or less trivial problems of communication turn up, or can be expected to turn up.[4] The reason why the use of the words 'mean' and 'understand' is limited in this way is *not* that it would be pointless to assert the trivial truth that speakers normally *mean* something, or that hearers normally *understand* utterances. Like the notions of truth and falsity, the notions of meaning and understanding are latecomers in our language: their sophisticated use is *conditioned upon* concrete practices and techniques of language use, such as the language game in §11.2, or the use of clock-machines described in Part I, §§1.4–1.5.

11.7 CONCLUDING REMARKS

It is tempting to compare the notion of speech acts with Wittgenstein's notion of language games. We are now in a position to see that this comparison is essentially wrong: speech–act theory is an attempt to *explain* language games which are conceived of as regularities. What I have called a language game, or a rule in a language game, is characterized by standing in no need of explanation. It is not a question of regularities caused by underlying linguistic mechanisms, but of established practices; familiar ways of acting. The notion of speech acts is a theoretical conception designed for the purpose of explanation. The notion of language games is not. It is designed for the purpose of description and recollection.

12

Language vs Languages and Philosophy vs Linguistics

12.1 SEARLE'S CONCEPTION OF THE RELATIONSHIP BETWEEN LANGUAGE IN GENERAL AND PARTICULAR LANGUAGES: CONVENTIONAL REALIZATION OF UNDERLYING RULES

If someone requests that I do something and expresses the request in French, I will only be confused and shrug my shoulders: I do not know French. But I still know what a request is, and I would not be confused if the request was expressed in Swedish or in English. Described in such a brief manner, this fact makes it very tempting to say that there must be a general notion of requests that *underlies* the different ways in which requests can be *expressed* in different languages. The following investigation will be concerned with this idea, and the nature of the fact that prompts it.

Searle's view is that requests and promises are normally made according to the same underlying rules in all human languages. The difference between two languages, according to his view, is to be found in the *conventional realization* of the underlying rules: the difference concerns the linguistic means that are used in the two languages as devices for indicating requests and promises. Searle illustrates this with an imaginary example:

> ... imagine that chess is played in different countries according to different conventions. Imagine, e.g., that in one country the king is represented by a big piece, in another the king is smaller than the rook. In one country the game is played on a board as we do it, in another the board is represented entirely by a sequence of numbers, one of which is assigned to any

Language vs Languages and Philosophy vs Linguistics   137

piece that 'moves' to that number. Of these different countries, we could say that they play the same game of chess according to different conventional forms. Notice, also, that the rules must be realized in some form in order that the game be playable. Something, even if it is not a material object, must represent what we call the king or the board. (Searle 1969: 39)

According to Searle, then, performing illocutionary acts in different languages is, in important respects, similar to the chess example:

> Different human languages, to the extent they are inter-translatable, can be regarded as different conventional realizations of the same underlying rules. The fact that in French one can make a promise by saying 'je promets' and in English one can make it by saying 'I promise' is a matter of convention. But the fact that an utterance of a promising device (under appropriate conditions) counts as the undertaking of an obligation is a matter of rules and not a matter of the conventions of French or English. Just as in the above example, we can translate a chess game in one country into a chess game of another because they share the same underlying rules, so we can translate utterances of one language into another because they share the same underlying rules. (Searle 1969: 39–40)

It is true that a French child and an English child, in a certain sense, learn *the same thing*: to make requests and promises.[1] And in a different sense, it is true that the two children learn *distinct things*: the one child learns French, while the other child learns English. But is it therefore correct to say that there are identical *underlying* rules of requests and promises which are *realized* in different ways through different *conventions* in different languages? Before investigating Searle's account of the relationship between language and particular languages, I must describe his notion of underlying rules more closely. In Searle's formulation of the underlying rules for promising, these rules concern the use of an expression specified merely as a *promising device*, denoted Pr. Let me give one example of the form of underlying rules, the sincerity rule:

> *Rule 4.* [Promising device] Pr is to be uttered only if [speaker] S intends to do [future act] A. (Searle 1969: 63)

The conventional realization of the underlying rules within some particular language is, if I understand Searle correctly, basically the same set of rules, but now *attached* to elements in a linguistic description of a particular language. A linguistic description of some element in French, for example, would take the place that the variable *Pr* has in the underlying rules. What kind of an account of language is this? Searle evidently thinks that he can describe the general phenomenon of language (as opposed to particular languages such as English or French) by simply *leaving out* the details that make the difference between English and French and, instead of 'I promise' or 'je promets', introduce a variable *Pr* for promising devices in particular languages.

This shows not only a most particular conception of the relation between language in general and particular languages; intended as a philosophical account of promising, it also shows a most particular conception of the relation between *philosophy* and *linguistics*. According to this conception, Wittgenstein's *Philosophische Untersuchungen*, which is concerned with the way our language works, would be interpreted as investigations using *word variables*, that is, they would be interpreted as investigations into the use of 'pain indicating devices,' 'colour indicating devices,' 'knowledge indicating devices,' and so forth. Otherwise, it would seem, these investigations would not have the generality of a philosophical study, but would concern only Wittgenstein's own German!

> ... I am not especially concerned with the particular conventions one invokes in speaking this language or that (and it is primarily for this reason that my investigation differs fundamentally from linguistics, construed as an examination of the actual structure of natural human languages) but the underlying rules which the conventions manifest or realize, in the sense of the chess example. (Searle 1969: 41)

Within such a way of thinking, a philosophical study of language would differ from a linguistic study of English, French or Swedish by having an *abstraction from particular languages* as its object of study. This 'abstract language' is obtained from particular languages in the same sense as an abstract algebraic structure in mathematics is obtained from particular mathematical structures, and it is *general* in the same sense.

My problem in this chapter does not only concern the kind of generality that characterizes the notions of requests, promises, questions and statements. My problem also concerns the kind of generality that distinguishes philosophical issues on language from the generality of, for example, Searle's linguistics-oriented approach to notions of language. It might be said that a philosophical investigation such as the present one concerns what is general *within the use* of a particular language. Searle, however, attempts to *reconstruct* this generality within the linguistic notion of particular languages as a study of a *variable* particular language.

12.2 A COMPARISON: ROAD SIGNS

Since the functions of road signs are similar in most countries, it would be possible to describe the uses of road signs *in general* by describing the use of signs that we specify merely as 'speed limit indicating signs,' 'one-way indicating signs,' or 'freeway indicating signs.' This description could be combined with a table which specifies the *particular* speed limit indicating, one-way indicating, or freeway indicating signs that are used in different countries. A book containing these two component descriptions could be said to contain a parallel to Searle's account of the relation between language and particular languages.[2]

Consider a young Frenchman and a young Englishman who are learning to drive a car in traffic. An aspect of what they learn is what we might call 'the language of traffic': the system of road signs. In what sense do they learn the same thing, and in what sense do they learn distinct things? According to Searle's way of thinking, the *identical* part of their learning is expressed in that part of our imagined book of the world's road signs which describes the use of signs specified merely as 'X-indicating signs.' What *distinguishes* the two cases of learning the road signs from each other, on the other hand, is expressed in the other part of the book, in the table that specifies the particular French and English road signs.

I am not opposed to this way of expressing the similarities and differences between the Frenchman's and the Englishman's learning of the road signs. But I would say that it is a rather schematic description which *draws on* our familiarity with road signs rather than *accounts for* their ways of functioning. I will try to explain what I mean. We could just as well say that what is identical in the two cases of learning is the *uses* of road signs, and that what is different is the *signs* that have these uses. But how do we learn the *uses* of road signs?

The point of many road signs is to regulate our behaviour in traffic. A road sign can often be paraphrased in the form 'Do this here,' 'Do not do such and such a thing here,' etc. But what is the nature of these actions that I should sometimes do, and sometimes not do? To learn the use of road signs, I must of course learn that too! What does it mean to change lanes, to overtake another car, to pace down the speed, or to stop the car? And how do I know what 'here' means: how do I know where I should pace down the speed of my car? Immediately, when I see the speed limit sign, or at passing it, or perhaps ten meters after the sign? Can I increase the speed again, when the sign is out of sight? How far from the stop sign should I stop the car? Must I stop the car even if there is no other car in sight? How long must the car stand still?

When someone learns road signs for the first time, it is important that these questions concerning the meaning of road signs are resolved in some connection with actual traffic situations. What we call 'overtaking a car,' for example, is a very particular thing and it is not defined by the result of ending up in front of the other car. The use of verbal expressions for describing traffic situations, events and actions is established in connection with these very situations, events and actions. It is true that someone might verbally explain to me how overtaking another car should be done even though I have never actually witnessed such an event. But such an explanation would have to draw on *some* previous familiarity with the actual phenomenon of traffic. More important is the fact that even if I react with 'I understand' to the verbal explanation, it would still make sense even for myself to *test* my understanding in an actual case: 'Is *that* an acceptable overtaking?' I would not be confused if it turned out that I had misunderstood the explanation: it is in connection with the actual practice of overtaking cars that the use of the word 'overtake' is finally established.

It is true that the beginner is often given verbal instructions for how to perform an action he has not done before: 'Stop the car *just before* the white line.' But these instructions require *some* previous familiarity with the phenomenon of traffic, for what is meant by 'just before the white line'? One millimetre, or one meter, or perhaps ten meters? It is important to note that these verbal instructions can be (and often are) misunderstood. The following kind of instruction has an important role when similar questions are resolved: *'That's* perfect,' *'Now* you did it correctly,' 'Pace down the speed – not now ... now – yes, that's good.' And these instructions have a use only in actual traffic situations. (If these instructions are misunderstood too, the teacher has his own brake pedal to use.)

I am not saying that you must be a competent driver to know the meaning of road signs and verbal expressions for traffic phenomena. You might never have driven a car. The point is that the meaning of road signs and of verbal expressions for traffic phenomena cannot be abstracted from actual traffic situations, because that is where what constitutes an acceptable *following* of the rules is determined. What I am saying is that when you learn the road signs for the first time, that learning is *essentially an aspect of a more extensive learning of the over-all phenomenon of traffic.* What you learn is how signs and words function *within* the courses of events and actions that constitute traffic.

In light of these reminders about traffic and road signs, how do we look at the similarities and the differences between the Frenchman's and the Englishman's learnings of road signs? We were so concentrated on the signs and the differences between signs in different countries that we did not *properly* see the obvious identity: the *everyday* phenomenon called 'traffic' as it is concretely given to us with its signs.

We were staring at the different road signs in France and in England, and could not see that which is identical – which *surrounds* the signs. We had a tendency to see the signs and their meanings as autonomous in relation to the unsurveyable features of actual traffic. Now we see that road signs are a *part* of what we call 'traffic.' The identity between the Frenchman's and the Englishman's learning is not perceived as something we would like to describe as being, in any sense, 'underlying,' or 'abstract.' We are now in a position to see that what is the same in the two cases of learning is found in *the situations and practices of traffic* in France and in England.[3]

Someone might still be tempted to object: 'You did say that the point with road signs is to *regulate* our behaviour in traffic. If that is so, then road signs, together with laws and rules of traffic, must *explain* why traffic has the features it has – explain these features in basically the same sense that Searle talks about explaining regularities in language use in terms of rules!' This objection is caused by the temptation to think that the general phenomenon of traffic can be explained by the totality of individual followings of laws, rules and signs. But I have tried to show that road signs have their meaning determined only within their use in traffic. In an important sense, traffic must have the features it *actually has* in order for road signs to have the meaning they *actually have*.

But if that is so, why do we need the signs at all? Because in a different, trivial sense, signs *do* explain features of traffic, for example, a *particular* stop sign explains why cars stop at the *specific* place where that particular sign is situated. What I want to draw attention to is the fact that such an explanation works only against the background of the established use of the stop sign in traffic, that is, it draws on the phenomenon of traffic as it is known to us, with its cars, crossings *and* stop signs.[4]

It might be fruitful to exploit this example as a background for a comment on the notion of 'use': it is quite common in the philosophy of language to conceive of the use of language as a totality of *particular utterances on particular occasions* (parole). Language use, conceived of as such a totality, is then thought to be explainable in terms of abstract meanings and pragmatic rules of use, these factors being thought to have a logical priority in relation to actual use. My remarks on the use of signs (and verbal expressions) in traffic show that use cannot be conceived of merely as such a totality, but must be seen as a fundamental *activity* in which we are *trained* to participate. I follow road signs the way I do because I am trained to do exactly what I do.

'But in order to be *able* to follow this road sign now, I must already know its meaning.' Yes, but when you learnt that meaning, you were taught to do exactly what you are about to do now.

Both Chomsky's well-known distinction between *competence* and *performance* and Saussure's distinction between *langue* and *parole* are misleading philosophical schematizations of the simple fact that you must be trained in an activity in order to perform it on a particular occasion. In place of those common distinctions, I would propose a distinction between *established use* (a technique, a practical method) and *use on a particular occasion*. My knowledge of language is at the level of my use of language.

12.3 FIRST LANGUAGE LEARNING VERSUS SECOND LANGUAGE LEARNING

Consider learning the road signs for the first time in your native country, and learning a system of foreign road signs at a later point in life. There are enormous differences between these two cases of learning! You can learn the foreign signs completely from instructions in a book, but it would be nonsensical to imagine such a way of learning road signs for the first time in your life. A book of instructions may be useful when you learn road signs for the first time, but it is only one of the components in a wider training in which you *become at home in traffic as a whole*. When you learn the meaning of road signs in a driving school, for example, you are actually led through a myriad of traffic phenomena in order to get a closer familiarity with traffic and the multifarious ways in which signs (and verbal expressions) work there.

When you learn the meaning of road signs for the first time, you cannot do *only* that: *you must learn it all*. When you learn the road signs for the first time, that learning is just *one aspect of a more extensive learning*. When you learn *foreign* signs, on the other hand, you *draw on* what you have already learnt about how to move in traffic. You do not have to learn that again from scratch. The learning now takes place at another level, at the level where everything can change without changing the nature of traffic, or the nature of the meanings and functions of road signs. Only if a foreign sign is part of a new kind of traffic situation or practice is it necessary to learn that sign within a more extensive learning of that situation or practice.

Why does it normally sound strange to say that a two-year old English child is beginning to learn to speak *English* (except, perhaps, if the child has bilingual parents)? We would rather say simply that the child is learning to speak. At the age of one, the child could not speak at all. Should we say that the child then could not speak any *particular* language, that he could speak neither *English* nor *French* nor . . .?

Consider once again the child who learns to participate in the game of passing toys that the parent requests. What does he learn? Does he learn a particular language such as English; if so, is it his learning *English* that explains why he later on begins to pass toys? Is the *practice* of requesting and passing toys a *result* of following the rules (or the conventions) of a particular language?

If I call one of my friends and invites him for tea, I would normally not say that I use *Swedish* to express this invitation. Is that so only because it would be pointless to assert something which is so obviously true? When we look at the phenomenon of speaking from the point of view of the *activities* of which speaking is a part, the notion of particular languages appears *out of place*.

A child who is learning to speak learns basic patterns of acting and reacting of which speaking is a part. The particular language is what can be exchanged within these patterns. That is why it is absurd to say that a one-year old child knows neither English nor French: the child has not even learnt the *activities of language use* in which English can be substituted for French. It would be like analysing the statement 'That child cannot drive a car' as meaning 'That child cannot drive a VW, or a Volvo, or a Mercedes, or a ...': it would be to describe the child's lack of knowledge at the wrong level.

To say that a human being masters a *particular* language or does not master a *particular* language makes sense only if he already masters *language*. 'But if he masters language, he masters the particular language he learned as his first language.' Yes, but when he learned that particular language, he learned a myriad of practices, activities, reactions and situations that cannot be said to belong to this particular language. The learning of the particular language was a *part* of a more *extensive* and *unsurveyable* learning. So to say that a person who knows language knows the particular language he learned as a first language is extremely misleading: it takes our attention away from the deepest and most fundamental aspects of his mastery of language, from the activities *in which* the system of words and sentences which we call 'his first language' *works* as a language works.

What you already know when you learn a second language is not only another particular language that can be exchanged for the new particular language. *You know the activities of language use in which it is possible to use either particular language.* This is a parallel to learning foreign road signs: the unsurveyable situations and practices of traffic which we learned when we learned about road signs the first time are already mastered: we do not have to learn them again from scratch. Only if a foreign sign is part of a situation or a practice with which we are unfamiliar from our native country is it necessary to extend the learning to include that situation or practice. Similarly, if a word in a foreign language has a use within a language game with which I am unfamiliar, then I must learn that word together with being trained in the new language game. This is what happens when a student of a science is taught the terminology of that science: he is taught the terminology *together with* being trained in the scientific methods and techniques *within which the terminology has its life*.

12.4 IF USE IS ALL THAT MATTERS, WHY CAN I NOT INVENT WORDS AND EXPRESSIONS AT THE MOMENT OF SPEAKING?

What is the commonplace sense of the fact that I do not understand a request in French? I would compare the fact that I do not know French at all with the fact that I do know Spanish roughly, and English better: not knowing a foreign language is more akin to knowing a foreign language badly than to not knowing language at all. (Remember that we would not say that a one-year old child knows neither English, nor French, nor. . . .)

Suppose that a French tourist approaches me in my hometown and begins to talk to me with a polite facial expression. The situation is clear enough: he wants to know how to find one of the sights in town. Suppose I hear a word that resembles the word 'cathedral'. I lean forward, open my mouth – and find that I do not know how to continue. Everything seems prepared for describing the way to the cathedral, but to my own surprise, I do not find the words. It is as though someone had grabbed me at the last moment, preventing me from reaching a goal that had seemed so extremely close to me. Then I say, 'Do you speak English?', and receive a reluctant 'Yes.' The strange feeling of being prevented from doing the most obvious thing in the world vanishes and is replaced by a feeling of ease and mobility. But what is it that makes me feel this way?

It is *to some extent* as though I were about to make a certain move in a game of chess, but found that the chess piece I was about to move was missing. Then I ask my opponent if it is all right with him to use another object instead, a coin or whatever, and to make my move with that object according to the rules of the missing chess piece.

The 'Yes' I receive from the Frenchman is a 'Yes' to using the *English* words 'go', 'that', 'there', 'direction', 'left', 'hundred', 'meters' and so on. But why am I suddenly stressing the fact that these words belong to a *particular* language? Because unlike the chess example, I cannot describe the way to the cathedral by trying to use any kind of noise according to the rules for the use of words. Wherein does the difference consist? Is it that the words of a language, unlike the pieces of chess, have 'meanings'?

One difference is that in the chess example I am missing *one* piece, while in the communication example, I am missing almost every word in French. But suppose that *all* the pieces were missing in the chess example. The first moves would not present any problems; here the position of the objects on the board identify their roles in chess. Later on, however, many kinds of problems would turn up.

Another difference is that the use of chess pieces consists in moving them according to a limited set of well-known and easily identifiable patterns on a familiar board and, in our example, the board is *not* missing. What corresponds to the board in the communication example is the surroundings in the street. But the *relevant features* of this 'board' change depending on what I want to say. To know how to use the 'board' in listening to what I say, the Frenchman would have to *recognize* the expressions that I use, such as 'over there', or 'that yellow building at the end of this street'. But before I saw the possibility of using English, it was impossible for me to use words that the Frenchman would recognize. So in a certain sense, the 'board' is missing in the communication example as well.

The Frenchman's 'Yes' tells me that if I use English words and sentences, he will recognize *their place* within the basic patterns of acting in language. He is familiar with moving around within the patterns of language *with English words*. When I say 'After the yellow building over there you turn to left,' he is almost on his way already: he *reacts* to my words in the fundamental sense investigated earlier in this inquiry.

Words work against the background of their established and learnt use. That is what it means to say that words, unlike chess pieces, have 'meanings,' and that is why I cannot invent noises or use Swedish words to describe the way to the cathedral to the Frenchman: the noises do not have established uses *at all*, and the uses of Swedish words have not been established *for the Frenchman*. The puzzlement over how to describe the fact that I cannot understand a request in French is caused by a failure to appreciate the relation between *established use* and *use on a particular occasion*.

Finally, why is it so difficult to learn a foreign language if almost every essential feature of the use of words in the foreign language is identical with, or at least similar to, what I already know? Why do we have to go through any training at all? Because we must learn *where the words of a foreign language belong in the activities of language*. That is a big task, even if it is not comparable to learning language for the first time, where we learn these activities *as a whole*. We must learn to recognize the language games *in* the foreign expressions. We must come to be at home in the old patterns of acting in language while using those foreign expressions.

12.5 A PROBLEM CAUSED BY A MISUSE OF THE LINGUISTIC NOTION OF PARTICULAR LANGUAGES: THE PROBLEM OF LINGUISTIC RELATIVITY

Many philosophical problems concerning language arise from conceiving the actual and complete phenomenon of language from the limited and technically cultivated point of view of linguistic theory. The aim of this inquiry is to describe and investigate *everyday* facts of language for the purpose of solving philosophical problems that arise in linguistically framed ways of thinking about language. The problem of so-called linguistic relativity is an example of such a philosophical problem. This problem is often expressed in terms of a dualism between language (conceived of as an unspecified particular language) and thought (conceived of as some sort of mental abode of concepts). This dualism is fundamental in Edward Sapir's reasoning:

> We see this complex process of the interaction of language and thought actually taking place under our eyes. The instrument makes possible the product, the product refines the instrument. The birth of a new concept is invariably foreshadowed by a more or less strained or extended use of old linguistic material; the concept does not attain to individual and independent life until it has found a distinctive linguistic embodiment. (Sapir 1921: 17)

The problem of linguistic relativity can be viewed as the problem of how to conceive of the following simple fact: there are forms of expression in certain languages which fulfil functions that are *unique* to these particular languages, and these expressions are not easily translatable into other languages. The subtle vocabulary for describing different forms of snow in Innuit is a famous example of this fact. Scientific languages, or terminologies, offer other examples.

The hypothesis of linguistic relativity (often referred to as the Sapir-Whorf hypothesis) is the hypothesis that features of a particular language, its vocabulary, for example, determine the way that speakers of this language think about the world, perceive the world, remember features of the world, and so on. I will investigate this idea by considering the hypothesis in its modern weak interpretation, in which one talks about a limited *influence* of language on mental processes, rather than about determination:

> It may not be surprising that it should be easier to draw certain distinctions in one language than it is in another. But this is nevertheless true; and this difference seems to have a limited influence on perception and memory among languages, and on our day-to-day thinking. (Lyons 1981: 307)

Imagine a country with many different types of road surfaces. The country may be poor, so instead of renewing and standardizing the road surfaces, one has designed, say, ten different kinds of warning signs for different forms of bad road surface. A foreigner in this country will not be able to drive his car with the subtlety of a native driver. He will not easily see the relevant differences between road surfaces; if he is asked to recall what road surfaces he has driven on within a mile, he will have difficulties that the natives do not have. Why are the natives so much better at this? Is it because their road-sign language *encodes* distinctions between road surfaces?

What does codification mean here? In what way does codification in a language make it easier to perceive and recall the codified features? Let us put the question like this: what does the foreigner have to *learn* in order to understand the signs and to drive according to them? What he lacks is not only the particular *signs* that these people have, but also the *training* they have gone through! The nature of this training has already been investigated in previous sections and the result was that learning a new kind of road sign is essentially a part of a more extensive learning-process. Thus, in an important sense, the signs for different road surfaces do not *facilitate* the natives' ability to perceive and recall features of the road surface. The natives were introduced to and trained in these abilities *when they learned the signs*. The signs become part of their road-sign language only through this extensive training.

Perceiving, recalling and reacting to different road surfaces are not general mental processes of some kind that are *facilitated* by the signs: they are most particular acts *belonging* to the use of the signs, and he who has learnt the signs has also learnt to perceive, recall and react in certain ways to certain features of road surfaces. If he has not learnt that, then he has not learnt the signs either. In light of this example, consider the following remark by Lyons:

> ... the absence of numerals of higher value than four in many Australian languages has often been taken as evidence of the inability of speakers of such languages to cope with the concept of number. But it turns out that Australian Aborigines who learn English as a second language have no difficulty with the numerals and can use them to count and perform calculations as readily as the average native speaker of English. (Lyons 1981: 308)

Why is it that Australian Aborigines who learn English as a second language 'have no difficulty with the numerals and can use them to count and perform calculations as readily as the average native speaker of English'? Is it because the English vocabulary has this influence on their thought, or perhaps because they already knew how to count in some abstract or mental sense, but had not realized that they could calculate concretely, until they encountered English and its vocabulary? There is a strange tendency in this way of thinking to constantly *avoid* seeing things in their normal daily surroundings: Aborigines who learn English as a second language learn to calculate to the extent that they are given the same training that English children normally receive at school in a subject which is taught under the name 'mathematics' – and *not* under the name 'English', nor under the name 'Thinking'.

Words in dictionaries of foreign languages can be viewed as *remote symptoms of very different human activities*: the words are actually *taken from* these activities. Numerals in a foreign dictionary tell me: numerals exist in this book because the people who speak this language *actually do count*. A book which contains the terminology of an advanced science tells me: this terminology is a sign of an enormous number of very different and very complicated activities in which these words *are actually used and play very different roles*.

Similarly, a linguistic description of a particular language can be seen as a *limited and remote reflection of existing language game activities*. If we conceive of language use as being merely the use of a particular language, as the production of grammatically well-formed sentences of a particular language, then we have confused the reflection with what is remotely reflected, and we are faced with the problem of relating this delimited *image* of language with the unsurveyable number of very different human activities, such as counting, which now seem to go on as *parallel* processes 'in the mind.'

The problem of linguistic relativity belongs to a dualistic schematization of the activities of language use, a schematization which manifests a misuse of the linguistic notion of particular languages.

12.6 PHILOSOPHY VERSUS LINGUISTICS

Searle's general speech-act theory is formulated by means of *variables* (e.g., Pr) for linguistically represented features of particular languages. It is an attempt to achieve philosophical generality *within* the linguistic conception of particular languages, and also an attempt to relate the philosophy of language to the empirical, linguistic study of particular languages.

Let us call words and sentences 'forms of expression.' Then we can say that the linguistic technique of representing language is the technique of representing (within formal calculi) forms of expression in isolation from the *use* of these forms in the activities of language, that is, in isolation from the place where they *belong and are at home.*

I have tried to give reminders of the original surroundings of these forms of expression. In other words, I have tried to give reminders of the *activities in which words and sentences have their life*. The point of these reminders is to make it possible to see two important but generally overlooked features of the dominating trends in modern theoretical linguistics:[5]

1. The linguistic notion of particular languages has as its basis certain *formal systems* employed as representations of languages.

2. The linguistic technique of representation treats only *forms of*

expression which are thereby *isolated* from their original places in language activities.

Suppose a philosopher is interested in language. He is determined to work as a philosopher and not as a linguist, so he knows that his efforts should concern 'deeper and more general' features of language than those he knows linguists to study almost by routine. But he also knows that theoretical linguistics has become a sophisticated science that has made important findings about human language. So if his work in the philosophy of language is to have any value, he thinks, it must start out from the modern scientific conception of language. This is met with enthusiasm by many linguists who now begin to see the possibility of gradually expanding their scientific endeavours to cover, bit by bit, those fundamental problems of language that have become known as philosophical problems.

Not every philosopher and not every linguist reach out for each other in this way, of course, but those who do actually do meet, and they meet in disciplines such as semantics, pragmatics and cognitive science. The point of reminding the reader of the activities of language is to disclose the problematic character of this collaboration. *Formal representations of forms of expression isolated from existing activities of language use, are employed as though they could form a basis on which the original activities of language use could be explained or reconstructed.*

The collaboration between linguistics and philosophy in semantics and pragmatics has in this way resulted in a logically *reversed* picture of facts of language – as has been shown throughout in this investigation.

The attempted collaboration between linguistics and philosophy consists in trying to reconstruct the generality that characterizes philosophical work within the technical linguistic notion of particular languages.[6] Let us take a closer look at the form this collaboration takes in Searle's speech-act theory:

> To which elements, in an actual linguistic description of a natural language, would rules such as 1–5 [underlying rules with a variable, *Pr*, for promising devices] attach? Let us assume for the sake of argument that the general outlines of the Chomsky-Fodor-Katz-Postal account of syntax and semantics are correct. Then it seems to me unlikely that the illocutionary act rules

would attach directly to elements (formatives, morphemes) generated by the syntactic component, except in a few cases such as the imperative. In the case of promising, the rules would more likely attach to some output of the combinatorial operations of the semantic component. (Searle 1969: 64)

In this way of thinking, the relationship between the fact that I know what a request is but do not understand a request in French would be schematized as a relationship between knowing rules with a *variable* for the illocutionary force indicating device, and *not* knowing how to replace this variable with a *French* form of expression.

By claiming that the rules for making promises and requests *attach* to linguistic representations of forms of expression of particular languages, Searle is trying to *remanufacture* that activity which is simply going on in language and *from which* linguistics has isolated its conception of language by applying formal means of representation. That is putting the cart before the horse.

A less misguided description of the fact that I know what a request is, but do not understand a request in French, might be the following. Making promises and keeping them, making requests and complying with them, are activities in which we are trained to participate. That I do not know French does not mean that I lack some alleged linguistic mechanism necessary for *producing* these patterns of acting with French 'tools,' so to speak. The fact of the matter is that I cannot *participate* in these activities in French because I have not learnt to which part of which language game a French utterance *belongs*. I cannot respond in the language game because I cannot *recognize the game* in French forms of expression.

12.7 CONCLUDING REMARKS

I have tried to remind the reader of the actual *surroundings* of functioning signs and expressions. I have tried to show that signs and expressions work only as *parts* of more extensive human activities. I have tried to recall the home of signs and expressions, the place where they belong and live – but to which we tend to become blind, as a result of confusing actual language with its limited theoretical representation in linguistics.

13
Intentions and Beliefs as Conditions for Use

13.1 THE ROLE OF BELIEFS IN MAKING STATEMENTS

In Searle's analysis of speech acts, a number of psychological states are taken for granted and presented as mental conditions for language use. The analysis represents beliefs and intentions as kinds of biological, natural facts to which a language is attached through rules and conventions. It is a picture of language as a linguistic mechanism connecting the minds of the speaker and the hearer. It is an idea of language as an extension (for the purpose of communication) of more fundamental capacities of the mind:

> The capacity of speech acts to represent objects and states of affairs in the world is an extension of the more biologically fundamental capacities of the mind (or brain) to relate the organism to the world by way of such mental states as belief and desire, and especially through action and perception. (Searle 1983: vii)

This picture of language has led Searle to develop a foundation of the theory of speech acts within the philosophy of mind: 'A basic assumption behind my approach to problems of language is that the philosophy of language is a branch of the philosophy of mind' (Searle 1983: vii). It seems to me that this conception of beliefs, desires and intentions as primitive mental phenomena is necessitated by the attempt to develop Austin's (1962) remarks into a *theory* of meaning and of language use. If Searle's analysis of speech acts is to be non-circular, then the beliefs and intentions treated in the analysis as *conditions* for use must be conceived of as being more primitive than the forms of language use that are analysed. The analysis would otherwise depend on what it purports to explain, namely our promises, requests and statements as everyday linguistic practices.

Consider the following fact. If we look at a newborn child who is lying in his bed next to the kitchen in which his mother is talking loudly, it would never occur to us to say that the child *believes* that his mother is in the next room. Why is that so? Is it because the child's *mind* is still so undeveloped that it cannot form such a complex, inner mental state? Let us investigate that question by studying certain obvious facts of the child's development.

When the child grows older, he will begin to say, first 'Mummy!,' then 'Mummy is in the kitchen,' and later 'I believe that mum is in the kitchen.' What kind of development does this reflect? Does it reflect a development in the child's mental capacity for certain psychological states which then form more and more subtle conditions for his use of language?

If we want to understand what development is reflected in the child's successive mastery of these sentences, we must look more closely at the different ways the sentences are used. 'Mummy!' is used when directly confronted with the mother, and as a reaction to the fact that the mother shows herself (as smiling in a particular way is another reaction). The child's behaviour is, to some extent, similar to that of a dog recognizing his master.[1]

The use of 'Mummy is in the kitchen' is different. Normally, this sentence is used in situations in which the mother is not present and is used to *inform* an ignorant person of the fact that the mother is in the kitchen. But the child who uses the sentence is obviously not ignorant of the fact that the mother is in the kitchen: he states it as a *fact*. How did he establish that fact? Well, we can imagine, for instance, that the child has recently been in the kitchen to show his mother a drawing, or that he has heard his mother's voice coming from the direction in which the kitchen lies. That is, the child may either have *observed* the mother in the kitchen, or he may have *conclusive evidence* for the fact that the mother is in the kitchen. If we wanted to, we could go on describing a whole family of different ways of observing the mother in the kitchen, and of situations containing more or less conclusive evidence for the fact that the mother is in the kitchen. It is this family of home circumstances that forms the conditions for the statement that the mother is in the kitchen. A child who learns to use the sentence 'Mummy is in the kitchen' must become acquainted with this family of home situations. (The child might not be able to judge his mother's location so easily in a strange house, since the evidence is, to some extent, foreign to him.)

If we say about a child who listens to his mother singing in the kitchen, that he *knows* that his mother is in the kitchen, then we presuppose that the child masters home circumstances in a way that a newborn child does not. He can move around in the home, search for his mother, fetch her, show her a drawing, ask for ice cream, and so on. But that presupposes nothing less than that the child masters activities to which uses of 'This is the kitchen' and 'Mummy is in the kitchen' *belong*.

To say that the child knows that his mother is in the kitchen is therefore not to say that the child is in a prelinguistic inner state of *knowing* which then can form a basis for a sincere linguistic *statement* that his mother is in the kitchen. His knowledge that his mother is in the kitchen is the very fact that he finds himself in a particular home situation that has a *verifying function within a mastered use of the sentence 'Mummy is in the kitchen'*.

Let us finally take a look at the use of the sentence 'I believe that mum is in the kitchen'. Someone might propose the following conception of such belief statements: 'A speaker who states the belief that his mother is in the kitchen is not making a direct statement about his mother's location. He is stating a fact about his mind: he is describing his own *attitude* toward a certain proposition. Only indirectly is the statement about the mother's location.' To investigate this conception, let us first consider another example.

If someone asks me about the weather and the situation is such that I cannot actually observe the weather (or do not bother to look out the window), then I might do something that could easily be mistaken for a process of introspective searching for my own beliefs or attitudes: I try to *remember* facts that can be used as evidence, for example, a weather forecast from yesterday's TV-broadcasting. The process I go through here, however, is not a search for some hidden beliefs or attitudes, but a search for *facts that point in some direction* (i.e., evidence). Thus it is only as a *result* of this process that I might come to have a certain belief about the weather.

What this shows is that the judgement 'I believe that it is raining' is not made through the identification of an inner mental state, but through ordinary albeit inconclusive observations or information about the weather. The use of the sentence 'I believe that it is raining' is *very* similar to the use of the sentence 'It is raining': to say 'It is raining' is to make a judgement about the weather on the basis of *conclusive* evidence or a direct observation of the weather; to say 'I believe that it is raining' is also to make a judgement about the weather, *but in this case on the basis of inconclusive evidence.*[2]

Let us return to our original example. How does a child come to *believe* that his mother is in the kitchen? He does so in ways that are very similar to the ways in which he comes to *know* that she is in the kitchen. The difference is that the evidence is no longer conclusive. The evidence may be the fact that it is lunch time soon, or that the mother is not in the bedroom, or that sounds are heard coming from the kitchen area, although the sounds are not the ones typically heard from the kitchen, and so on. This kind of evidence, and the correct distinction between what is conclusive evidence and what is merely inconclusive evidence, is something that children learn only late in their development.

To have a belief about simple matters of fact of the kind exemplified is not to be in a primitive mental state, but to be in a *situation* which contains inconclusive evidence as determined within a technique of inconclusive verification. Beliefs exist only within the patterns of language and life that I have been trying to focus on with the aid of the notion of language games, the notion of inconclusive evidence and the notion of verifying functions of situations.

These semi-technical notions may give the impression that I am trying to construct a new philosophical theory of what beliefs are. That, however, is not the function that these notions are intended to have. If you say that belief is a mental capacity, then I will remind you of the relevance of *commonplace* features of *ordinary* situations in which we say 'I believe that my mother is in the living room.' I am trying to make you relate to facts of daily life, instead of relating to some philosophical discourse or representation of life. That is the intended function of these notions. They might appear technical, they might give the impression of belonging to a philosophical system of notions, but the attitude in which they are employed in this investigation is the following: there are no 'philosophical facts,' aside from the ordinary facts of our life.

The fact that a newborn child cannot be said to believe that his mother is in the next room is not a hypothetical fact about the child's undeveloped 'mind': it is not a philosophical or a psychological theory about infants' inner, mental life. It is an ordinary and given fact, interwoven with the child's undeveloped *way of living*.

Beliefs are, of course, associated with feelings of certainty or doubt, but these feelings do not constitute the basis for the use of 'I believe' or 'I am not sure'. A person who is about to make a journey may feel uncertain about whether he has the ticket in his pocket even though he just recently 'verified' that it is there. But if asked whether he is really uncertain about having the ticket in his pocket, he would most probably answer, 'No, I'm just a bit nervous.'

The conclusion is that it is a mistake to conceive of beliefs as prelinguistic mental states, and it is a mistake to conceive of beliefs as conditions for use. Beliefs are *interwoven with* forms of language use and, as such, they cannot belong to a general explanation of language use. But Searle's analysis is problematic also for another reason, which will be shown through an inquiry into Moore's paradox.[3]

13.2 SEARLE'S EXPLANATION OF MOORE'S PARADOX

There is nothing paradoxical about the sentence 'He believes that it is raining, but it is not raining': it describes a kind of situation which is not uncommon or strange in any way. But notice what happens by substitution of 'I' for 'he': 'I believe that it is raining, but it is not raining.'

This sentence seems contradictory in some way. But still, the two component sentences are *not* contradictory according to the rules of formal logic. This is what is known as Moore's paradox. Searle thinks that his analysis of statements explains Moore's paradox, since the analysis is that a speaker's statement that *p* (whether it be sincere or not) counts as an *expression of his belief* that *p*.[4] The contradictory feature of Moore's sentence would then be explainable as a formal conflict between the *stated* belief that it is raining and the *expressed* belief that it is not raining.

I am prepared to concede that Searle's analysis gives a formal explanation of the paradox – but then it is important to note that the explanation is based on a formal *interpretation* of the nature of the paradox. This formal interpretation *contains and furthers* what I consider to be the essential features of the paradox. To see this, we must recall the result of my investigation into the difference between saying 'It is raining' and saying 'I believe that it is raining.'

If my previous investigation is correct, then the paradoxical feature of Moore's sentence is due to the fact that it demands of the speaker that he rely on inconclusive evidence – 'I *believe* that it is raining' – when he obviously has conclusive evidence about the weather – 'It *is* not raining'.

Searle's analysis of statements contains a similar confusion of these language games in that the speaker's commitment to the *belief* in the truth of the proposition he expresses, *p*, is analysed as one of the conditions for the *stating* that *p*. Searle's analysis consequently assumes that the speaker plays two *exclusive* language games simultaneously; that he (expresses that he) relies on inconclusive evidence in *believing* the proposition, while simultaneously finding the matter *settled* on the basis of conclusive evidence or direct observation.

As a matter of fact, the sentence 'I believe that it is raining, *and* it is raining' already contains the confusion of conclusive and inconclusive evidence which underlies Moore's paradox, but in this formulation we do not get the feeling that there is a hidden conflict. However, the conflict is not formal and Searle's speech-act analysis contains the confusion underlying the paradox in a disguised form.

Moore's sentence, then, is not a formal contradiction or conflict in any sense: it just brings together the two exclusive language games played with its two component sentences – as does Searle's analysis of statements.

13.3 STATEMENTS CANNOT BE DIVIDED EXHAUSTIVELY INTO SINCERE AND INSINCERE STATEMENTS: THE NORMAL USE OF ORDINARY SENTENCES IS NEITHER SINCERE NOR INSINCERE

I find it relevant here to investigate the pragmatic employment of the notions of *sincerity* and *insincerity*, since this employment is based on the conception of beliefs that I have questioned above. According to the pragmatic point of view, the speaker's *belief* in what he says is what distinguishes sincere, rational uses of language from insincere uses.

Searle seems to conceive of every statement as being either sincere or insincere, depending on whether the sincerity condition (*S* believes *p*) obtains. Moreover he seems to think that *normal* use is sincere in this sense. This is related to Grice's maxim of Quality:

> try to make your contribution one that is true, specifically:
> (i) do not say what you believe to be false
> (ii) do not say that for which you lack adequate evidence
> (Levinson 1983: 101)

Grice and Searle take for granted that a speaker can simply have beliefs and access to evidence which *subsequently* form a basis for his (alleged rational and sincere) use of language. But as I have shown, to believe and to have evidence are already parts of language games and presuppose forms of language use. What one purports to analyse – language use – is consequently *concealed* in the beliefs that are taken as conditions in the analysis.

Possible objection: 'You make the boundary between lies and sincere uses of language impossible to draw. The speaker's belief in the truth of what he says must be what distinguishes a sincere statement from a lie, where the speaker believes what he says to be false.' I think that the received distinction between sincerity and insincerity is partly based on a tempting misuse of the word 'sincere'. We want to say that if a person does not lie, then he must be sincere. And since we normally do not lie, we are forced to conclude that normal use is sincere. This way of conceiving normal language use is then developed in the pragmatic conception of the role of beliefs in making statements.

Observe that you can lie with the sentence 'It is raining' only when you can establish whether it is raining or not. But establishing whether it is raining or not is already the normal, basic use of the sentence. It is not a *condition* (in the form of a prelinguistic belief) for the normal use of the sentence. The lie consists in a simple modification of this basic game: it consists in simply saying something about the weather that excludes what you already have established about the weather in a basic game. Lying is a modified language game.[5] The lie consists of a basic language game plus a last step, which we may call 'the insincerity step.' But *normal* use does not consist of *another* such last step: there is no 'step of sincerity,' if my previous investigation is correct. But such a step is exactly what is hypothesized in Searle's sincerity condition and in Grice's maxim of Quality.

A speaker who is just about to tell a lie may, of course, suddenly decide to be sincere. *Here* we might talk about a 'step of sincerity,' but this step is merely the decision to *play the normal language game,* which does not contain such a step. The distinction between sincerity and insincerity thus exists only against the background of normal language use. The normal case is that our speech is neither sincere nor insincere. The statements we make, consequently, cannot be divided exhaustively into sincere and insincere statements. *Normal language use is more basic than the distinction between sincerity and insincerity.*[6]

We speak about the sincerity of a speaker only when the situation is such that the speaker can be suspected of lying. This is a situation that frequently occurs when children try to describe events that they have not fully learnt to judge. We may react by saying, 'The child is sincere, he really believes that the shopkeeper gave him that toy.' But does this mean that children are capable of having beliefs for which adults lack the imagination, or perhaps that children's *minds* are so unbalanced that all kinds of beliefs may pop up?

Children do not master the subtler parts of the use of the word 'give'. They are not familiar with all the features of giving something to someone in our society. The ways in which children establish the truth of sentences lack many of the features that adults master. It is not the case that children have some kind of imaginative mental capacity for false beliefs. They just have a language and a life which is not yet fully the language and the life of an adult: children's strange beliefs often just reflect their limited mastery of the language and the life that surrounds them.

I said that we judged the child above to be sincere on the basis of the fact that he believed what he was saying. Then I said that the child's belief was determined by that limited part of language and ordinary circumstances of life which the child mastered, that is to say, by the way the child had learnt to use the word 'give'. This has an important consequence: in a sense, we judged the child to be sincere on the basis of the fact that the child simply *stated the facts the way he knew how to do it*. The child's sincerity was not a 'component' of his way of using language. It was *we* who talked about his sincerity and about his belief in a situation in which *we* could suspect him of lying.

Concerning the notions of sincerity and insincerity, I conclude: simply to state that it is raining and to lie that it is raining are two language games. To be sincere is neither a third language game nor a component of the first language game, but a notion that has a use in situations in which the speaker can be suspected of lying. We use the word 'sincere' in these situations to communicate the fact that the speaker is playing the first, basic language game, and not the second, modified language game.

Searle's speech–act theory represents sincerity as the normal language game and lying as a breaking of the rules of this game.[7] If my investigation is correct, this is a mistake: 'lie' is the name of a kind of language game, 'sincerity' is not. The normal use of language is neither sincere nor insincere, and we use the word 'sincere' merely in order to *distinguish* between ordinary, basic uses and lies.

13.4 THE ROLE OF INTENTIONS IN MAKING PROMISES: SPEAKER'S INTENTION TO PLACE HIMSELF UNDER AN OBLIGATION

We often speak of an obligation in connection with promises. It is normally sufficient to say 'You did promise me to repair that bicycle' in order to remind someone of the fact that he *ought* to repair the bicycle. The person who is reminded in this way will feel *responsible* for repairing the bicycle, and if he does not actually repair it, then he will probably give all kinds of excuses, good or bad, for not doing so.

But what is an obligation in connection with promises? Why does saying 'You did promise' have the effect it has on a person who, for some reason, has not kept a promise? Searle seems to take the existence of obligations for granted. His analysis just *connects* these taken-for-granted-as-simply-existing-phenomena to the correct making of a promise. The essential condition in Searle's analysis of promises is the following:

> [Speaker] S intends that the utterance of [sentence] T will place him under an obligation to do [future Act] A. (Searle 1969: 60)

Searle's speech–act theoretical answer to our question above must therefore be the following: obligations are connected with promises because a correct promise involves the speaker's intention to place himself under an obligation. Simply stated, it is in the semantic nature of promises to be connected with obligations.

But what *is* an obligation? Recall the example of a baptism discussed in a previous chapter. In that discussion, we imagined a child who was impressed by the way the baptism was performed. The problem with this child was that he did not continue to use the name he gave, or seemed to give, to some member of his family: he just played around with the words and gestures of baptism, which, for some reason, had made an impression on him. Now we might say that this child does not know that a baptism *requires* him to continue to use the name he suggests in saying 'I name you Jim'; he does not understand us when we say to him, 'But you named me Jim,' in a reproaching tone of voice.

Why *must* the child continue to use the name he suggests? Because a baptism, as a matter of semantic fact, involves such a requirement? No, the reason we say that the child *must* continue to use the name he suggests is that he does not master the wider pattern of acting to which 'I name you Jim' belongs. It remains to teach him to continue the game which he unwittingly initiated in his imitation of the game's first move. It remains to teach him that what he goes around saying actually belongs to a wider pattern of acting. So if the child *must* continue to do something specific, that is so only because the game is actually played in that way, not because the first move in the game *contains* a hidden 'must.' We may speak of a 'must' only against the background of the game. The sense of 'must' derives from the complete game as an established way of acting.

Searle, on the other hand, tries to derive the complete game of making and keeping promises from an obligation connected with the first move in the game. The 'must' – which exists only against the background of how the game is played – is something that Searle projects onto the first move of the game and presents as causally (or morally?) involved in producing the other move in the game. 'But we normally feel remorse when we break a promise, or simply fail to keep it, and that seems to contradict your notion of the obligation connected with a promise as being a purely logical "must".'

Compare reproaching a young child who is about to learn how

to use 'I promise' for not continuing in a particular way with reproaching a schoolboy for not keeping a promise. There is an important difference between these two cases. The first reproach is a way to teach the child a part of language: he does not master the use of 'I promise' until he has learnt how to *continue* in a particular way. The reproach might be paraphrased: 'No, you must act like this if you are to play the game at all.' But the other reproach is directed toward a child who already masters this part of language; it says no more than 'Treat that game with respect, it is an important one!' The schoolboy already masters promising when his parents and teachers induce in him a feeling of remorse for promises he does not keep.

That promises are connected with an obligation is something we learn only after we have learnt to make promises. It is something added, something secondary. Promising, as a basic practice in language, is not connected with an obligation: I just make my promise and do what I have promised to do.

Let us discuss an exceptional case then, in which we may speak of an obligation connected with a promise. Suppose that I make a promise because I want to show kindness to someone. Afterwards I react with the thought, 'What a fool I am! Once again I have made a promise I should not have made, just because I wanted to appear kind.' This is a situation in which I may say that I am obliged to do what I have promised to do. But why?

In making the promise, I embarked upon a course of action which I afterwards regretted as a mistake. Why do I consider myself obliged to continue anyway? A whole complex of different facts may be involved here: the other person expects me to do what I have promised to do, so if what I have promised to do is to be done at all, then it is I myself who must do it. It may cause trouble to many people if the action is not performed. The other person will be angry if I do not perform it, and I am afraid of him. I have an image of myself as a trustworthy person. I feel bad about unkept promises, I simply *cannot* break a promise.

But how can the other person *expect* that I will do what I have promised to do? Is it not because promises are connected with an obligation to perform the promised action? No, at least not in those very basic cases that interest me. His expectation is due to the fact that promises follow a certain well-known course in which he plays a part. The other person *adjusts* himself to the fact that I will perform the action that I have promised to perform: that adjustment is *his* task in the basic practice of making promises. So if I do not keep my promise, if I do not follow the course, it may lead to a variety of problems.

It is only against the background of the normal course of promises that we may say that we are obliged to do what we have promised to do, and only in situations in which we are considering not keeping the promise, that is, situations in which we consider departing from the normal course of action. The fact that problems will occur if we do not keep a promise is *contingent on* the basic fact that promises follow a well-known course to which people adjust themselves.

The notion of promising that I am questioning here is not peculiar to Searle, but is accepted quite generally in philosophy; it seems to play a fundamental role in ethics. Bernard Williams, for example, claims that:

> the institution of promising operates to provide portable reliability, by offering a formula that will confer high deliberative priority on what might otherwise not receive it ... Obligation works to secure reliability, a state of affairs in which people can reasonably expect others to behave in some ways and not in others. (Williams 1993: 187)

The basic idea seems to be the following: the normal use of a promise is connected with an obligation, and this obligation functions as a *source* of our expectations concerning the speaker's subsequent behaviour. But compare making a promise to using the blinker on a car in traffic: it is only because using the right blinker and then turning to the right is a basic, established pattern of acting in traffic that we, under certain circumstances, may speak of an obligation to turn to the right. It is a pattern of acting, and when you use the right blinker, other drivers and pedestrians adjust themselves to the fact that you will turn to the right (that adjustment *belongs* to the use of the blinker): if, having used the right blinker, you do not turn to the right, you might easily cause an accident. The obligation here is not involved in the normal use of the blinker, *but derives from normal use*.

Normally when I turn to the right, I just use the right blinker and turn to the right. It is only if I find out that I perhaps should not turn to the right at all and, consequently, should not have used the right blinker, that we may talk about an obligation to turn to the right *anyway*.

My conclusion is that the essential condition in Searle's analysis of the *first* move in promising presupposes not only the whole pattern of making and keeping promises, but also the attitudes we tend to take toward this pattern in situations where it makes sense to expect that the promise will not follow its normal course, and perhaps should not have been made at all.[8]

13.5 THE ROLE OF INTENTIONS IN COMMUNICATION: GRICE'S ANALYSIS OF MEANING IN TERMS OF COMMUNICATIVE INTENTIONS

Grice has suggested an analysis of meaning centred around the notion of communication and communicative intentions. The analysis is often presented as an alternative to more traditional, *semantic* conceptions of meaning. The basic idea is that meaning primarily should be explained as something that *speakers do*, not as something that *sentences have*. According to Grice's original analysis, a speaker means something by an utterance if and only if: (i) the speaker intends his utterance to cause some effect in the hearer; (ii) the speaker intends this effect to be achieved by means of the hearer's recognition of intention (i).

The analysis perhaps requires an illustration from Grice's own writings:[9]

> I have a very avaricious man in my room, and I want him to go; so I throw a pound note out of the window. Is there here any utterance with a meaning$_{NN}$? No, because in behaving as I did, I did not intend his recognition of my purpose to be in any way effective in getting him to go ... If, on the other hand, I had pointed to the door or given him a little push, then my behaviour might well be held to constitute a meaningful$_{NN}$ utterance, just because the recognition of my intention would be intended by me to be effective in speeding his departure. (Grice 1989: 219–220)

Grice's original analysis has been subjected to detailed criticism by philosophers such as Strawson (1964), Schiffer (1972) and Searle (1969), and by Grice himself (1969). Counter-examples have been invented for the purpose of showing that further intentions must be added to the analysis, and the analysis has thereby grown incredibly complex.

Perhaps *one* reason for the fact that Grice's analysis has been so influential none the less is that it may be felt to be *liberating*: what you mean is up to your own intelligence, as is the way you decide to communicate your meaning. You are not forced to mean according to prefabricated semantic rules or to communicate according to established language-game patterns (although relying on such 'conventions' facilitates communicating your intentions). It is, in the last analysis, your own intentions that decide what you mean, and you yourself make the final decision as to how to make your audience recognize these intentions. The analysis presents the individual speaker as being in complete intellectual control over the process of meaning and communication. However, it is precisely this aspect of the analysis that Searle finds unsatisfying: 'Meaning is more than a matter of intention, it is also at least sometimes a matter of convention' (Searle 1969: 45).

Let us set these differences aside. I want to draw attention to a way of thinking which seems to lie behind both Grice's and Searle's conceptions of meaning. Suppose that I visit a friend whose son is on his way out, and that I utter to the son, 'It is cold.' By uttering 'It is cold,' I communicate to the son that it is cold. What makes my utterance an act of communicating such a thing? Is it not simply the fact that I utter 'It is cold' when I arrive and meet the son on his way out?

Objection: 'No, your description of the situation excludes precisely what is *essential* to communication, namely, the fact that you make the utterance with certain communicative intentions.' Why is it not sufficient to say that I make the utterance under the circumstances described? 'Because what you have described is merely the *means* by which you communicate that it is cold. These means, taken by themselves, do not contain an act of meaning something and do not constitute an act of communication. You have just described the *external framework* of meaning, the utterance of a grammatically well-formed sentence under certain external circumstances.'

When I am talking about the utterance 'It is cold,' I am talking about the everyday situation of saying such a thing to someone. I am *not* restricting or redefining the utterance in technical linguistic or acoustical terms. That would be to *impose* a reinterpretation onto the ordinary utterance 'It is cold.' That imposed picture of the utterance is presupposed in the objection.

According to the physico-linguistic picture, it seems as though my saying 'It is cold' did not contain an act of meaning something or of communicating something to the son. My saying 'It is cold' now seems empty and pointless, and it fails to appear as that meaningful communicative behaviour we know it to be. It is almost as if I had not told the son anything at all in saying 'It is cold'! A mere sound, 'It is cold', just happened to be produced by my articulatory organs.

We do not find ourselves at home in this picture of the situation. We know that there is something more to it. We feel that the picture is not *wholly* wrong, and yet the most *essential* feature of the situation seems to be missing from the way it depicts the situation. But this means that when we try to remember this essential feature of the situation, *we are still under the influence of the picture*, and our recollection of the situation becomes distorted by it. The trivial fact that I tell the son that it is cold now tends to present itself primarily as *an attempt to overcome the limitations imposed by the picture of the situation; an attempt to overcome the imposed gap between the speaker and the hearer by a 'communicative intention.'*

Our focus of attention is shifted, and it no longer seems that what I am doing in this situation is simply what we ordinarily would say that I am doing, namely, telling the son that it is cold. The essential act performed must take place, we think, in a more concealed part of reality. In order to tell the son that it is cold, it seems that I must first do something more fundamental. The pointlessness and isolation of individuals salient in the imposed picture must be overcome by an act which is not captured in the picture: as a speaker, I must *direct my attention toward another human being*. I must try to come into some kind of *contact* with the *other* person. And the other person must direct *his* attention primarily to my attempt to come into contact with him: so it seems that we finally do meet in our attempts to overcome ... the *picture* of the situation! Communication presents itself as the underlying mutual attempt to overcome the isolation of individuals imposed by the picture.

Under the influence of the imposed picture, communication is conceived of as an *attempt* to do something almost impossible. It is as though we were trying to break through invisible barriers. On the other hand, success requires merely that our hearer recognizes our attempt:

One of the most extraordinary [properties of communication] is this: If I am trying to tell someone something, then ... as soon as he recognizes that I am trying to tell him something and exactly what it is I am trying to tell him, I have succeeded in telling it to him. (Searle 1969: 47)

At this point, having formed the idea of communicative attitudes and intentions directed toward a hearer (under the influence of the imposed picture), it is the imposed picture of the situation that is seen in a new light. Uttering 'It is cold' under the circumstances described is now seen as an *instrument* that I use in performing that more essential act of reaching out toward another individual human being. We arrive at the widespread picture of language as an instrument employed for communicative purposes.

Let us take a look at how Searle's analysis of promises is contingent on this imposed picture. Searle modifies Grice's original analysis in order to incorporate it into his speech–act theory. The modified analysis appears as one of the conditions in the analysis of promising:

S intends (i-I) to produce in H the knowledge (K) that the utterance of T is to count as placing S under an obligation to do A. S intends to produce K by means of the recognition of i-I, and he intends i-I to be recognized in virtue of (by means of) H's knowledge of the meaning of T. (Searle 1969: 60)

This analysis is a clear example of how the focus of attention is shifted from the ordinary making of a promise to some alleged attempt to produce in a hearer the *knowledge* that a promise is being made: according to Searle's analysis, the speaker intends to produce in the hearer the knowledge that the essential condition of promises obtains. It is as if the speaker were not primarily making a promise, but rather trying to make his hearer *understand* that he is making a promise.

The analysis is an attempt to bridge the gap between the speaker and the hearer which is suggested by the picture of the 'external facts' of the situation of promising a person something. The analysis, and its focus of attention, can be understood only against the background of the imposed picture of the situation.

My previous investigations show that the picture is misleading and *responsible* for the basic problems of meaning and communication. The imposed picture is misleading not only because it conceals what belongs to the language games as wholes, and erroneously emphasizes only their *first* moves, it is misleading also because it makes us forget that the points of view of syntactic, phonetic, acoustic and physical representations are *imposed reinterpretations* of the ordinary communicative situations. Grice's concept of communicative intentions is a philosophical construction *prompted* by this misleading picture of communication. The idea that an intention must be connected with an utterance in order for the utterance (or the speaker) to mean and communicate something, presupposes an original misconception of the utterance and its surroundings in language activities.

13.6 CONCLUDING REMARKS

Speech–act theory is *dualistic* in the sense that it presents communication as consisting of an 'outer side' which, in itself, seems pointless, and an 'inner side' which is supposed to contain underlying mechanisms of communication:

> People don't speak merely to exercise their vocal cords. Generally, the reason people say what they say when they say it is to communicate something to those they are addressing. That is, in saying something a person has a certain intention, and the act of communicating succeeds only if that intention is recognized by the hearer. (Bach & Harnish 1991: 231)

I have remarked that the alleged outer side of communication is just an imposed reinterpretation belonging to syntactic, phonetic, acoustic and physical representations. This picture is recognized as being in and of itself insufficient as a complete picture of communication. But since the picture is supposed to represent what is immediately given in communication, one is forced to hypostatize a specifically *inner* side of communication, one which can bestow upon utterances the communicative functions we know them to have in ordinary communication.

Since the picture of the outside of communication is the picture of vibrating vocal cords, acoustic blasts, phonemes and syntactic constructions, in plain English, a reality which seems lifeless and desolate in comparison with our experience of talking to each other, the communication theorist is confronted with the problem of relating this dead outside of communication with a more lively inside. Once inside what is outside, the theorist finds all he needs: he finds beliefs, desires, thoughts and above all intentions. It is all *in* there, related (in ways we only can theorize about) to the speaker's utterance *out* there.

This dualism is necessitated by the original misrepresentation of language use. The medley of linguistic and physical representations of facts of language use forces the communication theorist to postulate beliefs and intentions as more primitive, specifically 'inner' phenomena. Why? Because the representation of the immediate facts of language use is alien to these notions; and, since we are not prepared to deny the existence of these phenomena, they are driven into a specifically mental realm of reality.

I have shown that beliefs are interwoven with forms of language use and that the obligation which is sometimes connected with promises is contingent on the ordinary making and keeping of promises. To see this, however, it is absolutely essential to resist the medley of representations of language use, and look instead at language use as the common-or-garden activity with which we all are familiar. In doing this, I have also questioned the tempting sender–receiver picture of communication, that is, the idea that a speaker utters a grammatically well-formed sentence which a hearer receives and understands, or behind which he recognizes the speaker's intention.

14
The Semantic Reading and the Notion of Indirect Speech

14.1 THE NOTION OF INDIRECT SPEECH IN SPEECH–ACT THEORY IS A TECHNICAL NOTION

Would every person immediately understand us if we told him that when he requests salt by saying 'Can you pass the salt?', he is in fact speaking *indirectly*? I do not think so. And neither do I think that the meaning of the following claim is clear to everyone: 'In everyday speech, we often use one sentence to convey the meaning of another' (Gordon & Lakoff 1975: 83).

Nor do I think that it is clear to everyone how it is possible to react in the following way to the utterance 'Can you pass the salt?': 'How do I know he has made a request when he only asked me a question about my abilities?' (Searle 1979: 57). The reason for my doubts is that *this* notion of indirect speech is a *technical* notion. It is not the ordinary notion of indirectness that we use when, for instance, we say that someone who is insinuating something is speaking indirectly.

The *sense* in which the normal use of the sentence 'Can you pass the salt?' is claimed to be indirect in the statements above, presupposes the technique of reading the sentence as a question about the hearer's abilities. That technique is not applied when we say that an insinuation is a case of speaking indirectly.

To introduce the technical notion of indirect speech to someone, it is necessary to teach him a particular way of conceiving utterances: he must be taught to conceive of utterances according to the technique of semantic reading, and he must be led to conceive of this reading as a way of specifying a literal content of utterances. The person must be taught to paraphrase the utterance

'Can you close the window?' as a *question about the hearer's abilities*, to paraphrase the utterance 'You could be a little more quiet' as a *statement about the hearer's abilities*, and to paraphrase the utterance 'Do you want to hand that book over' as a *question about the hearer's desires*.

Someone might perhaps object that 'Can you close the window?' *is* a question about a person's abilities. That is true, when it is conceived of in isolation from its normal use, and according to a common technique of reading. It is not difficult to learn this technique of paraphrase, and it probably does not require much instruction to teach a (literate) person how to employ it. As a matter of fact, a variant of semantic reading is learnt already in school, when we learn how to read and write.[1] A simple form of this technique is spread in every literate society, and I do not question this technique of paraphrase itself; rather, I intend to investigate the philosophical claims that are normally connected with the technique in semantics and pragmatics.

14.2 INVENTING DIFFERENT READINGS: THE GAME OF INDIRECTNESS

We can easily imagine a game of inventing readings of expressions: the participants of the game are supposed to invent ways of reading linguistic expressions so as to make their normal use seem indirect or metaphorical. The players are given the problem of inventing readings of expressions such as 'loudspeaker', 'a solid argument', 'The prices went up' and 'Can you open the door?' which make their normal uses seem deviant from what their reading might suggest. The first player who can explain his reading to the others has won the game. Let us call this game 'the game of indirectness.'

What is it the players are doing in inventing these readings? It seems to me that the technique is to split expressions into components, then recall *other* uses of the components as they occur within other expressions and, finally, *project* these other uses onto the first expressions. Let us take an example: the sentence 'The prices went up' is split into components. Another use of the component expression 'went up' is recalled, namely, its use in expressing a movement in physical space (for instance, 'I went up to the top floor'). Finally, the latter use is projected onto the expression under consideration. If an expression happens to have two uses as it stands, as is the case with 'Can you open the door?', it suffices to project one use onto the other without splitting the expression.

How is one use projected onto another? Normally through a paraphrase that accentuates the projected use in one way or another (*a question about the hearer's abilities*), or through imagining a context which suggests the projected use of the expression (*there have been complaints about this door: can you open the door, or is it impossible?*)[2]

What is the literal meaning of expressions within the game of indirectness? The literal meaning is the use which has the function of *being projected*. The literal meaning is the use that works as an *object of comparison* with the considered use of the expression. This particular notion of literal meaning is technical in the sense that it presupposes the act of projection performed in these kinds of games. It is *not* the ordinary notion, according to which the literal meaning of an expression simply is its most common use, or the use that is specified in a dictionary, and not something that one *projects* onto other, less common uses of the expression. I am not questioning the ordinary notion of literal meaning.

By looking at a use of an expression against the background of another use of it which is projected onto the expression, the former use appears as indirect. But there is no end to the possibilities of projecting uses onto one another: a skilled player is, at least in principle, able to make almost any use seem indirect or metaphorical. George Lakoff and Mark Johnson, for example, seem to play the game of indirectness in their book *Metaphors We Live By*. A method of projection employed in that book is to italicize the component expression that is to be subjected to a reading, and to state in capital letters from where this reading is to be taken:

> TIME IS MONEY
> You're *wasting* my time.
> This gadget will *save* you hours.
> I don't *have* the time to *give* you.
> How do you *spend* your time these days?
> ... (Lakoff & Johnson 1980: 7–8)

Lakoff and Johnson present their views on metaphor as radically different from traditional views in semantics and pragmatics, in fact different even from what they refer to as 'the Western tradition since the Greeks.' I would rather stress what these two writers have in common with the tradition in semantics since the logical empiricists, namely, the technique of semantic paraphrase which they have developed into an entertaining game, played with the different uses of our language as building blocks.

14.3 THE FACTS OF USE WHICH THE GAME OF INDIRECTNESS DRAWS ON

This game obviously draws on the simple fact that an expression normally has different (although related) uses. The meaning of an expression is, in many cases, a *family* of uses, as Wittgenstein has shown. The game of indirectness consists in looking at one member of this family in light of another member of the family.

Something similar occurs naturally when a foreign language is so closely related to our native language that it is possible to *misunderstand* it. To a Swede, for example, Norwegian often presents itself as a peculiar metaphorical language. We cannot help comparing Norwegian with the uses of the corresponding Swedish expressions, and these uses are not always identical. We tend to measure Norwegian with a Swedish measuring stick, and this is often done consciously in jokes, that is, as a game.

This phenomenon, which happens naturally when we hear a language which is similar to our own, is *produced* in the game above within one language by the employment of paraphrases and imagined contexts. Different uses within one language are played off against each other, with the result that our own language appears foreign to us! By staring at the reading of 'Can you open the window' as a question about someone's abilities, its common use as a request appears strange and indirect to us. (This is the stunning effect of reading *Metaphors We Live By*.)

14.4 THE DIFFERENCES BETWEEN INVENTING READINGS IN THE GAME OF INDIRECTNESS AND THE EMPLOYMENT OF THE SEMANTIC READING IN SEMANTICS AND PRAGMATICS

The imagined game does not contain any restrictions concerning the projected use, and that is why almost any use of expressions can be perceived as being indirect or metaphorical within the game: that is the *point* of the game of indirectness. For *any* expression, the players are supposed to recall another use of the expression (or of a part of the expression), and then project this other use onto it. Despite the fact that the expression 'went up' has an *established* use in connection with prices, the players are supposed to read the expression 'went up' in 'The prices went up' as it is used to express a movement in physical space.

The semantic reading is not employed with such an aim. The way an expression should be read is predetermined, or at least guided, by techniques of analysis within two related disciplines: the techniques of grammatical analysis in linguistics, and the techniques of logical analysis in philosophy.

In semantics and pragmatics standardized forms of paraphrase are cultivated in close connection with a dogma of literal or linguistic meaning. As the reading is currently designed in semantics and pragmatics, the projected use is often taken from the predicate calculus (or some similar formal calculus), and the paraphrase is either a formula from this calculus, or a verbal reading of such a formula. An example of what the semantic reading has taken from grammatical analysis would be the technique of reading grammatically determined forms in different languages, such as the singular-plural reading and the tense reading. Grammatical analysis contains many methods of treating linguistic expressions in isolation from situations and contexts of use, and these methods are essential to the technique of semantic reading.

Furthermore, the employment of the semantic reading in semantics and pragmatics does not accentuate the *different* uses of one expression (e.g., of the expression 'up'), but usually attempts to abstract away from these differences.[3] The aim of the semantic reading is not to produce a sense of indirectness: the semantic reading is employed in connection with a basic idea of *expressing something directly*, or literally.

The effect of this abstraction is that semantic paraphrases develop, to a certain extent, a life of their own. One is satisfied with the familiarity of certain established forms of paraphrase, and with the ability to operate with them within an imposed calculus, for example, the predicate calculus. The relation of a semantic paraphrase to an actual use of it is often ambiguous and, in an important sense, the paraphrase is detached from actual use.[4]

A final difference between the game of indirectness and the normal employment of the semantic reading is that the semantic reading is not normally applied to current phrases such as 'hit the hay' (meaning, *to go to bed*) and 'kick the bucket' (meaning, *to die*). However, instead of representing the use of these phrases as indirect (as would be done in the game), the semantic reading nevertheless produces the impression that these uses are *exceptions* to the normal working of language, and consequently deserve a special term: *idioms*.[5] The meaning of idioms is often expressed by a typical paraphrase of the semantic reading, but the paraphrase is not based on the linguistic structure of the idiom in the way in which the semantic reading is generally performed.

Although the semantic reading is not employed with the aim of producing an appearance of indirectness, it will still produce that effect in many cases. In particular, that effect will be produced if we take into consideration the way semantically read expressions are used in different situations and contexts. Many fundamental pragmatic problems arise through this comparison between the semantic reading and facts of use.

Grice's invention of the notion of conversational implicature introduced a general method for treating these alleged forms of indirect meaning as pragmatic phenomena of use. It seems that Grice's primary aim with this invention was to justify the application of formal logical readings onto natural language, but the invention soon proved to have a much wider applicability. The semantic reading found a collaborator in pragmatics.

14.5 AN EXAMPLE OF HOW THE SEMANTIC READING MISCONSTRUES FORMS OF USE AS INDIRECT: METAPHOR

Two people are discussing the issuing of a box containing six compact discs of solo pieces for harpsichord. They are somewhat sceptical about the commercial value of such a box, and discuss the matter without being able to express their doubts in a satisfactory manner. Then one of them says, 'Not many people could stand so much *raindrop* music.' 'Exactly!', the other one replies, evidently eased by the metaphor. The discussion is over.

Anyone who has experienced how a metaphor solves problems of this kind knows that if anything presents itself as indirect, it is the fumbling for words that precedes the metaphor. The metaphor comes as a final solution – as the most *direct* way of expressing the matter.

How can we understand the claim, then, that the exemplified metaphor in fact expresses the matter in an *indirect* way? How would one explain to someone who is still in a state of happiness over how the metaphor finally expressed his doubts in such a direct manner, that, in fact, the metaphor was a form of indirect speech? One would have to invite him to perform a semantic reading of the utterance. He would have to bring the *common* use of the word 'raindrop' to this *invented* use of the word, and then measure the invented use by employing the common use as a standard. That is quite a technical procedure that people must learn. (A method of projection here could be to look up the word 'raindrop' in a dictionary.)

But why compare an invented use with the common use of the word? Is that not to misunderstand the metaphor? The theoretical justification for this procedure is, of course, the idea that words have literal meanings which follow them into almost any situation of use (the exception being idiomatic expressions). But these allegedly invariant and almost ever-present linguistic meanings are a philosophical construction deriving from the fact that the semantic reading is a *standardized* technique of paraphrasing utterances.

If an inventor of a metaphor measures the metaphor with the standard of uses cultivated in certain academic settings, he will indeed find that his use of words is indirect in the sense that it deviates from the applied standard. I do not deny that. What I want to point out is that this notion of indirectness is *imposed* on the metaphor through the employment of the cultivated standard. By treating this imposed feature of metaphor as the *nature* of metaphor, facts of use are misconstrued. The idea of an indirect meaning of metaphors belongs to this *treatment* of metaphors, not to their use in actual communication.[6]

The way in which metaphors work, it seems to me, does not differ essentially from the way that new uses of words are found in new situations, for example, our imagined new uses of the word 'open' in connection with blasting a tunnel through a mountain.[7] The difference is this: the metaphor employs an expression which we are not inclined to use in normal circumstances. We do not expect to find a concert announcement saying, 'Tonight, raindrop music by Joseph Haydn will be performed at the Albert Hall.' The word 'open' is often neutral to the general setting in which it might be used in a way that the word 'raindrop' is not.

If there is a feature of *contrast* in metaphors, that contrast is not a mechanism contained in the way the metaphor works in communicating something. The contrast resides in the fact that the metaphorical expression is so laden with one use of it that it might sound strange in its new use. The contrast, then, does not trigger an inference of a metaphorical meaning. It does not belong to the way in which the metaphor *works*. The contrast is not as basic as it may seem: it resides in fact that we are not inclined to use the invented expression outside the particular kind of communicative situation in which it was invented.

In sum, one might say that while the use of a metaphor does normally not rest on a contrast for its functioning, the use of the word 'metaphor' normally does. Theorists of metaphor tend to confuse the use of the word 'metaphor' with the use of metaphors.

14.6 THE RELATIONSHIP BETWEEN THE PRACTICE OF SEMANTIC READING AND THEORIES OF MEANING

What is the relationship between *reading* 'Can you hand me that pencil?' as a question about the hearer's abilities and *giving a semantic theory* of the literal meaning of the sentence such as Searle's speech–act theory?

Since the semantic reading consists of a standardized form of paraphrase and is designed to correspond to the multiplicity of *syntactic representations* of sentences, and not of *uses* of sentences, it seems to me that the theoretical notion of literal meaning rests on the semantic reading. The 'intuitiveness' of the theoretical notion of literal, linguistic meaning draws on a mastery of semantic reading. But what is the relationship between a technique of semantic reading and a theory of literal meaning? A technique of semantic reading *prepares the ground* for a theory of literal meaning. A technique of reading comes before the semantic theory in the landscape of uses of language. It levels off differences in use, delimits the multiplicity of uses of expressions, and makes the multiplicity of *readings* correspond to the multiplicity of syntactic representations.

To the extent that this preparatory work is impossible or difficult to complete, ordinary language is claimed to be ambiguous, vague, context-dependent and idiomatic; some theorists see the need for another form of preparatory work, namely, a regimentation of the syntactic representation of ordinary language. In regimentation, syntactic distinctions are introduced in the representations of sentences so as to correspond to distinctions in the developed readings according to general patterns. (One of the important functions that pragmatics is supposed to fulfil within a general theory of natural language is that of reducing the number of cases where such a syntactic regimentation would be necessary.)

Once this preparatory work is completed[8] it is possible, in principle, to formulate rules, based on linguistic structure, for how to perform a semantic reading of any sentence in the regimented representation of the language. The rules may be completely formalized (or mechanized), according to the pattern of, for example, Tarski's truth-theory, or they may be expressed in a more informal manner, as in Searle's speech–act theory.

A semantic theory is, if I am right, such a set of rules for a developed technique of semantic reading.[9] In semantics, however, these rules are not conceived of as rules for an *imposed* technique of reading. The set of rules are conceived of as a model for the way our language *actually works* with respect to meaning:

> A language (natural or artificial) consists of (a) a set of basic (i.e., unanalysed) expressions, termed a *lexicon*; (b) a set of rules for combining those expressions in well-formed constructions, termed a *syntax*; and, (c) a set of rules for deriving the meaning of each construction from the meanings of its parts, called a *compositional semantics*. (Green: 1989: 5)

Why does Green claim that a language – natural or artificial – consists of a lexicon, a syntax and a semantics? Because she is conceiving of our ordinary language according to the imposed, linguistic *representation* of language, which is an artificial language which indeed does consist of a lexicon, a syntax and a semantics.

A semantics of a natural language is a formal account of an imposed, standardized technique of reading the expressions of that language. The idea that a natural language *contains* a compositional semantics is based on a confusion of these imposed representations with our actual language.

14.7 INDIRECT SPEECH ACTS AND IDIOMS

The way the semantic reading is involved in representing the common use of 'Can you hand me that pencil?' as indirect is by now,

I think, obvious. What I want to discuss here is how a feature of this use gives rise to a problem concerning how to employ the reading. The problem is interesting because it is generally conceived of as a theoretical problem regarding the *nature* of indirect speech acts.

In contrast to the invention of metaphors, the use of 'Can you hand me that pencil?' is, in some sense, an *established way* of requesting a pencil. To say 'Do you at present have the ability to hand me that pencil?' is *not*, in this sense, an established way of requesting a pencil. This feature gives rise to the following problem: should we apply the semantic reading to these kinds of expressions at all, or should we perhaps treat them as exceptions to the reading, that is, as idioms?[10]

As remarked, this problem of how to employ the semantic reading is instinctively conceived of as a theoretical problem concerning the nature of indirect speech acts: 'According to idiom theories, the indirectness in many putative cases of ISAs [indirect speech acts] is really only apparent' (Levinson 1983: 268). Searle's theory, which is not an idiom theory, is based on applying the semantic reading to these expressions. He does not treat them as exceptions to the semantic reading, that is, as idioms. This employment of the semantic reading represents the common use of these expressions as indirect.

Although Searle's theory is not an idiom theory,[11] he too is aware of the above mentioned problem of the correct way to apply the semantic reading. Along with the idiom theorists, Searle instinctively conceives of the problem as being a problem about the way language actually *works*:

> If, as I have been arguing, the mechanisms by which indirect speech acts are meant and understood are perfectly general – having to do with the theory of speech acts, the principles of cooperative conversation, and shared background information – and not tied to any particular syntactical form, then why is it that some syntactical forms work better than others? Why can I ask you to do something by saying 'Can you hand me that book on the top shelf?' but not, or not very easily, by saying 'Is it the case that you at present have the ability to hand me that book on the top shelf?' (Searle 1979: 48)

Searle's summary of the problem shows that he is preparing for a theoretical compromise, a notion of idiomatic *uses* of expressions which are not themselves idioms: 'How, in short, can it be the case that some sentences are not imperative idioms and yet function as forms of idiomatic requests?' (Searle 1979: 49).

This compromise is presented by Searle as a *recognition* of the possibility of two different forms of conventions associated with the pragmatic distinction between meaning and use:

> It is by now, I hope, uncontroversial that there is a distinction to be made between meaning and use, but what is less generally recognized is that there can be conventions of usage that are not meaning conventions. I am suggesting that 'can you', 'could you', 'I want you to', and numerous other forms are conventional ways of making requests (and in this sense it is not incorrect to say they are idioms), but at the same time they do not have an imperative meaning (and in this sense it would be incorrect to say they are idioms). (Searle 1979: 49)

The only thing I want to stress here is that Searle's employment of the semantic reading, and the rules for this reading which he formulates in his speech–act theory, are not conceived of as parts of an *imposed technique of treating language*. He conceives of the effects of this treatment of language, not as effects belonging to the practice of applying a semantic reading onto language, but as the recognition of features of actual language. Searle is therefore forced to introduce a philosophical distinction between conventions of meaning and conventions of use in his theory of indirect speech acts. He is forced to do this in order to justify, not his employment of the semantic reading itself, but his wider employment of this reading as a philosophical theory about 'the mechanisms by which indirect speech acts are meant and understood.'

14.8 CONCLUDING REMARKS

I began this chapter by presenting the semantic reading as a technique of projecting uses onto expressions. In order to emphasize the fact that the semantic reading is an invented technique which is *imposed* on language, I imagined a game in which the point was to design semantic readings.

I listed a number of differences between the imagined game and the way the semantic reading is generally designed in semantics and pragmatics, and I showed how the feature of indirectness is contingent upon the semantic reading.

After having emphasized the semantic reading as a concrete practice which is imposed on language, I went on to investigate the role that the semantic reading plays in semantic conceptions of meaning. I remarked that a semantic theory consists of the formulation of rules for a developed technique of semantic reading. More importantly, I suggested that these rules are not understood in semantics as rules for an *imposed* technique of treating language, but are misconstrued as a theory about the way our language works.

I concluded the chapter by giving an example of how the technique of semantic reading is habitually entangled with this misconception of it: I showed how a problem concerning the employment of the semantic reading is instinctively conceived of as a theoretical problem regarding the nature of an ordinary, established use of 'Can you hand me that pencil?'

Part IV

Presupposition

15

The Notion of Presupposition in Pragmatics

15.1 PRESUPPOSITIONS AS BACKGROUND ASSUMPTIONS ABOUT THE CONTEXT

The notion of presupposition is perhaps the least established and least uniform notion of pragmatics that I look at in this investigation. The literature on presupposition is disparate, consisting mainly of articles that are either extremely programmatic[1] or of a purely technical nature.[2] However, in order to get a first approximation of what pragmatists characteristically mean by the term 'presupposition', consider the following exchange:

A: Do you regret having bought that apartment?
B: Do I regret *what*!? I haven't bought an apartment.

Here, A seems to have made a false assumption concerning B, namely, that B has bought an apartment. It seems that it is only against the background of this assumption that it makes sense for A to ask B whether he regrets his (assumed) transaction. And since the assumption is false, it does not make sense for B to answer affirmatively or negatively: he can only state that the assumption that A has obviously made is false.

Thus it seems that in making utterances, we first make certain background assumptions about the context, assumptions which do not belong to the semantic content of the utterances – at least not according to the way in which utterances are normally paraphrased within the semantic reading. It also seems that utterances work only against the background of these assumptions concerning the context: 'Presuppositions are propositions implicitly *supposed* before the relevant linguistic business is transacted' (Stalnaker 1972: 387–388).

If the assumptions are recognized as false, as they are in the example above, then the utterance becomes unacceptable or inappropriate. These considerations are, it seems to me, typical for a pragmatic approach to the notion of presupposition.

15.2 THE IDENTIFICATION OF PRESUPPOSITIONS IN LINGUISTIC TESTS

Pragmatics does not treat every kind of background assumption as a presupposition. The pragmatic notion of presupposition is a *technical* notion and, according to Levinson:

> the technical sense of presupposition is restricted to certain pragmatic inferences or assumptions that seem at least to be built into linguistic expressions and which can be isolated using specific linguistic tests (especially, traditionally, constancy under negation,. . .). (Levinson 1983: 168)

Levinson exemplifies how such a linguistic test might be performed:

> Let us start by taking the relatively simple sentence:
>
> (24) John managed to stop in time
>
> From this we can infer:
>
> (25) John stopped in time
> (26) John tried to stop in time
>
> Now take the negation of (24). . .:
>
> (27) John didn't manage to stop in time
>
> From this we *cannot* infer (25) – in fact the main point of the utterance could be to deny (25). Yet the inference to (26) is preserved and thus shared by both (24) and its negation (27). Thus on the basis of the negation test (and the assumption of its sufficiency), (26) is a presupposition of both (24) and (27). (Levinson 1983: 178)

Presuppositions are isolated in these kinds of linguistic tests as inferences that survive negation. What Levinson means by saying that presuppositions are *built into* linguistic expressions can be understood only in the context of an additional linguistic technique, that of substitution:

> Where does the presupposition in (24) come from? From the word *manage* of course. If we substitute the word *tried* in (24) the inference to (26) of course is the same, but this is now an entailment as is shown by considering the negative sentence (28):
>
> (28) John didn't try to stop in time
>
> So presuppositions seem to be tied to particular *words* – or, as we shall see later, aspects of surface structure in general. We shall call such presupposition-generating linguistic items *presupposition*-triggers. (Levinson 1983: 179)

The technical notion of presupposition, then, is defined on the basis of certain linguistic techniques of observation in which the operations of negation and substitution on linguistic representations of utterances play central roles.

Before taking a closer look at the notion of presupposition, I would like to exemplify some further presuppositions and presupposition triggers. My examples are selected from those listed by Levinson (1983: 181–184):

Example 1. Definite descriptions
John saw / didn't see the man with two heads
Presupposition: there exists a man with two heads
Trigger: 'the man with two heads'

Example 2. Factive verbs
Martha regrets / doesn't regret drinking John's home brew
Presupposition: Martha drank John's home brew
Trigger: 'regret'

Example 3. Implicative verbs
John forgot / didn't forget to lock the door
Presupposition: John ought to have locked, or intended to lock, the door
Trigger: 'forget'

Example 4. Change of state verbs
John stopped / didn't stop beating his wife
Presupposition: John had been beating his wife
Trigger: 'stop'

As already remarked, the identification of the presuppositions and the triggers listed in the presupposition dictionary above belongs to a specific technique for treating language. Inferences made on the basis of written sentences are listed and compared with inferences made from the negations of the sentences. By substituting items in the sentences, the surviving inferences can be connected with particular linguistic items or constructions within the sentences. Through this method, presuppositions and presupposition triggers are identified. Levinson's claim that presuppositions are inferences that can be 'tied back to' particular words or constructions that 'give rise to,' and function as 'sources' of, the presuppositions, can be understood only in the context of the imposition of these linguistic techniques onto language.

15.3 PRAGMATIC VERSUS SEMANTIC CONCEPTIONS OF PRESUPPOSITION

If I understand the history of the notion of presupposition correctly, the notion has its source of inspiration in Strawson's (1950) critique of Russell's theory of descriptions. Strawson's own account of descriptions is interesting, because its most basic innovation is the distinction between a *sentence* and the *use* of a sentence. It could almost be said that the characteristic idea of pragmatics, namely the distinction between language and use, arises out of Strawson's critique of Russell's theory of descriptions.

Although Strawson invented what I am inclined to call a *pragmatic* theory of descriptions, his theory contains an idea that was later developed by formal semanticists into a *semantic* notion of presupposition.[3] According to the semantic conception of presupposition:

A presupposes B if and only if
(a) if A is true then B is true,
(b) if A is false then B is true. (Van Fraassen 1968: 137)

The semantic notion of presupposition may be seen as a mirror image of the negation test insofar as it treats a formal feature of this test as a defining property of presuppositions. In order to account for the case of a false presupposition, semantic conceptions of presupposition introduce either a notion of a third truth-value[4] or a notion of truth-value gaps.[5]

Pragmatic notions of presupposition, on the other hand, do not treat the behaviour of presuppositions within linguistic tests as a *defining* property of presupposition. Linguistic tests are interpreted as external means of identifying presuppositions, the latter being defined by terms such as 'speaker', 'assumption', 'context' and 'appropriate'. In Chapter 16 I will show that, despite this interpretation, linguistic tests and methods of observation are fundamental to the pragmatic conception of presupposition. The function of linguistic tests for the notion of presupposition can be compared to that of the imposed technique of semantic reading for the notion of literal meaning.

According to Gerald Gazdar (1979: 103), the earliest attempt to define the notion of presupposition in pragmatic terms can be attributed to Keenan (1971), and Stalnaker (1972). We find in Stalnaker the idea that:

> presupposition is a propositional attitude, not a semantic relation. People, rather than sentences or propositions, are said to have, or make, presuppositions in this sense. (Stalnaker 1972: 387)

At the time when this pragmatic conception was suggested, it appeared to be merely an alternative interpretation of presupposition:

> There is no conflict between the semantic and pragmatic concepts of presupposition: they are explications of related but different ideas. In general, any semantic presupposition of a proposition expressed in a given context will be a pragmatic presupposition of the people in that context, but the converse clearly does not hold. (Stalnaker 1972: 387)

Since it seemed possible to account for the known facts of linguistic presuppositions within a semantic framework, and since the pragmatic definitions of presupposition did not introduce a new formal framework to work within, semantic conceptions continued to dominate.

Since then, however, pragmatists have become increasingly confident that presuppositions must be understood as pragmatic phenomena.[6] As in the case of deixis, conversational implicature and speech acts, pragmatists have recognized facts of language use that have turned out to be difficult to account for with traditional semantic techniques. Furthermore, since a semantic notion of presupposition would introduce either a third truth-value or truth-value gaps into the semantics of language, pragmatists often stress the fact that a pragmatic notion of presupposition would simplify semantics. Thus in 1983, Levinson was in a position to conclude that presuppositions: 'cannot be thought of as semantic in the narrow sense, because they are too sensitive to contextual factors...' (Levinson 1983: 167).

This claimed context sensitivity of presuppositions will be investigated in Chapter 17. Here it is sufficient to note that in place of simply suggesting alternative definitions of presupposition, pragmatists have now developed formal techniques by means of which they claim to account for the problematic facts. Pragmatists generally consider presupposition to be a *central* pragmatic phenomenon, along with deixis, conversational implicature and speech acts.

15.4 CONCLUDING REMARKS

The linguistic notion of presupposition is contingent upon techniques of linguistic representation and methods of linguistic transformation (e.g., negation and substitution). The presuppositions identified within the employment of these techniques can be interpreted in various ways. A semantic conception of presupposition defines presupposition in terms of certain formal entailment relations exhibited in the application of these techniques. A pragmatic conception defines presupposition within a wider, communicative setting, namely, in terms of the notions of speaker, hearer, context, belief, mutual knowledge and appropriate use. However, certain facts of presupposition have been difficult to account for within a semantic framework, and the notion is at present generally conceived of as pragmatic, at least among the pragmatists themselves.

16
Presuppositions and Methods of Linguistics

16.1 DESCRIPTION OF A LANGUAGE GAME

In §15.1 I remarked that the notion of presupposition is probably the least established and least uniform notion of pragmatics that I look at in this inquiry. This makes it a bit misleading to speak about 'the' pragmatic notion of presupposition, or even about a 'central idea' behind the pragmatic approach to presuppositions. This investigation does not belong to the field of pragmatics, however, but is rather an attempt to describe basic ways of thinking about phenomena of language use within pragmatics; therefore, I will simply select three common pragmatic ideas concerning the nature of presuppositions, and then investigate the basic ways of thinking manifest in those ideas. The three ideas that I have selected are:

(i) the idea that presuppositions are pragmatic *inferences* about the context,[1]

(ii) the idea that presuppositions are *assumptions* about the world made by the participants in a conversation,

(iii) the idea that utterances are *inappropriate* if the presuppositions are not *mutually known* (or assumed) by the participants in a conversation.[2]

The investigation will start with describing features of language use that are relevant to the pragmatic notion of presupposition. In order to distinguish these features of familiar practices in language from the technical notion of presupposition in pragmatics, in lieu of the term 'presupposition', I will talk about the *preconditions* for linguistic (and non-linguistic) practices.

With an eye toward these basic features of linguistic practices, I will investigate an example of a pupil learning exactly the features that I want to consider. Imagine that a driving school employed the following method in the beginning of their training program. The teacher drives the car and the pupil sits beside him. The pupil's task is merely to give correct reports on the teacher's actions and features of the traffic situation. The pupil must be very observant; if the teacher is using the choke when starting the car, the pupil must immediately report that to the teacher: 'You are using the choke now, when starting the car.' The pupil must also report the road signs as they approach: 'The speed limit sign says 60 miles per hour.' He should report the behaviour of other drivers: 'The car in back is trying to overtake us,' and of the teacher: 'You managed to change lanes.'

The question I am interested in is this: what role do the choke, the cars, the road signs, the teacher's attempts to change lanes and other features of traffic play within the linguistic practice performed by our pupil?

Let us imagine two mistakes that the pupil might make. First consider a mistaken identification of road signs. The pupil reports, 'The speed limit sign says 6 miles per hour,' when in fact the sign is not a speed limit sign at all, but contains information about the maximum weight allowed on a bridge. Teacher's reaction: 'A speed limit sign saying 6 miles per hour!? That was not a speed limit sign. It said that the maximum weight allowed on this bridge is 6 tons.'

Now consider a mistaken identification of the teacher's behaviour. The pupil reports, 'You didn't manage to change lanes,' when in fact the teacher did not even try to change lanes. Teacher's reaction: 'Didn't manage to change lanes!? I didn't even try to! I was concentrating on the rear-view mirror to keep an eye on the driver in the other lane, who must be drunk.'

When we consider these failures by the pupil and focus on his verbal utterances:

(1) The speed limit sign says 6 miles per hour

(2) You didn't manage to change lanes,

features of the traffic situation may appear as *contextual preconditions* for the normal and successful making of the reports – preconditions that do not obtain in the two examples. The first failure makes the existence of a speed limit sign appear as a contextual precondition for giving a correct report (1). The second failure makes the existence of an attempt by the teacher to change lanes appear as a contextual precondition for giving a correct report (2).

When these preconditions do not obtain, as they do not in our examples, the reports seem mistaken in a more basic way than if they were simply false (the teacher's reactions contain an element of surprise). It seems that by considering the causes of certain failures in language use, we have a method for isolating the contextual preconditions for the *normal* way of using language. From the fact that the mistakes under consideration are characterized by the absence of certain features of the context, we infer that normal use is characterized by the presence of these features of the context.

But if these features of the traffic situations are *contextual* preconditions for the pupil's linguistic behaviour, how do we then discern the pupil's specifically *linguistic* behaviour within his behaviour in general? Furthermore, is it not a bit dangerous to draw conclusions about the *normal* way of giving reports from these exceptional cases of mistakes? Might not a focus on mistakes place normal use in a distorted perspective?

16.2 A FORMAL NOTION OF PRECONDITION

Why am I saying that the pupil's mistakes make features of the context *appear* as contextual preconditions for his reports? Are they not preconditions? They are preconditions in the sense that we *do* treat the reports under consideration as mistakes made by the pupil, and in the sense that we *do* identify the mistakes in the pupil's misconception of certain features of traffic. I am suggesting that these features are preconditions in a sense that does not separate a linguistic practice in itself from a context in which the practice is exercised, namely, in the sense that the pupil makes certain familiar mistakes *within a well-known activity as a whole*.

What I am questioning is a philosophical notion of 'precondition' which results from abstracting certain formal features from the ordinary, non-philosophical use of the words 'precondition', 'failure' and 'success'. Influenced by the idea of language as an autonomous structure, it is tempting to construct a purely formal notion of preconditions underlying the failures in the examples. We tend to explain particular failures and successes as instances of a general logic of precondition. We tend to use the word 'precondition', and the words 'failure' and 'success', in a formal or grammatically twisted mode of use, and we tend to project this formal mode of use onto the foundations of linguistic practices.[3]

The examples of the mistakes may suggest a certain philosophical schematization of language use, but if we look closer at the examples, they do not justify such a schematization. The idea of the notion of precondition as a *general* and *explanatory* notion is mistaken, and mistaken in the same way as are the previously discussed notions of rationality, relevance and truth in their employment in pragmatics for explanatory purposes. These notions draw on the very phenomena that they are intended to explain, that is, various forms of familiar practices of language use.

Consider a non-linguistic example. Almost everyone knows how to drive a car: we place ourselves comfortably in the driver's seat, put the key in, turn on the ignition and so on. And we know that the absence of certain things involved in driving makes driving a car impossible. We may find that the car is stolen, that the key is missing, or that the tank is empty. We might call the car, the key and the filled tank 'preconditions' for driving a car. If one of these things is missing, it is not possible to drive the car – *impossible in an obvious, everyday sense*.

No general, formal notion of precondition explains why it is impossible to drive a car without a car, or without a key, or without petrol. These impossibilities are concrete, everyday impossibilities. It makes sense to talk about the key as a precondition for driving only against the background of the concrete function that the key has within the practice of driving a car. It is not an abstract philosophical notion, but a trivial everyday feature of a well-known activity.

Ordinary practices are more basic than the preconditions of which we sometimes speak in connection with these practices. The fact that a feature is a precondition for a practice presupposes the overall activity within which this feature *actually* functions as a precondition, in a trivial and obvious way. The philosophical mode of using this term, which I am calling into question, consists in fixing upon the formal connection between the word 'precondition' and the words 'success' and 'failure', a connection which is independent of the particular kind of practice that they are used to refer to. This formal mode of use is then interpreted as a general notion with explanatory powers.

16.3 A PRECONDITION FOR A LINGUISTIC PRACTICE BELONGS TO THE PRACTICE AS A WHOLE

Let us return to our linguistic example: the pupil who is reporting features of the traffic situation to his driving teacher. We imagined two different mistakes made by the pupil, and we described his mistakes by saying that certain preconditions for his reports did not obtain.

But how did we make the judgement about the existence of a speed limit sign in the first example, and about an attempt by the teacher to change lanes in the second example; how did we make the judgement that these features are typical preconditions for the two kinds of report that the pupil gives? Did we employ a mental dictionary that says that the existence of a speed limit sign is a precondition for using the definite description 'the speed limit sign' correctly, or that a precondition for using the word 'manage' correctly is an attempt made by the subject to perform the described action?

I am not questioning the possibility of writing such dictionaries: they actually do exist. My examples of presuppositions and presupposition triggers in Chapter 15 were taken from such a dictionary, written by linguists. My problem concerns the possibility of imagining such a dictionary in a mental form, underlying our judgements about the pupil's two reports. 'But if it is possible to write a dictionary, and even make a computer calculate the preconditions of the reports on the basis of such a dictionary, why should it not be possible to imagine that people worked out the preconditions in a similar manner, employing a mental dictionary?'

As already remarked, it is indeed possible to formulate general rules which, when applied to the expression 'My watch says 10:15', determine the following precondition: 'the speaker must have a watch.' Is this *formal* and *calculable* sense of precondition the sense in which having a watch is required for reporting 'My watch says 10:15'? It might be the sense in which a linguistically based dictionary, or calculus or computer program *represents* a feature of the normal use of this expression. But is it the sense in which we ordinarily say that having a watch is required for the report?

Think about the way a watch is employed in making the report. What kind of pattern of actions does one go through in making the report? One raises the left arm, takes a glance at the watch, and tells the time: 'My watch says....' The impossibility of performing this action without a watch resides in the trivial fact that we actually use a watch in performing it. The watch is a part of the language game. Thus the precondition we talk about here does not derive from the linguistic expression 'My watch says...'. It derives from the way that we, as a matter of fact, use watches when we report time in the form 'My watch says....' The notion makes sense only against the background of this linguistic practice *as a whole*.

The fact, then, that having a watch is a precondition for making the report 'My watch says 10:15' is not *worked out* or calculated on the basis of the linguistic expression 'My watch says 10:15', and it does not contain a *general*, formal notion of preconditions. Our knowledge of this particular precondition draws on our mastery of this particular practice of telling the time. However, it is possible to write a dictionary, or a calculus or a computer program, in which representations of preconditions are derived according to formal rules. In these representations, formal connections within linguistic practices are traced and exploited.

In what sense is an attempt by the driving teacher to change lanes a precondition for the report 'You didn't manage to change lanes'? Remind yourself of the way we actually make this kind of report. We observe an attempt by a driver to change lanes: he often glances in the rear-view window, turns his head to establish that the other lane is free, uses the blinker, but when he begins to turn, a hitherto unobserved driver honks, and the driver moves back to his lane. This is the kind of pattern of events we go through when we report, 'He didn't manage to change lanes.'

In what sense, then, is the attempt a precondition for the report? It is a precondition in the sense that the attempt *belongs* to the way the report is in fact made. One of the moves in this language game is the observation of an attempt. We actually go through that part of the language game when we make the report.

A consequence of this is that whenever a report of the form 'He didn't manage to...' is made, we can infer (with some confidence) that an attempt has been made by the subject – even if we have not ourselves observed the attempt. *That inference is based on our familiarity with these types of language games.* It is like inferring that a man has bought food from the fact that he comes out from the grocer's with two filled plastic bags. We recognize an action as a part of a wider pattern of acting.[4]

Furthermore, this formal feature of the practice of using the word 'manage' can indeed be expressed on a linguistic basis in a dictionary, under the heading 'Implicative verbs.' Nevertheless, it should be evident that the notion of such a dictionary cannot be employed, in a mental disguise, to explain features of the *original practices of language*. Such a notion cannot explain our ability to infer that a person P has made an attempt to perform an act A from the fact that someone utters, 'P didn't manage to do A.' The ability to infer preconditions, and the dictionary codifying preconditions, are both contingent upon language games as well-known human practices.

Let us sum up our results. I have remarked that the features of traffic that we have called preconditions *belong* to the linguistic practices performed by our imagined pupil, just as the football belongs to the practice of playing football. I have also remarked that our notion of the preconditions for certain linguistic activities draws on our familiarity with these particular practices. The idea of *contextual* preconditions having a *general* success-preconditioning property for linguistic utterances is a misleading, grammatically twisted mode of use, prompted by considerations of exceptional cases of failure, and employed with the questionable aim of explaining our practices of language use.

I will now go on to show how the three pragmatic ideas concerning presuppositions mentioned in the beginning of this chapter arise when methods of observation in linguistics are *imposed* on simple practices of language use.

16.4 MAKING INFERENCES FROM ISOLATED VERBAL UTTERANCES

Consider an ordinary way in which our pupil's verbal utterances might be isolated. A communication radio in the car is accidentally turned on, and the pupil's reports are overheard by the staff of the driving school. It is obvious that the people who overhear the reports are able to draw a number of inferences about features of traffic on the basis of the pupil's verbal utterances, for example, the following:

> the car is equipped with a manual choke,
> there is another car behind them,
> they are approaching a speed limit sign,
> the teacher has made an attempt to change lanes.

A result of the investigation of preconditions is that these inferences are drawn on the basis of a familiarity with the particular language games to which the overheard verbal utterances belong. We may say that the linguistic activity going on in the car is more basic than the drawing of inferences that takes place at the driving school.

This could be compared with the inferences about earlier civilizations drawn by archaeologists on the basis of tools preserved up to the present. It is evident that the people who once used these tools (e.g., blacksmiths), did not *infer* their occupations from the tools they possessed, as the archaeologist does.

Typically, these inferences are made on the basis of features that, through some process, have been isolated from the activities to which they belong. The inferences are not formal deductions (though representable as such), but *recognitions* of the *original* activities to which the isolated features belong.

16.5 LINGUISTS 'OVERHEARING' LANGUAGE USE

As a rule, pragmatic theories are based on, and discussed in relation to, written representations of utterances. Normally, the representations are not transcribed from observed utterances, but are constructed within a grammatical calculus for the purpose of illustrating properties of competing theories. For our present purposes, however, it suffices to note that most of the examples discussed *could* be found in actual communication and, even if some examples make a slightly artificial impression on us, their similarities to actual utterances *do* give rise to an act of recognition.

Thus in spite of the fact that many pragmatic examples of language use are not transcriptions of actually observed utterances, we may look at the linguistic method of observation as a

Presuppositions and Methods of Linguistics 199

way of 'overhearing' language use. The method of written representation contains a process whereby verbal features of linguistic practices are isolated and, on the basis of these isolated features, certain inferences can be made about the situation of use. Pragmatists draw inferences on the basis of linguistic material in essentially the same manner as the staff of our imagined driving school infers features of the traffic on the basis of what is overheard through the communication radio.

Levinson gives an excellent example of how inferences about the situation of use can be made on the basis of written representations of verbal aspects of conversations:

Here is the exchange:

(32) (i)   A: So can you please come over here again right now
     (ii) B: Well, I have to go to Edinburgh today sir
     (iii) A: Hmm. How about this Thursday?

It is not difficult to see that in understanding such an exchange we make a great number of detailed (pragmatic) inferences about the context in which (32) can be assumed to be taking place. For example, we infer the facts in (33):

(33) 1. It is not the end of the conversation (nor the beginning)
   2. A is requesting B to come to A at (or soon after) the time of speaking; B implies that he can't (or would rather not) comply; A repeats the request for some other time
   . . .
   4. A assumes that B knows where A is; A and B are not in the same place; neither A nor B are in Edinburgh; A thinks B has been to A's place before
   5. The day on which the exchange is taking place is not Thursday, nor Wednesday (or, at least, so A believes)
   6. A is a male (or so B believes); A is acknowledged by B to have a higher social status than B (or to be playing the role of a superior) (Levinson 1983: 48)

An important difference between overhearing communication through a communication radio and the linguistic method of observation is this: the linguistic way of observing use is *supplemented* by techniques of paraphrase and methods of linguistic transformation of data (e.g., substitution and negation). It is further supplemented by methods for comparing inferences from the original data with inferences from the linguistically transformed data. Through these supplementing methods, some inferences can be formally connected with linguistic items in the linguistic representation and, moreover, can be classified according to their behaviour under these treatments.[5] Thus Levinson can explain the inference of (33)–4 above, in the following manner:

> ... we know that (A believes that) B has been to A's present location before because of the word 'again': this can be claimed to be a pragmatic rather than a semantic implication just because, unlike semantic implications, those associated with 'again' are not normally negated by the negation of the main verb. We are inclined therefore to say that 'again' *presupposes*, rather than semantically entails, that some event referred to happened before as well.... (Levinson 1983: 52)

It is against the background of these imposed methods of observing language use that the distinction between the semantic contents, the conversational implicatures and the presuppositions of natural language utterances makes sense.

It should be observed that the inferences that the linguist treats in this manner have the same origin as in our imagined driving school example. The linguist's drawing of inferences on the basis of his material is less fundamental than the practices of language use that he purports to analyse. The linguist's inferences are parasitic on forms of use.

16.6 THE IDEA THAT PRESUPPOSITIONS ARE INFERENCES ABOUT THE CONTEXT

How does Levinson conceive of the inferences in his example? He first remarks that the inferences: 'reflect our ability to compute out of utterances in sequence the contextual assumptions they imply' (Levinson 1983: 49). This remark does not contain a clear statement of his view, since here the question of the *origin* of our ability to make the inferences is left open. His final statement about the example, however, is unequivocal:

Presuppositions and Methods of Linguistics 201

> In order to participate in ordinary language usage, one must be able to make such calculations both in production and interpretation. This ability is independent of idiosyncratic beliefs, feelings and usages . . ., and is based for the most part on quite regular and relatively abstract principles. Pragmatics can be taken to be the description of this ability, as it operates both for particular languages and language in general. Such a description must certainly play a role in any general theory of linguistics. (Levinson 1983: 53)

Levinson does not consider the situation of making inferences from the three sentences in his example as being parasitic on actual use. On the contrary, he treats this situation as a way of isolating abilities that *underpin* our ability to use language in ordinary situations.

In order to avoid a superficial interpretation of this function of linguistic methods for the pragmatic conception of language use, let us discuss a remark about the example made by Levinson in a footnote:

> There may perhaps be some equivocation here between inferences that the participants, i.e. A and B, might make, and inferences that observers or analysts – or readers of (32) – might make. For example, since A and B may well *presume* the facts in 4, 5, and 6, we might want to say that they didn't infer them (Levinson 1983: 48n)

Is Levinson trying to make the same point as I made above? Notice that he is not discussing the relationship between the inferences made in the situation of linguistic observation and concrete features of well-known practices of language use. He is not saying anything about the origin of these inferences. He is merely expressing his *natural reluctance* to saying that a speaker *infers* what is already given to him, namely, the day of the week, the identity of the person to whom he is speaking, and the fact that the other person already has visited the place where the speaker is.

But a reluctance to accept a particular consequence of a general picture of the situation does not necessarily lead to a questioning of that picture. The footnote continues:

yet, from the fact that participants would be expected to correct errors in such presumptions, we can conclude that they must nevertheless make the inferences to check that their presumptions hold. (Levinson 1983: 48n)

What conception does this footnote express? It expresses the view that *even* when a speaker or a hearer does not make a particular inference because he already presumes or is aware of the inference, the inference nevertheless *grounds the correct way of using language*. The inference is there – at bottom – and contains the norm for the practical use of language.

Levinson expresses the view that I am questioning, that is, the view that the inferences made in the situation of linguistic observation are not contingent upon forms of use, but do themselves condition these forms of use.

The situation of linguistic observation is instinctively confused with the situation of actual language use – as though the language user were in basically the same kind of situation as the pragmatist who infers features of the situation of use from linguistic representations. The pragmatist projects his activity onto the foundations of the ordinary activities of language use. This attitude toward linguistic methods of observation is necessary for the conception of pragmatics as a part of a general linguistic *theory* of language. But since the pragmatist's activity draws on the activities of language use he purports to analyse, the resulting picture of language use is logically reversed.[6]

16.7 THE IDEA THAT PRESUPPOSITIONS ARE MERELY ASSUMED TO BE TRUE

A number of pragmatic definitions of presupposition have been suggested.[7] I will discuss an idea that seems to be quite commonly accepted in these definitions, namely, the idea that presuppositions are merely *assumed* to be true by the participants in a conversation. I will trace this idea back to the way that examples are usually selected and employed within theoretical discussions of pragmatic issues.

An important reason for pragmatists to weaken the notion of presupposition in this way is to gain a theoretically general notion of presupposition. Consider the following typical situation of communication. A person informs someone about a mutual friend, John, by saying: 'John didn't manage to sell his apartment.' Assume that you are in a position to overhear this conversation. What inferences can you make? Well, it is probable that John has made an attempt to sell his apartment. On the other hand, it is not uncommon that people circulate reports that would surprise the person they concern, if he were to hear them. So a safer inference would be that the speaker *believes* that John has made an attempt to sell his apartment (as does perhaps also the hearer), and that the report about John is made against the background of this belief only.

A related justification for the pragmatic modification of the notion of presupposition might be that, even if the belief about John is false, the utterance about John *makes sense* for the participants in the conversation themselves. So it might appear that the utterance primarily involves the *belief* that John has made an attempt to sell his apartment, and not the actual attempt by John to sell his apartment, and that the pragmatic notion of presupposition must be modified accordingly.

This weakened notion of presupposition seems to contradict my investigation of preconditions, in which I remarked that the preconditions for the pupil's reports consist of *actual* features of the traffic situations in which they are made, for example, the following features:

> the car is equipped with a manual choke,
> a speed limit sign is approached,
> the teacher has made an attempt to change lanes.

The weakened notion also seems to conflict with our previous discussion of the situation in which the staff of the driving school overhears the pupil's reports through a communication radio: in our discussion, the staff infers *actual* features of the traffic situations, and not merely the pupil's *beliefs* about features of traffic. But suppose that the staff knows that the pupil is a genuine beginner who often misjudges features of traffic. Then we may imagine that their inferences will be slightly modified. Instead of drawing inferences about actual features of traffic, they will infer merely the pupil's *assumptions* or beliefs about features of the traffic situation:

the pupil believes that the car is equipped with a manual choke,
the pupil believes that they are approaching a speed limit sign,
the pupil believes that his teacher has made an attempt to change lanes.

Do these weakened inferences about the pupil's beliefs concern more basic features of use than do the inferences about actual features of traffic? Do the pupil's reports *primarily* involve his beliefs about features of traffic, and only *indirectly* (to the extent that his beliefs happen to be true) involve actual features of the traffic situation? It seems to me that the pragmatic conception of presupposition contains a 'Yes' to this question:

> A context is a psychological construct, a subset of the hearer's assumptions about the world. It is these assumptions, of course, rather than the actual state of the world, that affect the interpretation of an utterance. (Sperber & Wilson 1986: 15)

I think that this answer is mistaken; in order to see the problem clearly, let us consider a simple example of the use of the word 'realize'. Suppose that I have arranged to meet a friend at 9:30 a.m. At 9:25, I am still only preparing breakfast. Unintentionally, I glance at my watch and react: 'Oh, is it that late!' When I arrive a bit late, I explain to my friend: 'At 9:25 I was still preparing breakfast and I didn't realize how late it was until my watch caught my eye.'

This is a simple example of the way in which the word 'realize' is used. That I actually establish the time in some concrete way is fundamental to this use of the word 'realize'. Only against the background of this basic routine of use may we imagine particular cases of error. I may misjudge the time if, for example, my watch is broken; and when my friend explains to me that in fact both of us are a bit early, I respond, 'Oh, I *thought* that it was late, because my watch actually said 9:25.' When we consider my mistake, our attention is drawn away from the fact that an actual determination of time belongs to the basic routine of the game. Our attention is instead drawn toward this particular instance of use, and toward a false *assumption* made by me as a speaker. But my mistake was made *within* the basic routine of the game: I actually employed my watch in the usual manner, but my watch did not show the correct time.

The same considerations apply to the pragmatic justification of the weakened conception of presuppositions. By focusing on the possibility of making mistakes, our attention is drawn away from the basic routines of using words, to the possibly ignorant or mistaken participants in a particular conversation, and to their possibly false assumptions about the matter they talk about. But the possibility of failure in language use is, as our example shows, based on concrete routines of using words.

The pragmatic way of selecting examples shows how dangerous it is to draw conclusions about the general nature of a phenomenon by considering exceptional cases, such as examples of failure or of ignorance. The pragmatic conception of presupposition is not only a false generalization of the situation of linguistic observation, as remarked in the last section; the pragmatic conception of presupposition is also a false generalization of peripheral examples of use, examples of what might happen in conversations in which the participants happen to be ignorant of certain features of the matter under discussion.

This interest in exceptional cases belongs to a theoretical approach to language use, and is typical of pragmatics. The discussion within pragmatics is normally not based on simple and basic examples of language use: such examples are considered uninteresting for theoretical purposes, since they do not make apparent the differences between competing theories. The paradoxical result of this is that pragmatists shape their basic notions of language use by considering examples on the periphery of language, and features that might be salient in those exceptional examples are projected down onto the foundations of language use.[8] The focus on the individual speaker and his beliefs that is typical of a pragmatic conception of presuppositions is produced by the pragmatic approach to example selection.

We may sum up by saying that if you hear a person telling a friend that 'John didn't manage to sell his apartment,' then the inference that this person *believes* that John has tried to sell his apartment is indeed safer than the inference that John *actually* has tried to sell his apartment. However, the safer inference – the inference that will be true more generally – concerns a more peripheral feature of the use of 'manage' than the less safe inference does. In fact, the safer inference about the speaker's *beliefs* is based on the fact that the routine of use of the sentence revolves around an attempt by John to sell his apartment.

There is something which is more fundamental than the situations of conversation that pragmatists consider when shaping a general notion of presupposition: the basic routines of use of expressions. The demand for theoretical generality has the consequence that pragmatics inverts the logical order between features of language use.

16.8 THE IDEA THAT UTTERANCES ARE INAPPROPRIATE IF THE PRESUPPOSITIONS ARE NOT MUTUALLY KNOWN

According to Levinson, the following definition captures some of the basic ideas in the early attempts at a pragmatic theory of presupposition: 'An utterance A *pragmatically presupposes* a proposition B iff A is *appropriate* only if B is *mutually known* by participants' (Levinson 1983: 205).

This definition is interesting for the purposes of this investigation, because it manifests certain general traits of pragmatic thinking. Observe that the mutual knowledge condition is employed in the definition as a *general* 'appropriateness-conditioning' property, and is supposed to be a defining property of presuppositions.[9] What kind of considerations may have motivated introducing such an idea into the definition of presupposition? Probably examples of the following kind:

A: I suggest that you talk to the headmaster of the driving school
B: Talk to *whom*?! I didn't know that the driving school had a headmaster
A: Oh yes, his office is on the first floor

This example not only explains why the definition invokes a notion of mutual knowledge. It moreover explains why the definition uses the weak notion of appropriateness: the example does not focus on a basic routine of use, *but on what might happen in a particular situation of conversation*.

Observe that *A* does not make the *fundamental* kind of mistake that our previously imagined pupil makes. His use of the expression 'the headmaster of the driving school' is perfectly in accord with its basic routine (since this unusual driving school has a headmaster). But in this particular case of conversation, *B* happens to be unaware of the fact that the driving school has a headmaster, and the result is a small disturbance in the conversation.

Why does the disturbance arise in the conversation? Why does B react as he does? Suppose that a football match is about to begin, but that the players do not know where the football is: what might happen here? A number of things might happen. We can imagine situations in which the players become confused, and do not know where to search for the football. We can imagine situations in which they simply go to a particular place and find the ball. We can imagine situations in which a particular person is asked why he has not brought the ball, and is told to retrieve it, and so on. It is clear that these different situations are contingent upon one very simple and basic fact: football is played with a football.

Similarly, we might imagine B to react in many different ways to A's suggestion, other than with the particular reaction we have exemplified. He might not become confused at all, but simply ask, 'Where is the headmaster's office then?', immediately accepting the fact that the driving school has a headmaster. These different reactions are also contingent upon one very simple and basic fact (besides B's ignorance): the use of the expression 'the headmaster of the driving school' is interwoven with the fact that the driving school has a headmaster.

The fact that B's ignorance gives rise to a disturbance in the conversation does not demonstrate that the mutual knowledge that the driving school has a headmaster has a *fundamental* function within the use of the expression 'the headmaster of the driving school'. For why should mutual knowledge of that fact be of any importance *in conversation*? Because the *routine of use* of the expression 'the headmaster of the driving school' involves that fact!

Pragmatists over-emphasize conversation, the situation of talking to someone about different matters. I would suggest that the attempt to *explain* this situation in terms of abstract meanings, pragmatic abilities and communicative intentions, be replaced by a careful *description* of basic techniques of use; a description of the small, everyday routines of language use on which conversation is based.[10] If I talk to someone about what I did yesterday at five o'clock, for example, this talk rests on our common mastery of the use of the expression 'It's five o'clock' in connection with actual clocks and their use in society (see Part I).

16.9 CONCLUDING REMARKS

I have described the features of language use that are relevant to the pragmatic notion of presupposition, namely, the preconditions of linguistic practices. Thereafter, I traced three basic ideas of pragmatic notions of presupposition back to the interaction between the *original* situations of language use, and *imposed* methods of observation in pragmatics (including the pragmatic approach to example selection). The pragmatic conception of presupposition can be seen as a *product* of this imposition. Taken as a picture of features of the original situations of language use, however, the pragmatic notion presents facts of use in a logically reversed order.

17

Defeasibility and the Projection Problem

17.1 EXAMPLES OF THE PROPERTY OF DEFEASIBILITY

In Chapter 15, I remarked that the notion of presupposition was originally developed as a semantic notion, and that the pragmatic notion investigated above was conceived of merely as an alternative interpretation of presupposition. That situation has changed, however, due to the recognition of facts of presuppositions which have turned out to be difficult to account for within semantics: presuppositions seem to be sensitive to the context, both to the external context of use, and to the intra-sentential context. They are context-sensitive in the sense that they seem to *disappear* in certain contexts: presuppositions are thus said have the property of defeasibility. Here are a few examples of this property, taken from Levinson (1983):

Example 1. Sue died before she finished her thesis

In linguistic tests of presupposition, 'before' is identified as a trigger of the presupposition that the proposition expressed by the *before*-clause is true (or is assumed by the speaker to be true). Consider, for example, an utterance of 'Sue cried before she finished her thesis', which presupposes that Sue finished her thesis. But the utterance exemplified above does not have this presupposition. Why has this presupposition, which is normally associated with the word 'before', disappeared in Example 1? According to Levinson, this is due to the fact that the presupposition clashes with a general background assumption about mortals: 'we generally hold that people (and we assume that Sue is a person) do not do things after they die' (Levinson 1983: 187).

Example 2. At least John won't have to regret that he did a Ph.D.

The word 'regret' is identified in linguistic tests as a trigger of the presupposition that the proposition expressed by the *regret that*-clause is true, and normally the use of the exemplified sentence has that presupposition. On the other hand, if the participants know that John failed to get into a doctoral program, an utterance of the sentence will not have this presupposition. The presupposition is cancelled, because it clashes with what is mutually known by the participants.

Example 3. John doesn't regret doing a useless Ph.D. in linguistics because, in fact, he never did one

In this example, the presupposition that is normally associated with the word 'regret' is cancelled because of the intra-sentential context: the presupposition is overtly denied.

Example 4. John didn't cheat again, if indeed he ever did

In a similar way, presuppositions may be cancelled by being questioned: the presupposition which is normally associated with 'again' is cancelled in the fourth example.

17.2 THE IDENTIFICATION OF THE PHENOMENON OF DEFEASIBILITY IS CONTINGENT UPON A GENERAL WAY OF READING PRESUPPOSITION TRIGGERS

It is evident that the idea that presuppositions *disappear* in certain contexts requires some kind of *expectation of their presence*. Or, to express the matter in a less psychological fashion, the idea of the phenomenon of defeasibility is contingent upon a general way of reading presupposition triggers.

The reading of presupposition triggers is a *generalization* of the results of the linguistic tests that I investigated in Chapter 16. Observe what has happened here: the inferences from linguistic material investigated in Chapter 16 were still *contingent upon* actual language, in the sense that the inferences were made on the basis of a familiarity with forms of use. By generalizing these inferences within a formal way of reading triggers, a *detachment* from actual language has taken place. Presuppositions are now *formally* associated with triggers within a general technique of reading that has begun to take on a life of its own. (This technique of reading constitutes the beginning of a formalization of the notion of presupposition, and exemplifies, I believe, an important preparatory step in the formalization of linguistic notions.)

When this detached technique of reading contradicts facts of use, as it does in the four examples above, the contradiction is *welcomed* as an interesting property of presupposition. This parallels what we have seen of how pragmatic phenomena arise in general. Facts of use that might be employed to question established (and often semantic) techniques and notions are interpreted as novel pragmatic phenomena.

The defeasibility of presuppositions is a 'technical' property, a property that is contingent upon the technique of reading presupposition triggers in a formal manner.

17.3 INVESTIGATION OF THE EXAMPLES: THE FIRST EXAMPLE

How do we normally make the judgement that one event happened *before* another event? Let us imagine that someone decides to report the succession of everyday events. We may imagine that he reports, for example, 'I had coffee before I dressed,' 'I met John before I met Sue,' 'Sue went to the library before she finished her thesis.' How are these reports made?

The use of the word 'before' in these reports contains the observation of two distinct, non-simultaneous events. The central point of the use, we may say, is the temporal order of the two actually occurring events. Look at this use as being almost like an experimental routine in a laboratory: one observes two events and reports their temporal order in the form 'X before Y'. What would be the result of applying this routine of use to the situation suggested by Example 1? Since Sue never finished her thesis, that is, since there is no observation of such an event, the report 'Sue died before she finished her thesis' would be a basic mistake within such a routine of using the word 'before'.

But since the report in the example does belong to our language, it is evident that there is also *another* routine of using the word 'before'. What characterizes this form of use? It is a more complicated form of use, as can be seen from the following consideration. Suppose that a child says, 'My grandfather died before he finished my playhouse.' What kinds of facts belong to this use? We are no longer simply dealing with two distinct events and their succession in time. In order to hint at some essential features of this use, we might imagine, for example, that the child's grandfather had promised to build a playhouse for the child. We might imagine that the grandfather and the child had often talked about the design of the playhouse, and perhaps the child had even witnessed the grandfather begin to work on the house, but the grandfather dies, and that puts an end to the project.

The child's use of the word 'before' is based on this complex kind of situation. The word 'before' is not used simply to report a temporal relation between two events, but to explain why a certain act was never finished. *This is a different use of 'before'.*

Let us consider the relationship between the two uses of 'before'. Does it make sense to say that the second form of use can be derived from the first use by dropping the requirement that the *before*-clause be true? But that requirement is not simply dropped in the second use; rather we have *another* requirement: it is essential to the use we imagined, that the grandfather *actually did not* finish the playhouse. This different requirement is internal to a wholly different way of using the word 'before'.[1]

It does not make sense to try to derive the second use from the first use by simply dropping a precondition for the first use. We must *drop the first use in its entirety*, and accept the fact that the second use is simply a different practice in language, performed in other kinds of situations and with other internal preconditions.

The two ways of using the word 'before' exist side by side in our language, just as different card games (using the same set of cards) exist side by side. The uniformity that characterizes the linguistic representation of language does not reflect a corresponding uniformity in the *use* of language.

Let us finally consider the question, 'Why does the exemplified use of "before" lack its normal precondition?'. The answer is that the exemplified use of 'before' does *not* 'lack' some alleged normal precondition – any more than the game of handball lacks a football, which belongs to another game. It is simply another kind of use of 'before', with other internal preconditions. The idea that this use of 'before' lacks its normal precondition has a *technical*

17.4 REMARKS ON THE SECOND EXAMPLE

Suppose that I am trying to comfort a friend who has bought an expensive apartment. I tell him that the prices of apartments are constantly rising, and that he will get his money back, with a small profit, when he sells the apartment. I conclude, 'You'll see. You won't regret that you paid 60 000 pounds for the apartment.' In this use, it is a precondition that my friend has bought an apartment for 60 000 pounds.

However, we do sometimes say, 'At least you won't have to regret that you paid 60 000 pounds for that apartment,' to a person who has backed out of a transaction. Observe that there is something 'strained' about this latter use, to say the least: as an attempt to comfort someone who regrets that he has lost an opportunity to buy an apartment, it might sometimes be felt as an insult. The exemplified use of 'regret' is a *play* with the normal use of the word. It is a nonsense joke. One *pretends* that the fact that a precondition for normal use does not obtain can be employed *within normal use* as a justification for saying that someone does not have to regret something.

The utterance in Example 2 might be looked upon as a *grammatical remark* about the situation, jokingly presented as though an actual fact about John's regrets corresponded to it. (This is almost akin to pretending to comfort a dwarf by saying, 'At least you have extension in space.') It is a joke with similarities to the way that metaphysical nonsense arises in philosophy. The second example, then, is of a *very* different kind from the first example. The specific use of 'before' in Example 1 is a healthy and autonomous form of use, while the specific use of 'regret' in Example 2 is a grammatical remark *derived* from the normal use of 'regret' and employed in a joke.

Example 2 demonstrates the opposite of what pragmatists claim: in the exemplified situation, the normal precondition for speaking about John's regrets has *not* disappeared. That is why it is a *joke* to say: 'At least you won't have to regret that you paid 60 000 pounds for that apartment' in this situation.

17.5 REMARKS ON THE THIRD EXAMPLE

The third example is also a grammatical remark, but a grammatical remark can be used in at least two ways: (i) as a remark about a feature of a use of a certain expression and, (ii) as a grammatical joke. In order to understand these two ways of using a grammatical remark, suppose that an ignorant person asks: 'Does John regret doing a useless Ph.D. in linguistics?'

(i) As a reply to that question, saying, 'John doesn't regret doing a useless Ph.D. in linguistics because, in fact, he never did one' can be employed as a remark about the use of 'regret' in this particular situation, for the purpose of informing the ignorant person of the fact that a precondition for his question does not hold, and that his question therefore lacks a normal yes / no answer.

(ii) by *pretending* to be a normal negative answer to the ignorant person's question, the sentence can be used as a nonsense joke. In this joke, the fact that a precondition for a normal answer does not obtain is presented as if that fact could be a justification for why the pretended answer is negative.

Example 3 demonstrates, as does Example 2, the opposite of what pragmatists are inclined to claim, due to their tendency to confuse grammatical remarks and jokes with *ordinary* uses of words. It is *not* meaningful to talk about John's regrets in the exemplified situation.

17.6 REMARKS ON THE FOURTH EXAMPLE

In the fourth example, we are obviously not dealing with a nonsense joke (as in the second and the third example). Neither are we dealing with a different, autonomous use of 'again' (comparable with the use of 'before' in the first example).

The utterance 'John didn't cheat again, if indeed he ever did' seems to contain two parts. First we use the word 'again' in the normal way, saying, 'John didn't cheat again,' which presupposes that John did once cheat. But then we add: '. . . if indeed he ever did,' which must be understood here as a reservation concerning the correctness of the first part of the utterance. So even if the linguistic representation of the utterance may present itself as a unit, the utterance contains two parts that are in some sense *contrary* to one another: the last part of the utterance contains a reservation that the first part might contain a mistake.

The fourth example contains a tension which is not captured in the pragmatic claim that 'again' has simply lost its normal presupposition. It has *not* lost its normal presupposition, and that is why the reservation is expressed.

Someone might object that 'the *complete* utterance, with the reservation, does not presuppose that John cheated.' This tendency to conceive of the utterance as a kind of linguistic machinery and the reservation as a lever braking the production of presuppositions is quite alien to me. I would rather look more closely into the utterance, and say that the first part of the utterance does contain an ordinary use of 'again' *having* its normal precondition, while the latter part of the utterance contains a *grammatical remark*, a reservation concerning the use of 'again' in the first part. The point of this grammatical reservation is, of course, the fact that the normal precondition for using 'again' has *not* disappeared. A similar remark can be made in connection with:

If John cheated, then he will regret it,

which would be treated by pragmatists as a further example of the defeasibility of presuppositions.[2] They would emphasize the fact that the *if*-clause contains the possibility that John did *not* cheat, and that that possibility cancels the presupposition due to 'regret'. But surely, the point of the *if*-clause is to focus on the possibility that John *did* cheat, and the subsequent use of 'regret' is made against the background of *that* suggested possibility.

17.7 INFERENCES FROM LINGUISTIC DATA VERSUS FEATURES OF ACTUAL USE

The last remark about Example 4 discloses the difference between the approach to presuppositions in pragmatics and the approach to presuppositions in this investigation: the pragmatist focuses on the possibility of *inferring reliable information from the fact that an utterance has been made*, while this investigation attempts to *recall facts that concern the situation of actual language use*.

Consider again the utterance:

If John cheated, then he will regret it.

If by the term 'presupposition' we mean a certain kind of reliable inference from linguistic data, then we might say that this utterance lacks the presupposition that normally is connected with the word 'regret' – since from this utterance, we can make *none* of the following two inferences:

(i) John had cheated.
(ii) The speaker believes that John had cheated.

On the other hand, if by the term 'presupposition' we mean a certain feature of the actual use of 'regret', then the utterance does not lack the presupposition that normally is connected with 'regret': the central feature within the situation of use is the possibility that John *did* cheat, not the possibility that John did *not* cheat. The latter possibility is central only when we attempt to infer safe information from the utterance.

17.8 THE PROJECTION PROBLEM

The defeasibility of presuppositions within the context of the sentence is part of a problem which has become known as the projection problem. This is the problem of giving a formal account, not only of how presuppositions are *cancelled* in certain intrasentential contexts, but also of how they *survive* in other intrasentential contexts: 'The projection problem is the problem of predicting the presuppositions of complex sentences in a compositional fashion from the presuppositions of their parts' (Heim 1991: 397).

The presupposition due to the word 'regret' (according to the generalized reading of 'regret'), for example, is said to be cancelled in the statement:

If John cheated, then he will regret it

but to survive in a modal context:

It is possible that John regrets cheating.

The idea that presuppositions *survive* in certain contexts is obviously based on the possibility that presuppositions may *not* survive in certain other contexts. But the latter is nothing but the defeasibility phenomenon of presuppositions. In other words, the projection problem is based on the conception of defeasibility that I have been questioning here. It is not justified by facts of use, since the notion of defeasibility is not. The enormous interest that this problem has aroused among pragmatists can only be explained by the fact that the problem has a formal nature, and has a similarity to the idea that the meaning of a sentence depends functionally on the meanings of its parts. The latter idea has a paradigmatic function within the philosophy of language.

The projection problem, properly understood, is a problem of *applied mathematics*. It is a problem of formalizing the information that can safely be inferred from linguistic data. A solution to the projection problem might have important applications in, for example, expert systems.

However, since this investigation is philosophical rather than mathematical, I leave the projection problem with the following remark. A mathematical breakthrough in pragmatics, which the treatments of the projection problem seem to represent, is not necessarily based on philosophically sound conceptions of facts of language use. The projection problem demonstrates that a mathematical breakthrough in pragmatics can even arise out of absurd conceptions of the ways our language is used.

17.9 CONCLUDING REMARKS

The phenomenon of the defeasibility of presuppositions is contingent upon an overgeneralized reading of certain expressions in language (the triggers) and a false conception of the way in which these expressions are used in the alleged examples of the phenomenon. Many of the examples actually consist of nonsense uses, and should not be treated on equal footing with ordinary language use. Levinson, on the other hand, would probably claim that the examples show that:

in being grossly inappropriate, one can nevertheless be supremely appropriate (Levinson 1983: 26)

and that, by departing from normal use in a striking way, the speaker communicates meanings in new ways that it is a task for pragmatics to describe. But certainly, grammatical remarks and nonsense jokes should not be treated on equal footing with ordinary language use, and I do not think that many pragmatists would make such claim that they should. The fact of the matter is that pragmatists tend to conceive of these grammatical jokes according to their semantic readings. They tend to think that, in some sense, a state of affairs is really communicated in Example 2: in some sense (namely, the literal sense!), John *really* does not have to regret that he did a Ph.D.

It is not surprising that pragmatists tend to misconceive of grammatical remarks and jokes in this way. In Part III, §10.2, I showed that Searle's formulation of the basic problems of speech–act theory involved such a misconception. Grammatical remarks on the notions of meaning and communication were confused with empirical statements about communication. The pragmatic misconception of Examples 2 and 3 reflects metaphysical instincts and attitudes about language within pragmatics and modern philosophy of language.

The projection problem can be described as the problem of giving a formal account of the ways in which various sentence-contexts prevent and permit the inferences that are formally connected with the presupposition-triggers. This problem, properly understood, is a problem of applied mathematics. Intended as a philosophical problem concerning a feature of our actual language, however, the problem is a misconception.

Notes and References

INTRODUCTION

1. A typical example of this attitude is Carnap's (1956) remark on the language of science: 'It is today still mainly a natural language.'
2. The word 'implicature' is a technical term introduced in order to distinguish a certain kind of pragmatic inference from the notion of logical implication.

CHAPTER 1   LANGUAGE AND CONTEXT

1. Bertrand Russell (1948: 100–108) claims that the system of indexical expressions can be defined in terms of the single indexical 'this'. Willard Van Orman Quine (1960: 201) claims that a deictic sentence such as 'The door is open', can be replaced (on an occasion of use) by a non-deictic sentence 'that is an appropriate elaboration of "The door is open" for the occasion concerned'.
2. In this connection it should be observed that one of the general theoretical issues of pragmatics is the problem of defining a boundary between pragmatics and semantics. As remarked in the Introduction, *some* theorists would claim that the truth-conditions of an utterance of sentence (B) presuppose pragmatic information (see Sperber and Wilson (1986), and Carston (1988)). This modified conception of the role of use for meaning, however, does not touch the *conceptual* problems concerning these issues with which my investigation into the use of clocks and time-expressions is concerned, and these problems are transferred to the suggested alternative conceptions of meaning and language use.

CHAPTER 2   THE PRAGMATIC ACCOUNT OF DEIXIS

1. Strawson (1950: 327), for instance, says: 'To give the meaning of an expression [which has a uniquely referring use] is to give general directions for its use to refer to or mention particular objects or persons.'
2. John R. Searle (1983: 218–230) emphasizes that the specification of the meaning of indexicals cannot reduce indexicality to something which is not indexical. My main point, however, is that such a specification confuses a general description of the use of indexicals with what is described, and moreover presupposes the concrete use of the description in ordinary situations.

CHAPTER 3   CONTEXT-DEFENDENCE

1. See Bar-Hillel (1970: 69–70).
2. An indexical element may be observed in this use too, since it can be said to contain an implicit *now*, but that feature of the use of 'The marble is at G9' does not interest me here. I am interested in a feature that separates the two forms of use from each other, namely, the reference of the expression 'the marble' and the notion of time expressed by saying that 'The marble is at G9.'

CHAPTER 4   IRONICAL USE OF INDEXICAL EXPRESSIONS

1. H. P. Grice (1975: 53), for example, attempts to reconstruct the language games of irony on the basis of a general ability to make inferences. In Part II we will investigate the theory to which Grice's conception of irony belongs: his theory of conversation.

CHAPTER 5   THE SEMANTIC READING AND CONVERSATIONAL IMPLICATURE

1. Compare: 'It is as if I were to say: "You surely know what 'It is 5 o'clock here' means; so you also know what 'It's 5 o'clock on the sun' means. It means simply that it is just the same time there as it is here when it is 5 o'clock"' (Wittgenstein 1974: §350).

CHAPTER 6   LITERAL MEANING

1. This problem is discussed by John R. Searle (1983). It seems that Searle's discussion is motivated by the fact that the diversified use of the word 'open', for instance, constitutes a serious problem for the traditional notion of literal meaning. His purpose, however, seems to be to *save* the notion of literal meaning through a modification of the notion. In this modified notion of literal meaning, Searle's concept 'the Background' plays a central role. See Segerdahl (1994) and Toolan (1991).
2. This is an aspect of what Ludwig Wittgenstein says about the following of a rule in *Philosophical Investigations*. See, for example, §198.
3. See Part I, §3.4, and also §9.4 in this part.

CHAPTER 7   THE PRAGMATIC NOTION OF ORDER

1. G. Gazdar (1979: 44–45) sketches a formalization of the sub-maxim of order in which he takes for granted a syntactic notion of order.
2. See once again Wittgenstein's *Philosophical Investigations*, §198.

CHAPTER 8 GENERAL PRINCIPLES OF RATIONALITY AS A BASIS FOR LANGUAGE USE

1. The relationship between normal language use and the notion of sincerity will be investigated in greater detail in Part III, §13.3.

CHAPTER 9 FORMAL PRAGMATICS

1. I will not demonstrate that mathematical notions are determined within techniques of use, since I consider that demonstration to have been performed once and for all by Sören Stenlund in his *Language and Philosophical Problems*. All that I want to do here is to make clear that Gazdar's justification of formal pragmatics is mistaken, since it rests on a false picture of the relation between mathematical notions and the use of mathematical symbolisms.
2. See §5.5 for a description of the notion of defeasibility.
3. My examples are mainly variants of those given by Levinson (1983).
4. A related kind of generalized Quantity implicature (see Levinson 1983: 136).
5. In Part I, Chapter 3, I made a similar remark about the sign 'a.m.' in the time-expression '9:45 a.m.'

CHAPTER 10 THE SPEAKER–HEARER SCHEME OF COMMUNICATION

1. An example of a conception of pragmatics based on the 'formal semantics' approach to meaning is found in Gazdar (1979). An example of the 'communication-intention' approach to the notion of meaning is found in Grice (1989).
2. Strawson (1950), for instance, distinguishes between the significance of a deictic *expression*, and the reference of a *use* of that expression by a speaker in a context. The significance is identified with a set of general rules or conventions that, together with a context, determine the reference of a use. His argument for this distinction is similar to Levinson's (ironical use of honorifics to children): the significance is, according to Strawson, what permits us to *pretend* to refer in make-believe or in fiction.
3. For a more detailed description of the relation between syntax and actual language, see Segerdahl (1995).
4. See §§65–77 of *Philosophical Investigations*, especially §75. See also my investigation of three different uses of the sentence 'The mountain is opened' in Part II, §6.4.
5. Philosophical analysis into necessary and sufficient conditions is inherently metaphysical, in a sense that I think corresponds to Martin Heidegger's characterization in *The End of Philosophy and the Task of Thinking*: 'What characterizes metaphysical thinking which grounds the ground for beings is the fact that metaphysical thinking departs

from what is present in its presence, and thus represents it in terms of its ground as something grounded' (Heidegger 1972: 56).

CHAPTER 11 SPEECH ACTS VERSUS LANGUAGE GAMES

1. Searle's way of thinking is an example of a general tendency in philosophy: the tendency to take a notion that belongs to a secondary, more sophisticated, more general form of use, and then apply that notion in an attempt to explain, or clarify, or account for the more primitive practices of which the sophisticated notion is an *extension*. (E.g., the following notions: fact, state of affairs, truth, meaning, reference, rationality, description, promise, request.)
2. When Wittgenstein speaks of 'forms of life,' he is trying to give expression to this attitude. (I wanted to describe the game of requesting and passing toys as one of our familiar forms of everyday life.)
3. With 'a baptism' I mean the act of determining a name, not the religious ceremony.
4. See Part II, §8.6.

CHAPTER 12 LANGUAGE VERSUS LANGUAGES AND PHILOSOPHY VERSUS LINGUISTICS

1. When I say that the two children learn the *same* thing in the sense that they both learn to make promises, I am *not* implying that there are no differences at all between promises in France and in England. It is well-known that a promise to be at a definite place at a definite time means different things in different parts of the world. These minor differences, however, are irrelevant for the purposes of this investigation.
2. In French-speaking parts of Canada, if I am correctly informed, the stop sign contains the French word 'Arrêt'.
3. I am not implying that the situations of traffic in France and in England are the same in some absolute sense. One important difference is, for example, that England has left-hand traffic, while France has right-hand traffic. But still, the most fundamental features of traffic are common, and that explains why the same traffic licence can be valid in the two countries.
4. For an elaboration of this point, see §11.5.
5. Sören Stenlund made me see these features of linguistics, and the way in which they are necessarily overlooked by linguists and philosophers who attempt to build theories of language in general upon linguistic notions. For a more complete treatment of the problems dealt with in this section, see Stenlund (1990), especially the following three chapters: *Confusion of the perspectives of linguistics and philosophy*, and *Sentences of a language versus formulas of a calculus* in Part 2, and *Languages and formal systems* in Part 3.
6. Another example of this attempt to reconstruct philosophical gener-

ality within the linguistic notion of particular languages is Chomsky's idea of a 'universal grammar.' See Öhman (1988) for a discussion of this feature of Chomsky's way of thinking.

CHAPTER 13 INTENTIONS AND BELIEFS AS CONDITIONS FOR USE

1. 'Mummy!' is of course used as a *call* for the mother too, but that form of use does not interest me here.
2. Imagine a language in which one expressed what we call beliefs by saying: 'I have access to facts which indicate that....' When we consider *this* form of expression, we are not inclined to conceive of it as an expression of a mental capacity, or of a mental attitude toward something. Still, this form of expression does indicate that the speaker is involved in a certain way in the statement. It is *he* who has access to certain facts and, in this particular sense, his statement may be said to contain a 'subjective' element. So observe that I am not claiming that the utterance 'I believe that it is so-and-so' is merely a weaker variant of the utterance 'It is so-and-so,' as though the difference between the two utterances were merely a difference of degree of certainty: the *grammar* (in Wittgenstein's sense) is different.
3. For a related critique of Searle's concept of belief, see Hacker (1992). Instead of recalling ordinary situations of language use, Hacker develops his critique in the form of grammatical remarks.
4. See Searle (1969: 65n).
5. For a more elaborated description of a modified language game, see my remarks on the ironical use of honorifics to children in Part I, Chapter 4.
6. In Part II, §8.4, it was shown that the same remark applies to the notions of 'truth' and 'falsity'. Normal language use is more basic than the distinction between truth and falsity. The two notions rest on practices of language use.
7. See Searle (1979: 67).
8. This latter feature of Searle's analysis is related to Habermas' attempt at a 'universal pragmatics,' in which he tries to reconstruct the ways in which communicative acts are grounded in a rationality which he claims is inherent in language use. See Wilhelmi (1991).
9. In the quotation, Grice extends the notion of utterance to cover also non-linguistic acts, and restricts the notion of meaning to cover only what he terms 'non-natural meaning' ('meaning$_{NN}$', as opposed to the notion of meaning involved in saying 'Those clouds mean rain').

CHAPTER 14 THE SEMANTIC READING AND THE NOTION OF INDIRECT SPEECH

1. I am thinking of the often very schematic ways in which children are supposed to render what a written sentence says, for example,

when the teacher tests for reading comprehension. I am also thinking of the use of dictionaries in the study of foreign languages.
2. Another technique of projection would be the method of componential analysis of lexical meaning (see Lyons 1977: 317ff). The meaning of the expression 'up' might, I suppose, be ascribed the semantic feature +[SPATIAL].
3. This feature of the semantic reading was investigated in Part II, §§6.2–6.3, with respect to John Lyons's reading of 'My mother is younger than I am'.
4. A clear example of this detachment from actual use was investigated in Part II, §7.1: the semantic reading of the sentence 'A boy went to the bus terminal and bought a ticket'.
5. This feature of the notion of idiom has been pointed out to me by Sven Öhman. The idea that idioms are exceptions is, according to him, conditioned by the principle of compositionality. The principle of compositionality is one feature of current techniques of semantic reading.
6. This seems to be the way in which Monroe C. Beardsley (1958) treats literary texts. It follows that his distinction between 'primary' and 'secondary' meaning belongs to the application of certain theoretical techniques on literature, rather that to the actual writing and reading of literature.
7. See Part II, §6.4, for a description of different ways of using the word 'open' in connection with tunnel work.
8. Sören Stenlund has shown that the very idea of a completed syntactic preparation and regimentation of this kind, for the purpose of a subsequent formulation of theories of meaning, is highly questionable. See Stenlund (1990: 78–85).
9. I am not suggesting that my distinction between techniques of semantic reading and theories of meaning is all that sharp in practice, i.e., once they have come to be intertwined in semantics. The semantic reading and the semantic theory develop together within semantics, and just as a semantic theory is often characterized by a technique of reading, so the technique of reading is often characterized by theoretical notions and considerations. Think, for example, of Bertrand Russell's treatment of definite descriptions, which is at the same time a theory of meaning and a technique of paraphrase.
10. A consequence of treating 'Can you hand me that book' as an idiom is that the sentence must be conceived of as being ambiguous between the literal meaning of a yes/no question and the literal meaning of a request. This is not considered a satisfying account because it restricts the universality that is strived for in the theoretical ways of thinking under consideration here.
11. Searle's theory of indirect speech acts employs Grice's theory of conversation, and treats the indirect illocutionary force of an indirect speech act as a conversational implicature.

CHAPTER 15 THE NOTION OF PRESUPPOSITION IN PRAGMATICS

1. See e.g., Stalnaker (1972).
2. See e.g., articles concerning the so-called 'projection problem' for presuppositions.
3. Van Fraassen (1969), for example, does not mention the distinction between a sentence and a use of a sentence in his summary of Strawson's notion of presupposition.
4. As in Keenan (1972).
5. As in Van Fraassen (1969).
6. See e.g., Kempson (1975).

CHAPTER 16 PRESUPPOSITIONS AND METHODS OF LINGUISTICS

1. It might appear strange that anyone would seriously consider the idea that a presupposition – something that is 'implicitly supposed before the relevant linguistic business is transacted' – should be *inferred* in the situation of use. The idea, however, belongs to the typically pragmatic problem of accounting for language users' *ability* to correlate utterances with contexts. (See §16.6 below.)
2. This idea has been dismissed as inadequate by Gazdar (1979), among others. For my purposes, however, *dismissed* pragmatic ideas are as interesting as *accepted* pragmatic ideas. Observe that my remarks about the idea (iii) in §16.8 are not even similar to Gazdar's (1979: 105–107) arguments against it. My remarks are directed against the *general pragmatic ways of thinking* that happen to be manifest in this idea, and in many other ideas of pragmatics.
3. For a more detailed description of 'grammatically twisted modes of use,' see Part III, §§10.2–10.3.
4. My remarks should not be interpreted as supporting the artificial intelligence approach to linguistic practices, an approach which has been developed partly as a reaction to the problematic distinction between linguistic knowledge and background knowledge about the world. I consider the so-called frames, the schemes and the scripts often discussed in the field of AI to be sophisticated *representations* of human activities. They are not even *approximate explanations* of these activities. What I am trying to show is that a theoretical explanation of human practices is *out of place*, regardless of how these purported explanations are designed.
5. One difference between presuppositions and conversational implicatures, for example, is that conversational implicatures are inferences that normally cannot be connected with particular linguistic items.
6. Similar remarks can be directed against J. Bruner's (1987) method of observing, or 'constructing,' people's lives on the basis of a study of written representations of their different ways of describing their

lives. His idea that we 'construct our lives' by telling stories is a projection of this method of observation (a method which utilizes techniques from, e.g., linguistic and literary theory) onto the persons under consideration. Bruner's notion of 'life as narrative' is, I think, logically reversed in a manner which is similar to the way in which the notion of 'pragmatic inference' is logically reversed.
7. See Gazdar (1979: 103–108).
8. Stalnaker (1991: 474) employs an example of small talk about trivialities with his barber, in arguing for an even weaker definition of pragmatic presupposition! According to Stalnaker's modified definition, presupposing something is not a matter of making a certain assumption, but of *behaving as if* one were making a certain assumption.
9. In the definition, the word 'appropriate' occurs in a grammatically twisted mode of use. Compare §§16.2–16.3.
10. I am thinking of the kind of investigation that I made of the use of time-expressions (in connection with the imagined clock-machines) in Part I, of the use of the word 'open' (in connection with various features of mountains) in Part II, of the use of the word 'request' (in connection with a basic practice in our language) in part III and of the use of the word 'manage' (in connection with features of the driving teacher's behaviour) in this part.

CHAPTER 17   DEFEASIBILITY AND THE PROJECTION PROBLEM

1. Compare the use of 'before' in Example 1 with the specific use of 'and' in 'The boy went to the bus terminal and bought a ticket'. In Part II, Chapter 7, I showed that this use of 'and' cannot be explained in terms of an interaction between semantic rules of meaning and pragmatic maxims of use. The investigated use of 'and' was shown to be an autonomous form of use that could not be derived from its use in predicate logic by adding a pragmatic maxim.
2. See e.g., Heim (1991).

Bibliography

Austin, J. L. 1946. Other Minds. *Proceedings of the Aristotelian Society*, Supplementary Vol. xx. Reprinted in: *Philosophical Papers*. Oxford: Oxford University Press. 1961.
Austin, J. L. 1962. *How to Do Things with Words*. Oxford: Clarendon Press.
Bach, K. & R. M. Harnish. 1991. Linguistic Communication: A Schema for Speech Acts. In: *Pragmatics. A Reader*. Davies, S. (ed.). Oxford: Oxford University Press. Originally published in: *Linguistic Communication and Speech Acts*. Cambridge, Mass.: MIT Press. 1979.
Baker, G. P. & P. M. S. Hacker. 1984. *Language, Sense & Nonsense*. Oxford: Basil Blackwell.
Bar-Hillel, Y. 1970. Indexical Expressions. In: *Aspects of Language*. The Hebrew University, Jerusalem: The Magnes Press. Originally published in: *Mind* 63, 359–79, 1954.
Beardsley, M. C. 1958. *Aesthetics: Problems in the Philosophy of Criticism*. Indianapolis: Hacket Publishing Company.
Bierwisch, M. 1970. Semantics. In: *New Horizons in Linguistics*. Lyons, J. (ed.). Harmondsworth: Penguin Books.
Bruner, J. 1987. Life as Narrative. *Social Research* 54, 11–32.
Carnap, R. 1956. *Meaning and Necessity*. Enlarged Edition. Chicago: The University of Chicago Press.
Carston, R. 1988. Implicature, Explicature, and Truth-Theoretic Semantics. In: *Mental Representations: The Interface Between Language and Reality*. Kempson, R. (ed.). Cambridge: Cambridge University Press.
Chomsky, N. 1972. *Language and Mind*. Enlarged Edition. Harcourt Brace Jovanovich.
Cohen, L. J. 1971. Some Remarks on Grice's Views about the Logical Particles of Natural Language. In: *Pragmatics of Natural Languages*. Bar-Hillel, Y. (ed.). Dortrecht-Holland: D. Reidel Publishing Company.
Cole, P. & Morgan, J. (eds). 1975, 1978, 1979. *Syntax & Semantics*, Vols 3, 9 and 11. New York: Academic Press.
Davidson, D. 1967. Truth and Meaning. *Synthese* 17, No 3.
Davies, S. (ed.), 1991. *Pragmatics. A Reader*. Oxford: Oxford University Press.
Gazdar, G. 1979. *Pragmatics: Implicature, Presupposition and Logical Form*. New York: Academic Press.
Gordon, D. & G. Lakoff. 1975. Conversational Postulates. In: *Syntax and Semantics*, Vol. 3, Speech Acts. Cole, P. & J. Morgan (eds). New York: Academic Press.
Green, G. M. 1989. *Pragmatics and Natural Language Understanding*. Hillsdale: Lawrence Erlbaum Associates Publishers.
Grice, H. P. 1969. Utterer's Meaning and Intentions. *Philosophical Review* 78, 147–77.

Grice, H. P. 1975. Logic and Conversation. In: *Syntax & Semantics*, Vol. 3, Speech Acts. Cole, P. & J. Morgan (eds). New York: Academic Press.

Grice, H. P. 1989. Meaning. In: *Studies in the Way of Words*. Cambridge, Mass.: Harvard University Press. Originally published in: *Philosophical Review* 67, 1957.

Hacker, P. M. S. 1992. Malcolm and Searle on 'Intentional Mental States'. *Philosophical Investigations* 15, No 3.

Harris, R. 1981. *The Language Myth*. London: Duckworth.

Heidegger, M. 1972. The End of Philosophy and the Task of Thinking. In: *On Time and Being*. Transl, J. Stambaugh. New York: Harper & Row Publishers.

Heim, I. 1991. On the Projection Problem for Presuppositions. In: *Pragmatics. A Reader*. Davies, S. (ed.). Oxford: Oxford University Press. Originally published in: *Proceedings of the Second West Coast Conference on Formal Linguistics*. Flickinger, D. (ed.). Stanford, Calif.: Stanford University Press. 1988.

Kamp, H. 1979. Semantics versus Pragmatics. In: *Formal Semantics and Pragmatics for Natural Languages*. Guenthner, F. & S. J. Schmidt (eds). Dortrecht-Holland: D. Reidel Publishing Company.

Kaplan, D. 1989. An Essay on the Semantics, Logic, Metaphysics, and Epistemology of Demonstratives and Other Indexicals. In: *Themes from Kaplan*. Almog, Perry & Wettstein (eds). New York: Oxford University Press.

Keenan, E. L. 1971. Two Kinds of Presupposition in Natural Language. In: *Studies in Linguistic Semantics*. Fillmore, C. J. & D. T. Langendoen (eds). New York: Holt.

Keenan, E. L. 1972. On Semantically Based Grammar. *Linguistic Inquiry* 3, 413–61.

Kempson, R. M. 1975. *Presupposition and the Delimitation of Semantics*. Cambridge: Cambridge University Press.

Kempson, R. M. 1977. *Semantic Theory*. Cambridge: Cambridge University Press.

Lakoff, G. & M. Johnson. 1980. *Metaphors We Live By*. Chicago: The University of Chicago Press.

Levinson, S. C. 1983. *Pragmatics*. Cambridge: Cambridge University Press.

Lyons, J. 1977. *Semantics*, Vols 1 & 2. Cambridge: Cambridge University Press.

Lyons, J. 1981. *Language and Linguistics. An Introduction*. Cambridge: Cambridge University Press.

Martinich, A. P. 1984. A Theory for Metaphor. *Journal of Literary Semantics* 13, 35–56.

Martinich, A. P. (ed.). 1990. *The Philosophy of Language*. Second Edition. New York: Oxford University Press.

Morris, Charles. 1938. Foundations of the Theory of Signs. In: *International Encyclopedia of Unified Science*, Vol. 1, No. 2. Neurath, O., R. Carnap & C. Morris (eds). Chicago: University of Chicago Press. Reprinted in: *Writings on the General Theory of Signs*. The Hague: Mouton. 1971.

Öhman, S. 1988. Empiricism and Universal Grammar in Chomsky's Work.

In: *Language, Speech and Mind, Studies in Honour of Victoria Fromkin.* Hyman, L. & C. Li (eds). New York: Routledge.
Quine, W. V. O. 1951. *Mathematical Logic.* Revised Edition. New York: Harper & Row.
Quine, W. V. O. 1960. *Word & Object.* Cambridge, Mass.: The MIT Press.
Russell, B. 1948. *Human Knowledge.* London: George Allen and Unwin Ltd.
Sapir, E. 1921. *Language.* New York: Harcourt, Brace & World, Inc.
Schiffer, S. R. 1972. *Meaning.* Oxford: Oxford University Press.
Searle, J. R. 1969. *Speech Acts.* Cambridge: Cambridge University Press.
Searle, J. R. 1979. *Expression and Meaning.* New York: Cambridge University Press.
Searle, J. R. 1983. *Intentionality.* New York: Cambridge University Press.
Searle, J. R. 1986. Meaning, Communication, and Representation. In: *Philosophical Grounds of Rationality.* Grandy, R. E. & R. Warner (eds). Oxford: Clarendon Press.
Segerdahl, P. 1994. Critique of Pure Capacity. Searle and the Background. *Philosophical Investigations* 17, No. 3.
Segerdahl, P. 1995, Linguistic Theory and Actual Language. *Language and Communication: an Interdisciplinary Journal* 15, No. 1, pp. 31–42.
Soames, S. 1991. How Presuppositions Are Inherited: A Solution to the Projection Problem. In: *Pragmatics. A Reader.* Davies, S. (ed.). Oxford: Oxford University Press. Originally published in: *Linguistic Inquiry* 13, 1982, 483–545.
Sperber, D. & D. Wilson. 1986. *Relevance.* Oxford: Basil Blackwell.
Stalnaker, R. C. 1972. Pragmatics. In: *Semantics of Natural Language.* Davidson, D. & G. Harman (eds). Dortrecht-Holland: D. Reidel Publishing Company.
Stalnaker, R. C. 1991. Pragmatic Presuppositions. In: *Pragmatics. A Reader.* Davies, S. (ed.). Oxford: Oxford University Press. Originally published in: *Semantics and Philosophy.* Munitz, M. K. & P. K. Unger (eds). New York: New York University Press.
Stenlund, S. 1990. *Language and Philosophical Problems.* London: Routledge.
Strawson, P. F. 1950. On Referring. *Mind* 59, 320–44.
Strawson, P. F. 1964. Intention and Convention in Speech Acts. *Philosophical Review* 73, 439–60.
Strawson, P. F. 1990. Meaning and Truth. In: *The Philosophy of Language.* Second Edition. Martinich, A. P. (ed.). New York: Oxford University Press.
Toolan, M. 1991. Perspectives on Literal Meaning. *Language & Communication: an Interdisciplinary Journal* 11, No 4.
Van Fraassen, B. C. 1968. Presupposition, Implication, and Self-Reference. *The Journal of Philosophy* 65, 136–52.
Van Fraassen, B. C. 1969. Presuppositions, Supervaluations and Free Logic. In: *The Logical Way of Doing Things.* Lambert, K. (ed.). New Haven and London: Yale University Press.
Wetterström, T. 1977. *Intention and Communication. An Essay in the Phenomenology of Language.* Lund: DOXA.

Wettstein, H. K. 1991. How to Bridge the Gap Between Meaning and Reference. In: *Pragmatics. A Reader*. Davies, S. (ed.). Oxford: Oxford University Press. Originally published in: *Synthese* 58, 1984.
Wilhelmi, J. 1991. *Språk och Rationalitet. En kritisk kommentar till Habermas språkfilosofi*. Uppsala: Institutionen för Lingvistik, Uppsala Universitet.
Williams, B. 1993. *Ethics and the Limits of Philosophy*. Fontana Press.
Wittgenstein, L. 1969. *The Blue and Brown Books*. Second Edition. Oxford: Basil Blackwell.
Wittgenstein, L. 1974. *Philosophical Investigations*. Second Edition. Transl, G. E. M. Anscombe. Oxford: Basil Blackwell.

Index

Aborigines, Australian 149
abstract language 138
activities
   language and languages 142, 147, 149–50, 150, 151
   mastery of activities of life 18–20
actual use *see* use
applied mathematics 217
appropriateness 186, 191, 206–7
artificial intelligence (AI) 225
ascribing meaning 22–4
assumptions, background
   defeasibility 209
   linguistic meaning 225
   presuppositions as 185–6, 191, 202–6
Austin, J. L. 4, 120, 153
Australian Aborigines 149
autonomous system 1, 18
   deixis and notion of language as 15–17
   see also calculus conception
autonomous uses 211–13, 226

Bach, K. 169
background assumptions
   see assumptions
Baker, G. P. 9
baptism 162, 222
   effect-independence 128–30
Bar-Hillel, Y. 4, 8, 220
   deixis 18

semantics 34
Beardsley, M. C. 224
beliefs 153–61, 169–70, 223
   Moore's paradox 157–8
   role in making statements 153–7
   sincerity and insincerity 158–61

weakened notion of presupposition 202–6
   see also assumptions
Bierwisch, M. 57
Bruner, J. 225–6

calculus conception 101–6
   pragmatics and 1–5, 6–7
   process of language use 100–1
Carnap, R. 3, 219
Carston, R. 8, 219
change of state verbs 188
character 29
chess 131
children 12
   beliefs 154–5, 156–7
   language game of evidence 87–8
   promises and obligations 162–3
   requesting/passing language game 122–7
   sincerity and insincerity 160–1
   use of honorifics to 45–9
Chomsky, N. 114, 142, 222–3
clocks 19–24, 32–5
   see also time-expressions
codification 25–6, 148
Cohen, L. J. 58
Cole, P. 9
communication
   formal semantics and communication-intentions 109–13
   notions defined in logically reversed order 117–19
   'outer side' and 'inner side' 169–70
   role of intentions 165–9
   Searle's conception of problem of 120–2
   speaker-hearer scheme 113–17, 119, 168–9, 170

231

using ordinary things in 41–3
communicative intentions
  109–13, 165–9
compositional nature of
  meaning/composition-
  dependence 37–8, 39, 74, 91
compositional semantics 179
  see also semantics
compositionality, principle of
  224
concrete arrangements 22–4
conduct-grounding 92–7
constant linguistic meaning
  110–11, 113, 119, 177
constitutive rules 121–2
'constructing lives' 225–6
content 29
context 2, 15–24
  ascribing meaning by
    establishing practice 22–4
  deixis and language as
    autonomous system 15–17
  linguistic perspective in
    pragmatics 17–18
  mastery of language and
    mastery of activities of
    life 18–20
  presuppositions as inferences
    about 185–6, 190, 191, 200–2,
    203
  how time-expressions have
    meaning 20–2
context-dependence 31–44
  compositional nature of
    meaning 37–8
  disambiguation 35–7
  distinction between pragmatics
    and semantics 31
  misuse of linguistic terminology
    40–1
  and other forms of functional
    dependence 39
  three uses of linguistic notions
    43–4
  time-expressions 32–5
  using ordinary things in
    communication 41–3
contextual preconditions
  see preconditions

conventions
  of meaning and use 181
  realization of underlying rules
    136–9
conversational implicatures 4–5,
  53–65, 176, 200, 219, 224, 225
  defeasibility 64–5
  examples of how the theory
    works 62–4
  meaning more than is actually
    said 53–4
  pragmatic notion 58–62
  semantic reading 58–62, 84–6,
    98
  see also formalization; literal
    meaning; order; rationality
cooperative principle 60–2
  and conduct-grounding 92–7,
  98

Davidson, D. 73–4, 134
Davies, S. 9, 227
defeasibility 209–18
  examples of the property
    209–10; investigation of
    211–15
  identification and reading
    presupposition triggers
    210–11
  of implicatures 64–5; scalar
    implicatures 102–4
  inferences from linguistic data
    vs features of actual use
    215–16
  projection problem 216–17
definite descriptions 2, 5, 187,
  224
deixis 4
  difference between deictic and
    non-deictic expressions 31
  and notion of language as
    autonomous system 15–17
  pragmatic account 25–30;
    grammaticalization 25–6;
    philosophy 28–30;
    projection of general
    description of speech events
    onto actual events 27–8
  see also context; context-

dependence; irony
delimitation of literal meaning 59
dependence, functional 36–9
   see also context-dependence
description and recollection method 10–12, 156
   examples 9–12, 114
   family resemblance 118–19
   language games 126–7, 135
descriptions 207
   definite 2, 5, 187, 224
   deixis 27–8, 219
   projected onto actual events 27–8
   Russell's theory of 188, 224
detachment from actual use 76–8, 175, 210–11, 224
dictionary, mental 195–7
disambiguation 35–7
discourse-dependence 36, 39
disregard of situation 57–8, 59, 59–60
distinct uses   see particular/ distinct uses
Dummett, M. 134

effect-independence 128–31
essential rule 125
established use/practice
   cooperation and rationality 92–7
   distinction from use in particular occasion 48, 80–3, 131–2, 142, 146, 204–5
   language vs languages 142, 146
   meaning and 22–4, 47–8
   preconditions for 191–7
   speech acts vs language games 124, 125–6, 131–3
ethics 164
evidence
   beliefs 154–6, 158
   language game of 86–8
   semantic reading and implicature 85–6
   sincerity 159
examples

selection of 202–8
use of 9–12, 118–19
exceptional cases   see particular/ distinct uses
explanation
   vs description 10–12, 126–7, 135, 207
   of particular use and general practice 82–3, 131–3, 141–2

factive verbs 187
family resemblance 118–19, 174
first language learning 12, 143–5
foreign languages   see particular languages
formal logic 54–5, 58, 59, 60
formal semantics 109–13
formalization 99–106, 211
   applicability 104–6
   calculus conception 100–1
   motives for 99–100
   scalar implicatures 101–4, 106
forms of expression 150–2
forms of life 127, 222
functional dependence 36–9
   see also context-dependence

garage work 92–6
Gazdar, G. 5, 8, 221, 225, 226
   formalization 99–100, 103–4, 106, 220, 221
   presupposition 189
generalization 210–11
generalized Quantity implicatures 101
   see also scalar implicatures
Gordon, D. 171
grammatical analysis 175
grammatical calculus 43, 44, 116
grammatical mode of use 120
   defeasibility 213–15, 218
   precondition 194–5, 197, 226
   speaker-hearer scheme 116–17, 117–19
grammaticalization 25–30
Green, G. M. 179

Grice, H. P. 8–9, 220, 224
  communicative intentions
    110, 111, 221; analysis of
    meaning 165–9, 223
  conversational implicature 5,
    53, 58, 59, 60, 176
  cooperative principle 60, 95,
    96–7, 98
  language and use 3–4
  maxims of conversation 60–1,
    76, 82, 159
  rationality 92, 96–7, 98

Habermas, J. 223
Hacker, P. M. S. 9, 223
Harnish, R. M. 169
Harris, R. 9
Heidegger, M. 221–2
Heim, I. 216, 226
honorifics: use to children 45–9

idioms 175–6, 179–81, 224
imperative, simple 88–90
implicative verbs 187
implicatures
  conversational *see*
    conversational implicatures
  scalar 101–4, 106
inconclusive evidence 155–6,
    158
independently defined notion of
    order 80–2
indexical expressions 2, 219
  autonomous system 16–17
  grammaticalization 26
  ironical use 45–9
  using ordinary things in
    communication 41–3
  see also deixis
indicator words 35, 39
indirect speech 171–82
  game of indirectness 172–6;
    comparison with semantic
    reading 174–6; facts of
    use 174
  idioms 175–6, 179–81, 224
  metaphor 173–4, 176–8
  semantic reading and theories
    of meaning 178–9, 224

technical notion 171–2
inferences 197–202, 225
  identification of defeasibility
    210–11
  identification of
    presuppositions 186–8,
    199–200
  from isolated verbal utterances
    197–8
  from linguistic data vs features
    of actual use 215–16
  linguists 'overhearing'
    language use 198–200
  meaning-inferences 97
  presuppositions as inferences
    about context 185–6, 191,
    200–2, 203
  see also conversational
    implicatures
insincerity 158–61
'institutions' 121–2
instrument, language as 168
intentions 161–9, 169–70
  communicative 109–13, 165–9
  role in communication 165–9
  role in making promises
    161–5, 168, 170
inventing readings 172–6
irony 45–9
  meaning and established
    uses 47–8
  modified language game 48–9
  pragmatic conception 45–6
  utterance as way of acting
    46–7
isolated verbal utterances 197–8

Johnson, M. 173–4

Kamp, H. 100–1
Kaplan, D. 4, 9, 29–30
Keenan, E. L. 189, 225
Kempson, R. M. 5, 9, 73, 225
knowledge, mutual 191, 206–7,
    210

Lakoff, G. 171, 173–4
language games 10–11
  of evidence 86–8

irony 46–7; modified
  language game 48–9
lying as modified language
  game 159–61
Moore's paradox 157–8
presuppositions 191–3
recognizing in particular
  languages 152
simple imperative 89–90
vs speech acts 120–35;
  baptism 128–30; meaning
  and understanding 133–5;
  requests 122–7
languages, particular *see*
  particular languages
learning
  first language vs second
    language 12, 143–5
  mastery of activities of life
    18–20
  see also training
Levinson, S. C. 4, 5, 9, 86, 221
  autonomous system 15
  conversational implicature 59,
    60–2, 64–5, 84–6
  defeasibility 64–5, 209–10,
    217–18
  deixis 16
  formalization 103, 104
  grammaticalization 25, 26
  Grice's maxims of conversation
    60–2, 82, 88–9, 92–3, 159
  idioms 180
  irony 45, 46
  order 76–7, 78
  pragmatics 7
  presuppositions 190, 206;
    identification 186–8;
    inferences 199, 200, 200–2
  semantic reading 55, 84–6
lexical reading 55–7, 59
lexicon 179
life-activities 18–20
'life as narrative' 225–6
linguistic data, inferences from
  215–17, 197–206
linguistic notions: ways of using
  43–4
linguistic relativity 147–50

linguistic semantics 8, 73
  see also semantics
linguistic terminology *see*
  terminology
linguistic tests 186–8, 189, 210–11
linguistically based methods of
  observation
  compositionality 37–8, 73–4
  context-dependence 32–5,
    39–41; disambiguation 35–7
  and formal pragmatics 105–6
  and pragmatic inference
    197–202
  and the problem of deixis
    17–18
  and technical notion of
    presupposition 187,
    198–202
linguistically codified meaning
  25–30, 55–7, 148–9
linguistics, philosophy and 138,
  150–2
literal meaning 2, 56, 66–75, 220
  attitude towards semantic
    reading 66–7
  delimitation of 59
  distinct uses 67–8; condensed
    into one paraphrase 68–70
  indirect speech 173, 175, 177,
    178–9, 224
  truth-conditional semantics
    73–5
  use following from meaning
    70–3
  see also semantic reading
lying 158–61
Lyons, J. 56–7, 224
  deixis 15–16
  linguistic relativity 148, 149
  literal meaning 66, 67, 67–8,
    68

Manner, maxim of 61–2, 76
  see also order
Martinich, A. P. 53, 59
mathematics
  applied and projection
    problem 217
  formalization 99–100, 221

maxims of conversation 60–2
  rationality 84, 86–92
meaning 2
  analysis in terms of
    communication-intentions
    165–9, 223
  ascribing to establish a
    practice 22–4
  compositional nature 37–8, 39
  constant linguistic
    meaning 110–11, 113, 119,
    177
  content and character 29
  formal semantics and
    communication-intentions
    109–13
  formalization and 105–6
  not grounded in linguistic
    structure 73–4
  linguistically codified 25–30,
    55–7, 148–9
  literal see literal meaning
  semantic and pragmatic
    dimensions 17–18, 109
  semantic reading and theories
    of 178–9, 224
  speech acts vs language games
    133–5
  how time-expressions have
    meaning 20–2
  use and 24, 46–7, 118–19, 181,
    219; established use 47–8,
    146; use following from
    meaning 70–3
  varying situational speaker-
    meaning 110–11, 113, 119
meaning-inferences 97
  see also inferences
mental dictionary 195–7
metaphor 173–4, 176–8
metaphysical thinking 213, 218,
  221–2
method see description and
  recollection method
mind, philosophy of 153–7
modified language games
  irony 48–9
  lying 159–61
Moore's paradox 157–8

Morgan, J. 9
Morris, C. 1
mutual knowledge 191, 206–7,
  210

names 128–30
negation 186–7, 190, 199–200
nonsense uses 213–14, 217–18
normal use see use

obligations 161–5, 170
Öhman, S. 223, 224
order 76–83
  determination of 78–80
  explaining particular uses and
    general use 82–3
  independently defined notion
    80–2
  possibility of reversed 76–8
ordinary things 41–3
'overhearing' language use
  198–200

paraphrase
  indirect speech 171–2, 175,
    176
  literal meaning and 68–70, 75
  semantic reading as technique
    of 54–8, 66
particular/distinct uses
  literal meaning 67–70, 70–3,
    75
  presuppositions 212, 214, 226
particular languages 136–52
  first language learning vs
    second language learning
    143–5
  learning where words belong
    in activities 145–7
  linguistic relativity 147–50
  philosophy vs linguistics
    150–2
  road-signs analogy 139–42
  Searle's conception of relation
    between language
    and 136–9
philosophical analysis 117–19,
  119, 221–2
philosophy 222

deixis 28–30
linguistics and 138, 150–2
philosophy of mind 153–7
physico-linguistic perspective 121–2
practice *see* established use/practice
pragmatics 12, 24, 211, 217
  account of deixis 25–30
  and the calculus conception 1–5, 6–7
  formal *see* formalization
  game of indirectness 174–6
  inferences from linguistic data vs features of actual use 215–16
  linguistic perspective 17–18
  notion of conversational implicature 58–62
  order *see* order
  presupposition 185–90, 201–2; pragmatic vs semantic conceptions 188–90, 190; weakened notion 202–6
  semantics and 17–18, 31, 109; boundary 7–8, 219
  universal 223
preconditions 191–3
  belonging to language practice as a whole 195–7
  formal notion 193–5
presupposition triggers 187–8, 209–10
  general way of reading and defeasibility 210–11
presuppositions 5, 185–90
  as background assumptions 185–6, 191, 202–6
  defeasibility *see* defeasibility
  identification in linguistic tests 186–8, 198–200
  as inferences about context 185–6, 190, 191, 200–2, 203
  inferences from linguistic data vs features of actual use 215–16
  and methods of linguistics 191–208; appropriateness and mutual knowledge 206–7; inferences from isolated utterances 197–8; language game 191–3; 'overhearing' language use 198–200; precondition 193–7
  pragmatic vs semantic conceptions 188–90
  projection problem 216–17
  technical notion 187, 198–200
pretending games 46–7, 48–9
projection 27–8, 172–3, 202, 224
projection problem 216–17, 218
promises 117–18
  role of intentions 161–5, 168, 170
  underlying rules 136–8, 222
promising devices 137–8
propositional logic 54
propositions 2

Quality, maxim of 60–2, 159
  rationality 84, 90–2
Quantity, maxim of 61–2
  rationality 84, 86–8
Quine, W. V. O. 34–5, 39, 75, 219

rationality 84–98
  conduct-grounding 92–7
  general notion of truth 90–2
  language game of evidence 86–8
  meaning-inferences 97
  semantic reading and conversational implicature 84–6
  use of simple imperative 88–90
recollection and description *see* description and recollection method
regimentation, syntactic 178–9, 224
regularities 122–4, 135, 141–2
Relevance, maxim of 61–2
  rationality 84, 86–90
representation 106, 112, 127, 150–1, 169–70, 178–9, 195, 212

requests 134
  effect-independence 128, 130–1
  intuitive justification of speech-act conception 131–3
  language game 122–7
  underlying rules 136–7
reversed order of events 76–8
road signs 139–42
routines of use
  defeasibility 211–12
  presuppositions 204–6, 207
rules
  constitutive 121–2
  essential 125
  following 145–50
  semantics and 179, 182
  underlying 136–9, 151–2
  of use and order 79–83
Russell, B. 188, 219, 224

Sapir, E. 147
Sapir–Whorf hypothesis 147–50
Saussure, F. de 142
scalar implicatures 101–4, 106
Schiffer, S. R. 110, 111, 165
Searle, J. R. 5, 7, 9, 59, 165, 223
  conception of relationship between language and languages 136–9
  explanation of Moore's paradox 157–8
  family resemblance 118
  indexicals 219
  indirect speech 171, 180–1, 224
  intentions 166, 168
  linguistics and philosophy 151–2
  literal meaning 220
  meaning and understanding 133–4
  philosophical analysis 119
  problem of communication 120–2
  promises 168; obligations 161–2
  requests 122–5, 126–7
  sincerity 159, 161

speech acts: philosophy of mind 153; speaker–hearer scheme 113–14, 116–17; units of communication 110
second language learning 12, 143–5
Segerdahl, P. 220, 221
semantic reading
  conversational implicature 58–62, 84–6, 98
  and indirect speech see indirect speech
  and literal meaning 66–70, 173, 175, 177, 178–9
  and meaning-inferences 97
  scalar implicatures 102
  three aspects 54–8
  and truth-conditions 73–5
semantics 109, 179
  conceptions of presupposition 188–90, 190
  context-independence 34
  employment of semantic reading and game of indirectness 174–6
  formal 109–13
  linguistic 8, 73
  pragmatics and 17–18, 31, 109; boundary 7–8, 219
  truth-conditional 8, 73–5
simple imperative 88–90
sincerity 158–61
sincerity rule 137
situation, disregard of 57–8, 59, 59–60
Soames, S. 5
specialized uses see particular/ distinct uses
speech-act theory 5, 109–19
  approach compared with formal semantics 109–13
  dualism 169–70
  notions of communication defined in logically reversed order 117–19
  speaker–hearer scheme 113–17, 119; intentions 168–9, 170

speech acts vs language
  games 120–35; effect-
  independence 128–31;
  intuitive justification of
  conception of requests
  131–3; meaning and
  understanding 133–5;
  requests 122–7; Searle's
  concept of problem of
  communication 120–2
  technical notion of indirect
  speech 171–2
Sperber, D. 8, 204, 219
Stalnaker, R. C. 5, 9
  presuppositions 185–6, 189, 226
states of affairs 85, 86–7
Stenlund, S. 12, 221, 222
  calculus conception 1
  syntactic regimentation 224
stopwatches 32, 32–3
  see also clocks; time-expressions
Strawson, P. F. 109–10, 165, 219
  descriptions 188
  pragmatics 3
  reference of a use 221
substitution 187, 199
syntactic regimentation 178–9, 224
syntactic structure 112
syntax 112, 179
system, autonomous see autonomous system

Tarski, A. 73
terminology, linguistic
  misuse and context-dependence 40–1
  notions of linguistics 44
  use as normative delimitation 43
thought, language and 147–50
time-expressions
  context-dependence 32–41
  context 19–24
Toolan, M. 220
toys: request language game 122–7
traffic 139–42, 222

training
  languages and language 142, 145, 148–9
  rationality 88, 90
  requests 124, 125
truth, general notion of 90–2
truth-conditional semantics 8, 73–5
truth-value 2–3, 189
truth-value gaps 189

underlying rules 136–9, 151–2
understanding 123, 129, 133–5
universal pragmatics 223
use
  as activity vs totality of particular utterances 142
  autonomous uses 211–13, 226
  detachment from 76–8, 175, 210–11, 224
  distinct uses see particular/distinct uses
  established see established use/practice
  explaining particular and general 82–3
  facts of and game of indirectness 174
  inferences from linguistic data vs features of 215–16
  meaning and 24, 118–19, 181, 219; established use 47–8; use following from meaning 70–3
  misconstrued as indirect 176–8
  nonsense uses 213–14, 217–18
  normal: honorifics 46; obligations 164–5; sincerity and insincerity 158–61
  pragmatics 3–5, 16–17
  projections 172–3
  routines of see routines of use
  rules of and order 79–83
  truth and falsity 91–2
  see also context
utterances
  isolated verbal utterances 197–8
  part of a way of acting 46–7

Van Fraassen, B. C. 188, 225
varying situational speaker-
    meaning 110–11, 113, 119
verifying functions 155–6

well-formedness 55, 56
    see also literal meaning
Wetterström, T. 128, 130–1

Wettstein, H. K. 4, 42, 43
Wilhelmi, J. 223
Williams, B. 9, 10, 164
Wilson, D. 8, 204, 219
Wittgenstein, L. 9, 12, 43, 116,
    118, 138
    forms of life 222
    lexical reading 220

OHIO UNIVERSITY LIBRARY

Please return this book as soon as you have finished with it. In order to avoid a fine it must be returned by the latest date stamped below. All books are subject to recall after two weeks or immediately if needed for reserve.

DEC 0 7 1999
JUN 0 9 2000
DEC 0 7 2000
DEC 0 4 2000

CF